The Arts of Contemplative Care

The Arts of Contemplative Care:

Pioneering Voices in Buddhist Chaplaincy and Pastoral Work

Edited by Cheryl A. Giles and Willa B. Miller

Foreword by Judith Simmer-Brown
Preface by Pat Enkyo O'Hara

WISDOM PUBLICATIONS • BOSTON

Wisdom Publications
199 Elm Street
Somerville, MA 02144 USA
www.wisdompubs.org

Library of Congress Cataloging-in-Publication Data

The arts of contemplative care : pioneering voices in Buddhist chaplaincy and pastoral
work / edited by Cheryl A. Giles and Willa B. Miller.
    p. cm.
Includes bibliographical references and index.
ISBN 0-86171-664-7 (pbk. : alk. paper)
1. Chaplains. 2. Pastoral care. 3. Pastoral counseling (Buddhism) I. Giles, Cheryl A.,
editor of compilation. II. Miller, Willa, editor of compilation.
BQ5305.C4A78 2012
294.3'61—dc23

                          2012012179

ISBN 978-0-86171-664-7
eBook ISBN 978-1-61429-037-7

16 15 14 13 12
5 4 3 2 1

Cover design by Phil Pascuzzo. Author photo by Jewel Gilbert. Interior design by
Gopa&Ted2. Set in ITC Galliard Pro 10.3/14.4.

Wisdom Publications' books are printed on acid-free paper and meet the guidelines
for permanence and durability of the Production Guidelines for Book Longevity of the
Council on Library Resources.

Printed in the United States of America.

This book was produced with environmental mindfulness. We have elected to
print this title on 30% PCW recycled paper. As a result, we have saved the following resources: 18 trees, 8 million BTUs of energy, 1,853 lbs. of greenhouse gases, 8,352 gal-
lons of water, and 529 lbs. of solid waste. For more information, please visit our website,
www.wisdompubs.org. This paper is also FSC certified. For more information, please visit
www.fscus.org.

To my spiritual mentor Dolores, who taught me to be mindful,
and Norah, the next generation of pioneers.
—Cheryl A. Giles

To the many pioneers in the field of contemplative care
that have uplifted and inspired us, past and present.
—Willa B. Miller

Publisher's Acknowledgment

The publisher gratefully acknowledges the ongoing generous support of the Hershey Family Foundation and in particular the contribution toward the printing of this book.

Table of Contents

Preface

Pat Enkyo O'Hara

THIS VOLUME comes at a perfect time. Two streams are converging: a current of recognition that something is missing in the secular, commercial approaches to caretaking, and at the same time, a wave of realization in Buddhist communities that our practices of contemplation, awareness, and presence render us uniquely suited to fill this gap—to provide compassionate caretaking.

What does that kind of care look like? I asked an oncology nurse this question—she smiled and said, "There's just something about the Buddhist chaplains—simply the way they walk down the hall seems to put people at ease."

A more ancient image of compassionate care is Avalokiteshvara, the bodhisattva of compassion, portrayed as having a thousand hands and eyes, which she uses to respond to the suffering of the world. In one ancient Buddhist tale, a seeker asks, "What exactly does she *do* with all those hands and eyes?" And the answer, simply given, is, "It is like reaching behind you to adjust your pillow at night." In other words, the way of compassionate care is as natural as your spontaneous gesture while at ease.

When we think of the training and practice required for intelligent contemplative care, we might object to the simplicity of this response. But looking a little more deeply, we can recognize the truth that it points to: effective caretaking originates from a rather ordinary quality that can be quite challenging to acquire—true presence, a grounding in the naturally arising reality of the moment.

Whether it is the anguish of a sickbed, the anger in a correction facility, or the fear beneath the order of a military life, contemplative care originates from a heart/mind that is clear and responsive, grounded in interdependence. And the healing goes both ways. Practicing contemplative care strengthens the caretaker's own Buddhist practice, offering moment-to-moment opportunities to face the suffering in oneself as well as in others, and to hold it in contemplative space.

I congratulate the editors for bringing together these trailblazing voices. Together, they express a path of practice that is opening for contemporary Buddhists to make a desperately needed difference in today's world.

Roshi Pat Enkyo O'Hara, PhD, is the abbot of the Village Zendo. A Soto Zen priest and certified Zen teacher, she received Dharma transmission in both the Soto and Rinzai lines of Zen Buddhism, through the White Plum Lineage. Roshi currently serves as the guiding spiritual teacher for the New York Center for Contemplative Care. She also serves as co–spiritual director of the Zen Peacemaker Family, a spiritual, study, and social action association.

Foreword

Judith Simmer-Brown

THE BOOK you hold in your hand is pioneering. It shares the work of courageous contemporary Buddhist practitioners in the West who bring the depth of their meditation practice into direct service and healing in their work as chaplains. Two skilled editors have solicited and selected chapters that illustrate how these chaplains are creating "secular parishes" in the midst of the most painful environments of our changing world, from the hospital to the prison, the military, and hospices. They counsel college students and parents raising Buddhist children, and they address issues of racism, classism, and ageism. For every setting, they describe how to be simply present, to not turn away from suffering, and to generate the heart of compassion in ways that heal.

Each chapter is fresh and immediate, full of experiential insights. We find ourselves beside these chaplains as they speak with patients ravaged by disease, with families who have just lost a child, with soldiers agonizing over the acts they are forced to commit, or with prisoners beset by regret. They share the wit and directness of the dying and the naked honesty of those who have lost everything. Humbly, they tell us of the lessons they themselves have learned. The inherent dignity, wisdom, and bravery of their clients come through on every page, and we can see that kindness is the greatest healing force.

These contributors come from a variety of Buddhist lineages, from Japanese and Korean Zen to Tibetan Vajrayana and Shambhala, to Pure Land, to Theravada vipassana; some are seasoned Buddhist teachers, others are more recent practitioners. A third of the contributors are my colleagues, friends, or sangha brothers and sisters; another third are my former students. Many others I know through reputation and through the lives of clients they have touched. Still, I learned deeply from this book about what it is actually like to be a Buddhist chaplain on the job.

In most settings, these chaplains are the only Buddhists in a Judeo-Christian or purely secular world. Sometimes they feel isolated or groundless, or fearful and inadequate, when they do not know what to do to help. Most clarify that it is not useful to think of themselves as "Buddhist"—they are interfaith chaplains who do whatever is needed. We can sense them stepping closer to their clients, holding their hands, and supporting them emotionally.

In pragmatic ways, they guide us in how to be chaplains. These chaplains teach the staple Buddhist practices, including loving-kindness meditation, listening skills, and "basic attendance." They provide slogans for caregivers and speak about "compassionate presence" as the chaplain's art. Several chapters contextualize this work in the timeless teachings of the Four Noble Truths and the selfless Mahayana path of the bodhisattva. Our chaplains show us how they draw sustenance from this ancient wisdom, finding fresh inspiration from their lineage teachers, from scripture, from meditation instruction.

Many know they are pioneers, and invite many other Buddhist practitioners to join them. What can be done to pave the way for others? They show that it is not enough to only "just sit" to learn to minister to a dying person; it is important to have academic study and professional supervision to develop the theological and pastoral skills to help such people. They speak of additional training they received from Clinical Pastoral Education (CPE), hospice, and the military as critical supports for their work. They highlight the importance of ordination, both monastic and lay, and make specific suggestions about how this could be supported by our communities.

For all of them, daily meditation practice is the primary support for the work. They acknowledge that the most important quality that the Buddhist chaplain can bring to any intense environment is clarity of mind, gentleness of heart, and a listening ear. The only way to continually do this, without resorting to formulaic techniques or a "pastoral persona" that masks our burnout or cynicism, is to return again and again to the immediacy of whatever is happening.

I am reminded of a pith teaching from Chogyam Trungpa Rinpoche:

"The everyday practice is simply to develop a complete acceptance and openness to all situations and emotions and to all people, experiencing everything totally without mental reservations or blockages, so that one never withdraws or centralizes into oneself." That is the essence of meditation practice and of Buddhist chaplaincy.

Judith Simmer-Brown, PhD, has been a professor of religious studies at Naropa University in Boulder, Colorado, since 1978. She was trained at Cornell College (BA), Florida State University (MA), Columbia University and Union Theological Seminary (ABD), and Walden University (PhD). She teaches Buddhist scripture, ethics, and philosophy, as well as interreligious dialogue, to Naropa's master of divinity students. She is an *acharya* (senior Dharma teacher) of the Shambhala Buddhist lineage of Sakyong Mipham Rinpoche and Chogyam Trungpa Rinpoche, and performs *upadhyaya* (Buddhist minister) ordinations for Shambhala. She's the author of *Dakini's Warm Breath: The Feminine Principle in Tibetan Buddhism* and *Meditation in the Classroom*.

Editors' Preface

WHAT YOU HOLD in your hands is a book that broadly explores an emerging field of contemplative care, from a variety of perspectives. The term "contemplative care" has its roots in the movement of Buddhist chaplains, care providers, and ministers that are beginning to turn their passion for Buddhist practice and view into a meaningful living. It is a close cousin to the term "spiritual care" which is now in wide use in the context of hospital and hospice chaplains—and yet we would like to distinguish between "spiritual care" and "contemplative care."

We understand spiritual care to refer to a wide swath of practitioners who provide emotional and spiritual support in a variety of contexts, both professional and informal. Contemplative care, on the other hand, refers to a kind of care that is informed by rigorous training in a meditative or contemplative tradition. If we were to hazard a definition of contemplative care, it might be:

> Contemplative care is the art of providing spiritual, emotional, and pastoral support, in a way that is informed by a personal, consistent contemplative or meditation practice.

Contemplative care therefore requires that the care provider is a practitioner of meditation. In most cases, the care provider is connected to a contemplative tradition or lineage, such as Buddhism. While contemplative care is not necessarily Buddhist care, in this book we are focusing on contemplative care as it is practiced and understood by Buddhists.

The contributors to this volume do not always use the term "contemplative care" but rather draw on a number of interesting terms and provide us with many definitions that are very useful as we explore the parameters of this field. For example, we find this definition in Jennifer Block's chapter in this volume: "Buddhist spiritual care means helping people access the stillness, clarity, and love existing within our hearts." We hope definitions such as this one will spark a conversation and add to our understanding of how the many practitioners in these fields understand their work. We also hope that these definitions will be held lightly, as this field deepens and grows.

We understand the term contemplative care as encompassing several subfields, including Buddhist chaplaincy, Buddhist ministry, and Buddhist pastoral care. While pairing the word *Buddhist* with *chaplaincy, pastoral care*, and other terms with Christian roots is a fairly new endeavor, the spirit of engaged Buddhist service of the ministry and chaplaincy ilk is quite ancient. For thousands of years, Buddhist religious specialists have offered services to their communities that include practical forms of outreach, such as tending the sick and educating children. Yet most convert Buddhists in the West were introduced to Buddhism not as a form of pastoral work, but as a form of personal practice. We turned to it as a tradition that offered a promise of enlightenment, greater wisdom, and greater peace for the individual practitioner. Buddhism was not, initially, introduced to many of us as a form of practical *service* to a wide and diverse sphere of people needing spiritual care.

In this light, the pioneering nature of the work of the people contributing to this volume becomes all the more manifest and bold. Their work is at once "mainstream" and revolutionary, naturally compassionate, occasionally difficult, and constantly trailblazing, in the spirit of manifesting upaya. These voices inspire us to imagine a meditation practice that takes meditation off the cushion and into the world, out of our temples and into the halls of mainstream institutions.

Exploring this field, care is taken to distinguish the difference between the terms *chaplaincy* and *ministry*. Chaplains provide spiritual, pastoral, and emotional care to patients, their families, and staff, and they are often employed by an organization, such as a hospital. He or she may well identify with a particular faith and draw from the tools of that faith, but he or she puts the patient's or client's spiritual needs front and center, regardless of that person's tradition. Ministers, on the other hand, tend to the religious needs of a particular faith group, or sangha. Both chaplains and ministers engage in various forms of "pastoral work." While there is certainly overlap in the roles and duties of chaplains and ministers, we find it useful to distinguish these two forms of pastoral work.

Nevertheless, chaplains, ministers, and other kinds of pastoral care providers also share much in common. Buddhist chaplaincy, ministry, and pastoral work are each practices of presence. We show up to be with those who are suffering, dying, or in need of care. We show up to listen, to be attentive, and to "come alongside" others. In the process, those dedicated to the practice of care grow and evolve spiritually. It is not all about the patient, or student, or the one who is cared for. It is about relationship and interbeing. And as you'll see in this volume, these caring relationships take many unique forms.

The seeds of this book were planted when we (the two coeditors of this volume) met in the summer of 2006 in the context of working within Harvard's nascent Buddhist ministry program. The more we talked, the more realized we had a lot in common, and we began working together, coteaching classes around the themes of chaplaincy, hospice, prison work, and various other kinds of pastoral work, from a Buddhist perspective.

In our conversations with each other and with students, certain types of questions arose often: How can we integrate our practice into engaged contexts related to spiritual care? How does one formulate a *Buddhist* ministry, when conversing with others who are involved in other types of ministry? How does one enter into the world of chaplaincy with a Buddhist background? What does it mean to talk about a Buddhist theology? What is the Buddhist equivalent of a "sermon," of "chaplaincy," of "ministry," of "liberation theology," of "social justice," of "medical ethics," of "congregation," and even of "clergy"? How do we guide students through the maze of becoming Buddhist ministers and chaplains? What does it mean to be a *vocational Buddhist*?

In seeking to address these questions, we struck up conversations with some of the pioneers in this book and sought books and articles that expressed the groundswell of interest in spiritual care we heard coming from our students. As we worked together, and reached out to people in this world of "engaged care" or whatever we might want to call it, it became clear that we are in the middle of a revolution. Buddhists are making inroads into institutions and their voices and actions are starting to transform those institutions—and transform what it means to us to be "Buddhist." In the process, some creative forms of theological reflection and application are taking place. These revolutionaries are reimagining practice along interpersonal lines and taking Buddhist practice into places where it has simply never been—at least in the West.

At the end of the compilation of this book, we realize we have just scratched the surface of this burgeoning field. We were only able to include a fraction of the people who could have been included here. Nonetheless, it is our hope that this book inspires the many people doing this work to put their work into writing and get it out into the world.

We continue to be fascinated and inspired by all those who follow this new path and blaze new trails in the field, as they skillfully use the powerful tool of language to find their place and "translate" their Buddhist practice into terms that others can understand. This book is also for them: to connect them to each other—to those of their generation, and to the generation that came before them.

This book organized itself on the basis of the submissions into six parts. *Part I—The Roots of Contemplative Care: Foundations of a Discipline* explores the definition, parameters, key issues, and educational foundations of contemplative care, from a number of perspectives. In this section, we find Jennifer Block's exploration of the definition of Buddhist chaplaincy, Daijaku Judith Kinst's consideration of issues of pedagogy in the training of chaplains and pastoral care providers, Wakoh Shannon Hickey's call for the training provided by Divinity Schools, Lew Richmond and Grace Schireson's description of their SPOT training for Zen Buddhist ministers, and Cheryl Giles' exploration of the role of race in spiritual care.

Part II—Serving the Sick: The Art of Hospital Chaplaincy explores the role, challenges, and experiences of Buddhist chaplains, as they navigate the institution of the modern American hospital and beyond. In this section, we discover how hospital chaplains are applying their practices of meditation and compassion to the caregiving context. We hear the story of Chodo Campbell's moving pastoral visit to another pastor with end-stage stomach cancer in Zimbabwe. We hear Mark Power describe, with deep honesty, his personal journey to adapt his Buddhist training to a Christian context. We see how Buddhist hospital chaplains, such as Trudi Jinpu Hirsch and Koshin Paley Ellison, are adapting ancient scriptures to inform the framework of their own caregiving.

Part III—Dharma Behind Bars: The Art of Prison Ministry describes the migration of the teaching of Buddhism into the deepest reaches of prison life. Here we find Dean Sluyter's inspiring story of Gary, a maximum-security inmate who pulls through twenty-eight years of prison to a life he never dreamed of. We find Penny Alsop's moving account of Mother's Day in a women's prison. We hear Richard Torres' story of Kosal, a survivor of the Pol Pat regime, who discovers a deep freedom in his understanding of interdependence.

Part IV—Wielding Manjushri's Sword: The Arts of College and Military Chaplaincy explores the life of chaplains in institutions of higher learning and the military. In this section, Danny Fisher and Ji Hyang Padma explore the unique challenges of offering pastoral support to students in their college years. We also walk beside Thomas Dyer as he forges a path as the US military's first Army chaplain.

Part V—Living with Dying: The Art of End-of-Life Care explores the pioneering work of Buddhists in end-of-life care. Here we find Joan Halifax's reflections on the importance of community as a means of support at the time of death. We find Randy Sunday's description of a "social model" hospice in Southern California. We look over the shoulder of Carlyle Coash as he finds the internal strength to sit with a patient with devastating jaw cancer as he learns to meditate.

The final section, *Arts of Ministry: The Pastoral Role of the Dharma Teacher*, explores the emerging discourse on the various aspects of providing pastoral care within a sangha. Here we find Lin Jensen's reflection on the role of "right speech" in the pastoral care context. We find Rebecca Johnson's reflections on Buddhist ministry in the inner city context next to Steve Ruhl's reflections on a rural Zen Buddhist ministry. And we hear Sumi Loundon Kim's description of the intergenerational challenges of a Buddhist ministry focused on children and families.

We have found every one of these chapters deeply inspiring and moving. And we hope you will find the material in this book as inspiring as we have. More importantly, we hope this book starts a conversation about the range of work that is becoming vocational Buddhism and acts as a resource for individuals seeking to become educated and to train in these areas. And finally, we hope it will act as a spark for people who have yet to know what their calling is, who might draw on the visions of the bodhisattva's work that we see reflected here in these accounts and reflections.

ACKNOWLEDGMENTS

Many wonderful friends and colleagues have contributed to making this volume possible. We are deeply grateful to Josh Bartok, our editor at Wisdom, for his hard work on behalf of this project and for understanding the vision of this book. We also would to thank Janet Gyatso, whose presence at Harvard sparked our early conversations about this topic. This volume also would not have been possible without the loving support of our partners Jewel and Mike. Finally, we would like to offer a deep bow of respect and the gratitude to the many pioneers in the field of contemplative care who inspired this volume.

PART I

The Roots of Contemplative Care:
Foundations of a Discipline

Toward a Definition of Buddhist Chaplaincy

Jennifer Block

BUDDHIST CHAPLAINCY is in the formative stage as a modern-day discipline and profession at the intersection between Buddhism, chaplaincy, and suffering. Buddhist chaplains join chaplains from other faith traditions in institutional settings such as hospitals, hospices, and prisons. In this essay I propose to sketch, in broad brushstrokes, what it means to me to be a Buddhist chaplain.

The seeds of Buddhist chaplaincy as a vocation begin, of course, with the Buddha. The three most common causes of people needing health-care in our day—old age, sickness, and dying—were the very same that inspired the Buddha to reach beyond the familiar into greater truth and happiness. In doing so, he eventually found a path to peace in the midst of all that is difficult, uncomfortable, and confounding. Reaching out to the men and women in his community who were seeking ways to allevi-ate their pain, the Buddha offered care through careful guidance and a myriad of teachings. In essence, the Buddha was a chaplain, or rather, Buddhist chaplains who comfort others are walking in the footsteps of the Buddha. For 2,500 years, Buddhists have contemplated sickness, old age, and death to find an end to suffering. Buddhist chaplains continue

Reverend Jennifer Block is an ordained interfaith minister and Buddhist chaplain. Since 2004, she has served as education director and chaplain for the Zen Hospice Project in San Francisco, California, creating curriculum, teaching workshops, offer-ing spiritual care, and providing community outreach. Jennifer also serves as adjunct faculty for the Sati Center for Buddhist Studies in Redwood City, California, and the Chaplaincy Institute for Arts and Interfaith Ministries in Berkeley. Jennifer has an undergraduate degree in communications from Boston University and a theology degree from Naropa University.

this practice in hospitals, hospices, prisons, and other facilities, helping people to reduce their pain and skillfully deal with what is happening to them, in the moment.

In a classically Buddhist sense, there is not a lot of emphasis on hope or intercession from an outside source or deity, but more on how to use one's intelligence and basic goodness to be skillful and more at ease right in the middle of what is difficult. Yet everyone needs encouragement, assistance, and direction on their life's journey; the role of a Buddhist chaplain is to accompany individuals as their awakening and freedom from suffering unfolds. This may mean simply being a good listener, an encouraging companion, an intelligent guide, or a piercing truth-teller. Overall, the purpose of a Buddhist chaplain is to alleviate suffering in its many forms: physical pain, difficult emotions, and confusing or disturbing thoughts, more commonly known as agony, fear, anger, guilt, depression, loneliness, grief, and so on.

All of the teachings of the Buddha can be summed up by the following phrase: Nothing whatsoever should be clung to as "me" or "mine." Interventions of chaplains exist to serve this goal, to aid in this realization, by either describing the situation or providing a skillful means for someone to perceive it. "To cling to nothing" is a guide to the proper relationship to experience, as well as a statement of the ways things are when the goal is reached. All difficult situations can be improved by applying intelligent perspective and loosening one's tight grasp on how things have always been, or should be right now. This means any of us can work internally with our suffering to change it for the better, even if what is happening outside of us does not change.

According to Buddhist tradition, in the latter part of the sixth century BCE, Siddhartha Gautama wandered through northern India. Local villagers became curious about his uniquely radiant character, and asked, "Are you a celestial being or a God? Are you a man?" To these questions he replied, "I am none of these. I am awake." He then became known as the Buddha, which literally means "the Awakened One." What does it mean to be awake? In the Buddhist tradition, it is taught that the answer to this question is found through deep insight into the interdependent nature of the world as we experience it. When we look at the world, we do not actually see things as they are, but rather we see through the lens of our individual hopes, fears, and dreams. The Buddha pointed to this lens as the root of suffering and taught that we each have the potential to awaken from what is imaginary to what is real.

The connecting theme of this approach as a chaplain is the possibility of awakening, as understood from Buddhist teaching. Our deepest desire is to have a sense of belonging, and when we are able to recognize ourselves in "others," we can then care for them in a fundamentally different way. The function of the various approaches and interventions is to offer tools that will enable people to open their hearts and minds so that they may develop greater awareness of their true nature and, from that awakening, truly heal and transform.

Although the Buddha neither taught about higher powers nor denied their existence, many Buddhists acknowledge a universal life force. Human beings are both unique selves and part of this great universal life force—but if we overidentify with who we are or what we believe, we suffer. Our tendency is to embrace one thing as right/pleasing and its opposite as wrong/unsatisfactory. Making such dualistic distinctions is natural to the human mind, and it serves people on many practical levels. However, clinging or aversion toward dualistic categories causes more suffering than benefit. A middle path between dualistic opposites offers peace and freedom; the Buddha called this the Middle Way.

According to Buddhist teaching, suffering arises from our ignorance of interconnectedness and change and our bondage to dualistic thinking. Every aspect of creation is a process of becoming, of moving into new, transformed states. Things fall apart and come together, fall apart again and come together again. If we clearly and deeply see that all objects and mind states are impermanent and without selfhood, we see that there is nothing worth clinging to, and when we stop clinging to (or averting from) things as they are, we experience liberation from suffering. Our very perceptions can change and everything can appear in a new and fresh light, leading to a more wakeful and skillful way of life.

With time, reflection, and compassion, Buddhist chaplains help people realize that there is beauty and safety in change. We can learn to dwell peacefully in "things as they are" and develop an unconditional openness to whatever arises, is born, and/or dies—within the self, others, and all of creation. We become increasingly aware of our True

Nature: wisdom and compassion. Realizing compassion and wisdom in our lives is awakening; a change of perception, like suddenly seeing a three-dimensional object, where previously one could only see it as flat. Wisdom means seeing creation and ourselves as they are through the practice of mindful, nonjudgmental attention to ordinary experience. Thich Nhat Hanh describes this wisdom as "awareness of the interbeing nature of all that one observes—seeing the one in the many, all the manifestations of birth and death, coming and going, and so on—without being caught in ignorance." Compassion can be defined as liberation from the illusion of separateness. A heart can be broken open to compassion through suffering, as well as through love. One experiences compassion as a great affection for creation as manifest in the self, others, and the nonhuman world. This is experienced as an urge to embrace the world. Nhat Hanh says, "with compassion in our heart, every thought, word, and deed can bring about a miracle." Compassion enhances our appreciation for things and assures us that we are embraced by a wider community, not forsaken as isolated individuals.

This healing process is not something mysterious. Awakening to our true nature is available anywhere and everywhere, at all times. It exists within all phenomena, right here and now. It is a matter of removing the layers of our own projections that obscure the pure vision of reality. However, to wake up is not necessarily easy. We must first realize that we are asleep. Next, we need to identify what keeps us asleep, start to take it apart, and keep working at dismantling it until it no longer functions. The good news is that as soon as we make an effort to wake up, we begin to open up to how things actually are. We experience what we have suppressed or avoided and what we have ignored or overlooked.

Over time, one can develop an unconditional openness to whatever happens, arises, is born, and/or dies within oneself, others, and all of life. Buddhist chaplains are motivated by loving-kindness, an opening of the heart through spiritual practice, and are characterized by love for, compassion toward, equanimity among, and sympathetic joy for others. As Buddhist chaplains we do not serve as intermediaries or authorities per se, but as capable, steady companions who have investigated suffering through our own life experiences. So from our spiritual practice, we learn to lend patients our spirit and stability of mind for the possibility for their own healing, awakening, and transformation. Specifically, spiritual support from a Buddhist perspective can be defined as:

- Willingness to bear witness
- Willingness to help others discover their own truth
- Willingness to sit and listen to stories that have meaning and value
- Helping another to face life directly
- Welcoming paradox and ambiguity into care—and trusting that these will emerge into some degree of awakening
- Creating opportunities for the people to awaken to their True Nature

As a Buddhist chaplain, I serve others in realizing that most of life's events are not solely within human control. Simple yet profound, life-changing universal truths are discovered or remembered to help people experience the deepest, authentic peace and satisfaction—a heart and mind relaxed and open to what is. Buddhist spiritual care means helping people access the stillness, clarity, and love existing within our hearts. I have a sense of accomplishment or success when a patient begins letting there be room for all of everything to happen: room for grief, for relief, for misery, for joy. Gone is the sense of separation, of internal nothingness, or of not being quite present. This is what I call the mystery of spirituality and healing.

Cultivating an Appropriate Response:

EDUCATIONAL FOUNDATIONS FOR BUDDHIST CHAPLAINS AND PASTORAL CARE PROVIDERS

Daijaku Judith Kinst

What is the teaching of the Buddha's entire life?
An appropriate response.

—ZEN MASTER YUNMEN

A four-year-old boy dies suddenly and inexplicably on a sunny Sunday afternoon. In a hospital emergency room his father, pushed beyond endurance, rages at the staff, the world, God. His mother sits stunned and silent, holding his hand. Their world is undone. I enter this scene with nothing but my own being. No formulas or stock phrases can possibly meet such a time.

What is an appropriate response? How does one meet such profound suffering?

THIS QUESTION lies at the heart of the effective training of chaplains and pastoral care providers. It is a question I have pondered as I consider the elements that best

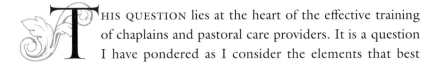

Rev. Daijaku Kinst is professor of Buddhism and Buddhist pastoral care and director of Buddhist chaplaincy at the Institute of Buddhist Studies, an affiliate school of the Graduate Theological Union Berkeley, California. Rev. Kinst is a Soto Zen Buddhist priest and teacher in the lineage of Shunryu Suzuki. Following her monastic training, she completed a master's degree in counseling psychology, a doctorate in Buddhism and psychology and trained as a chaplain at the University of California Medical Center, San Francisco. She has taught and led retreats widely and is guiding teacher, with Rev. Shinshu Roberts, of the Ocean Gate Zen Center in Capitola, California. She is actively involved in developing Soto Zen clergy as a board member of the Soto Zen Buddhist Association and enjoys supporting the Dharma in its many forms—as well as walks by the ocean and the practice of ordinary life.

support the education and training of Buddhist chaplains and pastoral care providers.

I believe that this rests on three essential elements: (1) living a life guided by and deeply engaged with Buddhist teachings, (2) academic study, and (3) supervised direct service in Buddhist and interfaith contexts. In this essay I will discuss one aspect of this tripartite training—academic study—how it shapes, supports, and sustains Buddhist chaplaincy and pastoral care, and how it relates to the other two.

Let's look at some aspects of each of these in turn.

BUDDHIST STUDY

The study of central Buddhist teachings is essential in Buddhist pastoral care education for several reasons. It provides a theological foundation for Buddhist chaplaincy, the basis from which the chaplain responds to others, and it sustains the chaplain in his or her work. Study can also clarify, for the chaplain, how these same teachings can be challenged and transformed in face-to-face meetings with another suffering being. Over time, study and reflection on the teachings strengthens the student's confidence that he or she has the Buddhist theological foundation from which to serve, and to act, in whatever way is required with openness, compassion, and flexibility. This in turn supports the ability to be simply and fully present and responsive, our greatest gift to a suffering other.

Based on my experience, central topics for study and reflection include, but are not limited to, Buddhist teachings on suffering, its cause and its alleviation; emptiness and interdependence; mind, perception, identity, and self experience; karma; wisdom and compassion and their relationship; the ethics of awakening manifest in such forms as the bodhisattva vow; and a familiarity with major schools and traditions. A sound knowledge of these areas provides a language and a conceptual base for considering questions of how these teachings are relevant to spiritual care. Such questions might include the following: How do we understand suffering and how is it relieved in the lives of ordinary humans? How do we understand the self and its relation to others in loss and death? How do we draw limits and set boundaries based in an understanding of wisdom and compassion? How do we interact with the diversity of human life with equanimity?

Bringing these topics closer to the day-to-day life of a chaplain, and their own experience, students investigate how the study of perception, identity, and clinging impacts their experience of listening to another. How does the teaching of dependent coarising apply to their experience of self, culture, society, family relationships? The Four Noble Truths are alive in each interaction for a chaplain. Suffering, its cause, and its alleviation are real to each person the chaplain meets—including, if he or she is paying attention, the chaplain. How do these teaching inform and shape these meetings? Depending on the circumstance and the needs of the person, such Buddhist teachings may be overtly present in a chaplaincy relationship, for example with a Buddhist patient in a hospital, or they may provide the basis for the Buddhist chaplain's effective response to a person from a very different faith tradition.

Training in and knowledge of ritual in multiple Buddhist and non-Buddhist traditions is also important. When meeting with Buddhists, it is vital for the Buddhist chaplain to have training in the role of services, rituals, liturgy, the use of written teachings, and other meaningful aspects of Buddhist traditions including, for example, the use of chants, beads, and Buddhist images. Knowledge of rituals commonly used in other faiths is equally important.

Assisting with ethical questions and dilemmas is common in the work of a chaplain. Therefore, developing skill in this area through substantial study of, and reflection on, Buddhist ethics is essential. For example, decisions about end-of-life care, pregnancy termination, organ donation, and professional responsibility are situations routinely faced by a hospital chaplain. Each of these circumstances, and many more, must be met with empathy and skill. In studying Buddhist ethics, our intention is not to find specific answers to each dilemma. However, such study greatly enriches our understanding of the process by which decisions, often painful decisions, are reached. The ability to be fully present with another at such a time, to listen to a person or a family in often confusing, conflicting, and deeply distressing circumstances, and to help clarify, with them, how a decision reflects their deepest values, increases the likelihood that the decision will be accompanied by a measure of peace. Respectful discussion and dialogue about ethical dilemmas in a classroom setting prepare the ground for this quality of companionship.

A sound Buddhist chaplaincy education should lead to effective functioning in an interfaith setting. A good working knowledge of other faiths and traditions is important—general knowledge as well as an understanding of specifics. However, what is most important is the quality of the chaplain's presence in an interfaith setting. The development of a respectful and easy stance when working with persons affiliated with other faiths or a Buddhist tradition other than his or her own is key.

The Buddha taught that all phenomena lack inherent existence and are dependently coarisen, including our own tradition and various points of view; nothing is absolute. If we align ourselves with these teachings, it is possible to stand comfortably in one's own experience (in this case one's tradition) while at the same time welcoming, respecting, learning from, and listening deeply to another. Grounded in these teachings, it is possible to stand with full confidence in the teachings of the Buddha and meet a person of any faith or tradition with curiosity and without defensiveness. Such an atmosphere creates openness and the possibility of genuine dialogue with colleagues across religious traditions. Also, and not insignificantly, this can contribute to a deeper understanding of the Buddhist chaplain's own tradition. The study of Buddhist teachings, therefore, supports the open and flexible stance with relation to others that is central to building viable interfaith, interdenominational, and culturally competent chaplaincy.

Within this environment questions such as whether or how to provide rituals from other faiths, for example Christian baptism, can arise with curiosity and openness and Buddhist chaplains can articulate a Buddhist interfaith perspective that does not presuppose that the Buddhist perspective is equivalent to no religious affiliation. It also allows for dialogue between Buddhist chaplains which, in turn, can enhance our understanding and appreciation of the field.

CONTRIBUTIONS FROM CONTEMPORARY
PSYCHOLOGY AND COUNSELING

Simplicity and depth of presence, the capacity to be still, to listen wholeheartedly and intelligently, and to respond appropriately, are the essence of the practical application of the Buddha's teaching. The ability to meet even the unthinkable with a fundamental sense of stability, kindness, and equanimity may be built from sustained Buddhist practice but it is also the area in which the study of contemporary Western psychology can make a fruitful contribution. Buddhist chaplaincy education and training is enhanced, through the development of basic counseling skills, an understanding of relevant Western psychological principles, and a sustained engagement in self-reflection.

The first step in any care or counseling relationship is being less anxious than the person one is serving. Learning to listen deeply, to attend compassionately and intelligently to another, is fundamental. Learning to notice what one noticed in an interaction and what one did not, and receiving direct feedback on the quality of one's presence, is invaluable. Practicing basic counseling skills in classroom and training situations develops these skills, promotes greater ease, reduces anxiety, and builds greater confidence and effectiveness.

A conceptual understanding of the psychological aspect of pastoral care relationships deepens and broadens the resources available to the chaplain. An understanding of transference, countertransference, and the impact of trauma, grief, depression, and patterns in family and relationships is helpful for the chaplain's work. A chaplain must be competent in assessing the psychological tone and needs of a circumstance quickly and with an open mind to engage complex interpersonal systems with a measure of calm. Pastoral counseling literature is particularly relevant in developing this understanding as are writings on clinical psychology.

For example Pamela Cooper-White, in her book *Shared Wisdom: Use of the Self in Pastoral Care and Counseling*, provides a history and contemporary definition of transference and countertransference as well as a very useful model for understanding the difference between pastoral care and pastoral counseling and psychotherapy. The work of Harvey Aronson and Jeremy Safran and many others provide not only relevant psychological principles but also include a discussion of the interface of Buddhism and psychotherapy. Griffith and Griffith, in *Encountering the Sacred*, give a nuanced and well-informed discussion of the interface of psychotherapy and spirituality.

Knowing when and how to refer to and develop professional resources is essential for any chaplain. Developing an understanding of child and elder abuse, domestic violence, and suicidality, being able to identify indications that it may be occurring, and being familiar with the legal and ethical guidelines and requirements for responding are all also critical.

Education and training in applied psychology and counseling is not limited to the development of a theoretical understanding of the material. Even the development of counseling skills and empathic listening, though important, can leave untouched an unexamined anxiety about the human condition that can undo efforts to be of service. Theory must take root in the person to bear fruit in the work.

Amid all this, sustained engagement in Buddhist practice is of course essential. Equally important, though, is the necessity for a commitment to clear-eyed and compassionate self-reflection and an understanding of how it is accomplished. Undertaking an honest, kind, and intelligent investigation of characteristic personal and interpersonal patterns allows the training chaplain to develop a familiarity with his or her strengths, vulnerabilities, and habitual tendencies as well as an ability to track useful and distorting inner responses that may impact the care of the person in need.

For the most part this process occurs when the training chaplain enters a supervised training site such as Clinical Pastoral Education (CPE). However a foundation for effective self-reflection can be established in graduate education through the study of relevant psychological literature and an emphasis on the development of self-knowledge. This foundation is also supported by including, in the curriculum, training programs such as the Sati Center for Buddhist Studies in Redwood City, California, which, over the course of one year, provides the enrolled cohort with a structure and a community in which self-reflection and interpersonal awareness can grow, as well as training in a wide variety of pastoral skills.

PASTORAL CARE LITERATURE

The practice of pastoral care has been extensively explored in non-Buddhist traditions. Topics such as the identity and role of the chaplain, the range of circumstances in which pastoral care occurs, the needs of specific populations, interfacing with the community, and models of spiritual and pastoral care have been fruitfully explored in the pastoral care literature. For example Duane Bidwell, in his book *Short-term Spiritual Direction*, considers the needs and opportunities of brief encounters and details concrete, specific guidance in bringing meaning and depth to such encounters. Margaret Guenther's classic text *Holy Listening* provides a discussion of listening and responding to the spiritual needs of another that is practical, grounded, and deeply caring.

There is also much to be found in this literature about the importance and impact of racism, sexism, homophobia, poverty, and other societal ills. Understanding the profound impact these and other factors have is crucial, and non-Buddhist pastoral care literature makes a significant contribution to this understanding. Such literature also covers many other topics such as what is often called "compassion fatigue," the exhaustion experienced by caregiving professionals who focus on others at the expense of their own self-care. Chaplaincy is taxing; understanding self-care and knowing how to intelligently address one's needs are integral parts of the successful chaplain's life.

The study of pastoral care literature also provides an opportunity to develop uniquely Buddhist understandings of the topics covered, to find points of contact and difference, to deepen the ability to provide competent interfaith care, and to simply learn from those who have been providing such care for many years. With adequate intellectual care, Buddhist textual sources can be adapted to pastoral applications and non-Buddhist pastoral care literature can be integrated in a Buddhist context. Including literature that is based in a Buddhist tradition, such as Seigen Yamaoka's account and discussion of pastoral care as a Jodo Shin Shu minister, *The Transmission of Shin Buddhism in the West*, is of particular value.

THE GROUND OF PRACTICE

Without an ongoing and committed engagement with Buddhist teachings and practices, as well as a vital relationship with a Buddhist teacher, minister, or guide, Buddhist chaplaincy training will not have the foundation it requires, nor will it be sustainable. Simple, compassionate awareness is an activity that, I believe, can be shared by Buddhists of all traditions and is a central element in the work of a Buddhist chaplain. Beyond that, the specifics of further practice commitments would depend upon the tradition and needs of the student and would be worked out in dialogue with his or her teacher, minister, or guide, ideally in the context of a sangha. A Zen practitioner will create supportive activities that will likely vary, perhaps greatly, from those of a practitioner of Tibetan Buddhism, and those could be markedly different from a follower of Jodo Shin teachings. What is key is that these activities exist, that there is a commitment to them, and that they are carried out in dialogue with a trusted elder of that community.

Although there may be classes introducing a variety of Buddhist practices, teaching in an academic setting is not well suited to providing this type of relationship. The relationship between a Buddhist minister, teacher, or guide and a practitioner is deeply personal and takes place in a different atmosphere and according to different models than the academic teacher-student relationship. In order for this relationship to function fully, in my opinion, it is best kept separate from the academic system. Academic teachers may be fully authorized to teach in their tradition, and they will naturally share their understanding; however, thoughtfully considered boundaries create an environment in which the student can engage deeply with a variety of teachings in an accepting and inclusive classroom setting.

As the field of Buddhist pastoral care and chaplaincy develops, ongoing conversations among those providing education and training in academic settings, nonacademic training centers, and practicum sites, will result in a greater understanding of the field. From these conversations, questions will emerge that will deepen our ability to respond to the evolving field of Buddhist chaplaincy and pastoral care and make valuable contributions to our understanding of Buddhist studies, the general field of chaplaincy and pastoral care, and contemporary psychological, psychotherapeutic, and counseling theory and practice.

With such a foundation of education and training, a Buddhist chaplain, meeting the parents of a four-year-old who has died unexpectedly and inexplicably, will have the intellectual, personal, ethical, emotional, ritual, and spiritual resources needed to be present for those parents, to hear, absorb, and embrace with deep compassion their fear, anger, grief, and great suffering—and in that and many other ways to make an appropriate response.

Meditation Is Not Enough

Wakoh Shannon Hickey

M Y PAGER goes off in the middle of the night, and I am called to the neonatal intensive care unit. A stillborn child has been delivered. The parents, Roman Catholics who speak no English, want the baby baptized. Catholic priests are not permitted to baptize dead bodies, but the priests of the local parish understand parents' emotional need for the rite, so they do not object to hospital chaplains performing the rite. I'm the chaplain on call, so the task falls to me. Reading a liturgy in Spanish, I lead family members in a traditional Catholic rite of emergency baptism, sprinkling holy water on the lifeless forehead of a tiny girl. *Yo te bautizo en el nombre de el Padre, y el Hijo, y el Espíritu Santo.* It's not my first time. The parents invariably ask: "Why did God do this? Is He punishing me?" How does a Buddhist chaplain answer that?

On another call, a lifelong Jehovah's Witness is bleeding out in the emergency room. Surgery involving blood transfusions would be necessary to

Rev. Wakoh Shannon Hickey, PhD, is assistant professor of religion at Alfred University in New York and a Soto Zen priest. She has practiced Soto Zen since 1984. She earned an MA in Buddhist and Christian studies in 2001 and an MDiv in 2003 from the Pacific School of Religion, an ecumenical Protestant seminary belonging to the interfaith Graduate Theological Union (GTU) in Berkeley, California. She studied Buddhism at the Institute of Buddhist Studies, also a member of the GTU. Dr. Hickey completed a PhD in religion and modernity at Duke University in 2008, specializing in American religious history, Buddhism in East Asia and the US, and religion and medicine. She has worked as a chaplain in both medical and university settings. Her current research explores medical uses of meditation, the education of American Buddhist clergy and chaplains, and the challenges of translating Asian Buddhist traditions to American religious culture.

repair his aneurism and save his life, but the doctrine of his church forbids transfusions from donors, because they are believed to violate the Biblical prohibition against consuming blood. If he were at a hospital near his home, he could use "banked" units of his own blood, but he and his wife are far from home. The wife is in denial. My job is to help her say goodbye in the minutes remaining, help him die with some measure of calm, and find someone at the local Kingdom Hall who can accompany the wife as she arranges to have her husband's body transported home. She asks me to pray, but in my zendo, we never do extemporaneous prayer. From somewhere beyond me, a prayer to Jehovah emerges from my lips. The moment I stop speaking, the man flatlines.

A Mormon woman is suicidal over her siblings' insistence that she participate in a Temple ritual that will seal her to her family for eternity. She isn't ready. The psychiatrist has no idea how to help her deal with this, so he calls me. Down the hall, a psychotic woman is certain that Jesus wants her to starve herself to death because she is such a terrible sinner. How does the Dharma help me to help these women?

I'm a Soto Zen priest who has worked as a chaplain in both hospital and university settings. Now I teach undergraduates in a rural village in western New York. I have been trained in American Zen temples and in the academy. I have given a lot of thought to what these institutions do—and what they don't do—to help prepare people for religious leadership and service. I'd like to share some of the conclusions I have drawn so far.

Years of zazen practice certainly helped me to approach the situations I describe above—and countless more—with some measure of calm and clarity. I found my way in each case, and each time I learned something new about the Buddha's teaching of no separate self. But zazen alone was not enough to help me navigate through the theological issues that each case presented, and zazen alone could not help me respond to the agonized questions that people asked me.

These are the kinds of situations chaplains deal with every day. They were not contemplated by the Buddha 2,500 years ago, when he and his disciples wandered across north India, begging for alms. Nor were they contemplated by Dogen, the thirteenth-century founder of my Zen lineage, when he established his monastery in the mountains of Japan.

The work of ministers, priests, and chaplains—Buddhist or otherwise— is always interpretive: we must continually make ancient traditions and teachings relevant to new cultural and historical contexts. In the reli- giously pluralistic situation of twenty-first-century North America, we must also collaborate with and serve people whose religious perspectives differ hugely from our own. While I believe meditation training is essen- tial to the preparation of Buddhist chaplains, it is not enough. Additional tools are needed for the job.

During my own preparation for ordination as a priest, and my training as a chaplain, I spent six years in seminary, earning a master's degree in Buddhist and Christian studies and a master of divinity degree. (I also spent six months in cloistered monastic training.) Academic training was not a requirement for ordination in the Zen lineage with which I was affiliated at the time, but I believed that if I were to take on the respon- sibilities and authority of priesthood, I needed training that American Zen communities are not fully equipped to provide. I had practiced Soto Zen for nearly fifteen years, in both residential and nonresidential settings, before I entered graduate school, and had observed that the training of American Zen priests consisted of meditation, participation in rituals, and informal (i.e., nonacademic) study of Buddhist texts and history. I had also witnessed a number of scandals involving clergy mis- conduct, both in my own lineage and in other Buddhist organizations. I wanted to study both Buddhism and Christianity academically, and I wanted professional training to help me avoid some of the pitfalls of religious leadership.

I entered graduate school in 1997, and in the years since then, I have seen huge shifts in seminary education. The mainstream model of clergy education—a three-year, residential master of divinity program—dates to the nineteenth century, and does not work as well as it once did. Seminarians these days are older; many are second-career professionals with families who have more difficulty relocating for graduate school than young, single people do. Mainstream Protestant denominations are also shrinking, and have less money to support seminarians, while the cost of graduate education has dramatically increased. Schools find it very costly to maintain aging buildings, upgrade libraries, incorporate new research and classroom technologies, offer competitive salaries, etc. In response to such changes, seminaries are developing new models of education, as will be discussed below.

Everything is changing, as the Buddha taught. And to use a modern metaphor, we must either learn to surf the waves of change, or sink.

My master's thesis—which was longer than my doctoral dissertation—examined a number of issues in the training of American Zen clergy. I studied the functions priests perform, and the ways they are trained, in three American Zen lineages, which ranged along a spectrum from highly monastic to nonmonastic. I compared the training in these communities to the typical training path of Soto Zen priests in Japan and to seminary education in the American Protestant mainstream. I considered the differing roles of Japanese and American Zen priests: in Japan, they are best known for performing culturally prescribed funeral and memorial services. In the American organizations I studied, three of the largest Zen communities in the United States, priests were typically called upon to do four things, which are normal expectations for mainstream Christian clergy as well. First, their religious communities expected them to be exemplars: that is, representative practitioners of their Zen traditions. (Clergy have feet of clay, of course, but in general we are expected to uphold the ideals of the traditions we practice, in a public way.) Second, they were ritual leaders: they performed various rites of passage and the regular liturgies of their traditions and improvised other ceremonies as circumstances required. Third, they were religious educators and public theologians, teaching the texts, stories, and disciplines of their traditions and reinterpreting them for new circumstances. Finally, they provided what Christians call pastoral care: they helped people grapple with questions of meaning during times of struggle and offered spiritual and ethical guidance. However, I found significant gaps between these role expectations and the formal training of American Zen priests and lay teachers. In all three organizations, training tended to focus on meditation and ritual, and frequently left leaders underprepared for the roles of religious educator, public theologian, or pastoral counselor.

Since my seminary days, as I have watched Buddhist, Christian, and Jewish colleagues move into various forms of professional ministry, I have come to realize that they also do many more things than I had considered in my master's thesis. They manage staff, budgets, and volunteers in the nonprofit organizations they serve. They work with boards of directors and government agencies. They do fundraising, publicity, and community organizing. And many operate in an American religious culture that blurs the line between clergy and laity. Although chaplaincy is a unique form of ministry, because it is explicitly ecumenical and interfaith, and because it takes place in institutions such as hospitals, prisons, and schools, chaplains are nevertheless called upon to perform many of these complex and demanding tasks as well.

For some years, I have participated in discussions about clergy training within the Soto Zen Buddhist Association (SZBA), a fledgling professional organization for American Zen clergy. I also have participated in many conversations, in person and online, with Buddhist chaplains and aspiring chaplains. It seems to me that participants in these Buddhist discussions fall into two broad camps.

Many—perhaps a majority—are what I would call monastically oriented, even if they live as laypeople. They believe that training for religious leadership and service should be centered in the meditation hall. Many argue that Zen training should consist primarily of daily meditation, liturgy, and temple work, particularly in traditional, ninety-day periods of intensive practice called *ango*. Some monastically oriented people express suspicion or disdain for academic training and professional certification, arguing that it can hinder religious insight, while others are much more supportive of formal study, in academic or temple settings, even as they stress the primacy of temple practice and long apprenticeship with one's Zen teacher.

Folks approaching the issue of chaplaincy training from the other side, including the organizations that certify professional chaplains, advocate a professional model of training. This includes a master of divinity degree or its equivalent. At the seminary I attended, that meant at least two years of coursework and a year of internship. In coursework, students learned to interpret scriptures critically, think theoretically and theologically, preach sermons, analyze congregational systems, do historical and ethnographic research, grapple with legal and ethical problems, and so forth.

Many of these academic and theological skills are essential for professional chaplains. In 2006 the Association of Professional Chaplains (APC), the largest and most influential certifying body for professional chaplains, decided that Buddhists seeking to become board certified chaplains—the highest level of professional certification, and necessary for employment in many settings—would be required to hold a bachelor's degree from an institution accredited by the Council for Higher Education Accreditation and to document the equivalent of 72 units (7,200 hours) of graduate-level training in each of nine areas: sacred literature, theology/philosophy, ritual/liturgy, religious history, comparative religions, religious education, institutional organization and administration, pastoral care and counseling, and spiritual formation. Up to 1,500 hours of meditation and/or chanting experience could apply to the 7,200-hour total, but only if it involved documented supervision, an educational component, and evaluation to determine whether educational objectives were being met.

In addition, all candidates for APC Board Certification must complete four units (1,600 hours) of Clinical Pastoral Education (CPE) at an accredited training site; be ordained or otherwise commissioned for ministry involving pastoral care; be endorsed as a chaplain by "a recognized religious faith group"; and have 2,000 hours of work experience as a chaplain, after completing CPE. These are rigorous standards, which I believe are appropriate for people serving vulnerable populations such as hospital patients, students, and inmates.

Both monastic and professional training are designed to instill certain ways of thinking, to shape character and identity, and to teach particular skills. I am a product of both kinds of education, and I can see the merits of both. I can also see some limitations of both.

One advantage of Zen monastic training is that one learns Dharma with the whole body. One moves, sits, chants as a member of the group body, dropping the self and harmonizing with others. This (ideally) helps to cultivate both character and religious insight. The rituals of Soto Zen *are* its primary pedagogical method. Long hours of meditation also teach one to be present with suffering, without trying to escape it, or justify it, or "fix" it, or explain it away. This quality, which chaplains call "nonanxious presence," is what suffering people need: someone who can be with them compassionately in the midst of their suffering. The only way to be fully present with anyone else's suffering, without squirming, is to practice being present with one's own. This ability to be fully present in the moment is one of the great gifts that Buddhist chaplains offer. It is not a skill typically taught in seminaries.

I think this kind of monastic formation is at the heart of the famous aphorism attributed to Bodhidharma: Zen is "a special transmission outside the sutras, not dependent upon words and letters, a direct pointing to the human mind, seeing one's true nature and becoming Buddha." There is no way to learn it but to do it, in year after year of patient practice. In this, I agree with monastically oriented Zen Buddhists.

At the same time, Dogen, the founder of my own Zen lineage, called this aphorism a "fallacy" and fiercely criticized those who used it to argue that Zen training need not entail rigorous study. In a treatise called "Buddha's Teaching" (*Bukkyo*), Dogen wrote:

> Fellows like this, even hundreds or thousands of years ago, were proclaiming themselves to be leading authorities; but we should know that, if they had such talk as this, they neither clarified nor penetrated the Buddha's Dharma and the Buddha's truth.

For Dogen, absolutely everything is Buddha and preaches the Dharma— so to call scholarly study "outside" the Buddha's teaching is to fundamentally misunderstand the central Mahayana doctrine of nonduality.

Furthermore, throughout Buddhist history, monks and nuns have been responsible for writing, preserving, and commenting upon Buddhist teachings. Educated monks and nuns composed the *nikayas, agamas,* and *vinayas,* the philosophical and psychological treatises, and the transmission stories unique to Zen known as koans. Until recently, meditation was the specialty of a few monks and nuns. Even in modern Japanese Soto Zen, formal education can and does substitute for some monastic training. The more academic training one has in Buddhist studies, the less time one is required to spend in a recognized training monastery (*senmon sodo*) in order to move through the ordination ranks. Clergy receive both monastic ranks (novice priest, head trainee, full priest, abbot or abbess of a temple) and academic ranks, which determine what and where a priest can teach other priests or laypeople.

I think the American Zen emphasis on personal religious experience and intuition, "heart" over "mind," is not so much a product of ancient Zen as it is a product of *American* religious history—specifically, of evangelical Protestantism since the early nineteenth century. Evangelicalism shifted religious authority away from clergy who gave learned expositions of scripture toward those who could testify to powerful, personal religious experiences (e.g., being "born again")—including those who were not formally ordained. Likewise, German Romanticism, which influenced Transcendentalists and other early promoters of Buddhism among white Americans, stressed intuition rather than rationalism. Although mainstream American denominations do require academic training for clergy, American religious culture has been shaped decisively by what John Wesley, the founder of the Methodist movement, called "the religion of the heart."

In order to reinterpret religious traditions of the past, to keep them relevant for present realities, we must understand where we have come from, where we are now, and where we are headed. Our historical and cultural situation is vastly different from those of our spiritual ancestors, at home and abroad. Different circumstances call for different skills. Professional seminary training is no panacea, but it does offer some useful training for our time.

For example, seminaries teach people to read sacred literature critically, and to interpret it for new circumstances. Even Biblical studies can help Buddhists understand a key source of religious authority for a majority of Americans and can help us learn to read any scriptures, including Buddhist ones, more thoughtfully. In some ways, modern Biblical studies are far ahead of Buddhist studies, particularly in English. For Biblical studies, a broad range of exegetical tools are available in English: myriad translations, commentaries from a wide range of perspectives, concordances, etc. Few such tools are available to English-speaking Buddhists, and only a fraction of the vast corpus of Buddhist literature has yet been translated from Asian languages into English (although the Pali Canon has been available in English since the 1920s). Biblical scholars have developed a wide variety of hermeneutical methods for analyzing scriptures from multiple angles as well: historical, literary, cultural, rhetorical, feminist/womanist/*mujerista*, and so forth, which Buddhist scholars can (and some do) employ.

Furthermore, many of the people Buddhist chaplains encounter in their work have been wounded by the toxic theologies of fundamentalists who read the Bible selectively and superficially. These theologies can worsen the suffering of people who are ill, grieving, or incarcerated, and countering them requires theological training and skill.

In addition, professional education can guide chaplains in dealing with legal and ethical problems that arise in counseling situations, and in making appropriate referrals to agencies dealing with problems such as domestic violence, addiction, sexual abuse, or suicide. Such skills are essential for chaplains and other religious professionals.

Another valuable aspect of formal theological education is that it obliges one to discuss one's own religious assumptions with people who do not share them. Exposure to people of different religious and cultural backgrounds can help one clarify where one stands and relate more empathetically to those who stand elsewhere. This combination of personal clarity and openness to difference is an essential pastoral skill.

But seminary education is expensive, for both students and schools. Many people who would like to be ministers or chaplains cannot afford to relocate for three years of graduate school, then enter jobs paying moderately at best in a very limited market. Given the relationship between race and economic class, these problems are especially acute for people of color.

Similar problems apply to extended monastic training—a complaint my American Zen peers repeatedly raise. Most Zen clergy must support themselves financially, and it is difficult to leave one's job and home for several months of *ango* training. Even in Japan, monastic training is increasingly problematic, because the medieval monastic ideal is not well adapted to the needs of modern, urban temple families or the parishioners they serve. Both monastic and professional modes of training also pluck people out of the contexts of their ministry and reinforce a split between theory and practice, clergy and laity, that may no longer serve. We must adapt to these realities.

These problems are pushing some seminaries to experiment with new models of education. Some are partnering with secular institutions to teach skills such as nonprofit management, in addition to the traditional subjects of theology, scripture, religious history, ethics, pastoral care, and preaching. Some are pooling resources and collaborating with other seminaries instead of competing. Increasingly, seminaries are offering nondegree certificate programs, and combinations of online teaching, distance education, and short-term residential intensives. These methods can also serve Buddhists well, and a few organizations are beginning to experiment with them. We just have to be willing to engage in the necessary conversations: between scholars and practitioners, among Buddhists of different types, and across religious lines.

This is how we cultivate *upaya paramita*, the perfection of skillful means.

Upaya means discerning what a particular person or situation requires and responding appropriately, so that we can all move together along the path to awakening. I cannot think of a better description of what a Zen priest or a chaplain does.

SPOT: A Training Program for Buddhists in America

Lew Richmond and Grace Schireson

SHUNRYU SUZUKI, founder of San Francisco Zen Center and Tassajara monastery, once wrote, "Here in America we cannot define Buddhists the same way we do in Japan. American students are not exactly priests and not exactly laypeople . . . [so] I think we must establish an American way of Zen life."

What did he mean by this? Who and what did he hope we might become?

Suzuki Roshi had a vision for America—a courageous and creative call for a universal Buddhism based on tradition, but not limited by it. From the time he arrived here in the late 1950s, Suzuki realized that

Lewis Richmond was ordained as a Zen Buddhist priest in 1971 by Shunryu Suzuki Roshi. He is the author of four books, including the national bestsellers *Work as a Spiritual Practice* and *Aging as a Spiritual Practice*. He is the cofounder with Grace Schireson of Shogaku Zen Institute, which sponsors the SPOT Buddhist priest three-year training program. Lewis is founder and presiding teacher of Vimala Sangha, a Zen Buddhist meditation community in Marin County, California, and blogs on Buddhist topics in the Buddhism religion section of *The Huffington Post*.

Grace Schireson is a Zen abbess, president of Shogaku Zen Institute (a Zen training seminary), and a clinical psychologist. She is the author of *Zen Women: Beyond Tea Ladies, Iron Maidens, and Macho Masters*. She received Dharma transmission from Sojun Mel Weitsman Roshi of the Suzuki Roshi Zen lineage in California. She has also been empowered to teach koans from the late Fukushima Keido Roshi of Tofukuji Monastery, Kyoto, after practicing over ten years in Japan. She has been married for forty-three years and lives with her husband at her Zen retreat center, Empty Nest Zendo in North Fork, California. She has two grown sons and four grandchildren.

Grace Schireson and Lewis Richmond are president and provost, respectively, of Shokagu Zen Institute.

for Zen to truly take root in America, it could not just be an imitation or extension of the Japanese style of practice in which he himself was trained, but it would have to be transformed by his American successors into something indigenous to our country and culture. It's been fifty years since Suzuki Roshi's arrival, so we might ask: What is the state of this vision? Does it hold relevance for other Buddhist traditions in the West? Are we truly making the Asian traditions our own, or are we still imitating Asian ways?

A MEETING OF ZEN MINDS

Several years ago, a group of about fifteen American Zen teachers in the Suzuki Roshi lineage came together to take up this and other questions. We had a lot in common. We had been trained in one or more of the residential practice places of the San Francisco Zen Center; we wore the priest robes of Soto Zen; we had received Dharma transmission, giving us authorization to teach; and we had struck out on our own to start our own Zen sitting groups just as Suzuki Roshi had done. Yet we were still wondering about Suzuki Roshi's vision and were brimming with questions.

What were we actually teaching our students? What new ways had we found to teach Zen meditation to Americans raised in a Judeo-Christian society with an individualistic Western mind set? In practicing outside of formal centers or temples, how had we changed the Asian forms of practice in which we were trained, and what were the implications of those changes? How were we leading our emerging practice communities, and helping them deal with conflict and difficulty? How were we addressing, for ourselves and for our sangha members, the questions that deeply mattered to all of us—questions about emotions, relationships, psychological problems, life crises, money, health, family, and children? How well were we taking care of our own emotional, psychological, and physical needs? What was inspiring our sangha members to practice Zen and keep at it? Were we actually creating that "American Zen way of life" that Suzuki Roshi spoke of? We each seemed to be inching our way along by feeling and intuition, but without, as yet, a shared systematic approach.

As we continued meeting, we agreed that all of our years of Zen training—leading a regimented life, keeping a strenuous meditation schedule, ringing bells, and bowing at altars—had given us understanding of Dharma, and improved our focus, concentration, and sense of Buddhist ritual, but it did not seem to have prepared us very well for what we were actually doing as American Zen teachers training Western laypeople to meditate and to appreciate the Buddhist view. We were not in a monastery or retreat center any more but were helping ordinary people with jobs and families live their lives more richly and productively. Were we increasing their own sense of liberation through meditation and the mindful practices and helping them to enrich the lives of others? What was the connection between our own training and this emerging vocation to share Buddhist practice with our lay sanghas?

These early peer group sessions were the first time that most of us had ever given public voice to these concerns. Each of us had gone off on our own to teach Zen—the first generation of graduates from the training centers that Suzuki Roshi had founded—and now, coming together after so long on our own, it was comforting and a bit surprising to find ourselves all in the same boat. We began to think about how we could develop a shared compass, standards and goals for teaching in settings outside of Zen centers. We wanted to teach students what they needed to know to practice and share Buddhism in their own lives rather than teaching them the skills necessary for sustaining a large Zen center. Teaching students to recognize their blind spots, to develop their teaching and speaking skills, and to learn how to guide others in study and practice describes training that develops the individual. Our own training in learning how to ring bells, wear robes, and follow Zen rituals was useful in furthering and continuing the institution, but it did not address our specific developmental needs. The former is a teaching that meets each person where s/he is, the latter, the teaching curriculum developed to insure the smooth functioning of schedule and ritual at a large training center.

As our discussions evolved, we realized that perhaps it was unrealistic to think that our own training—based on Asian models of practice and pedagogy—could actually have prepared us fully for the work we were now doing. On reflection, our residential training at Zen Center and Tassajara were not really representative of the many ways that Zen priests in Japan receive training. First of all, every Japanese person is reared and nurtured in a society and family that is deeply infused with Buddhist imagery, attitudes, and values. In that way the training of a priest-to-be in Japan—particularly in the realm of feelings and emotions—begins at birth. Second, the monastic training of Japanese Zen priests is not the whole of it. Most of them also continue a long apprenticeship with their primary teacher, assisting in the care of the home temple and performing the myriad tasks of a temple priest. And last, most Japanese Zen priests attend a Buddhist university, and receive an academic degree.

In the light of all this, why should we have assumed that we had received the whole package? Suzuki Roshi only had time during his twelve years in America to give us the essentials of Zen practice; the rest, as he exhorted, was up to us.

THE BIRTH OF SPOT

These very discussions became the next step in our teacher training, and the next chapter in Suzuki Roshi's invitation to "establish an American Zen way of life." We also recognized our dialogue as having a more compelling and immediate purpose—training the next generation of priests and teachers. Not only were we training lay practitioners, but many of us were already preparing to ordain our own priest disciples, who would take vows to make Buddhist practice the center of their lives. What were we going to teach them about keeping these vows in the midst of family and work? How were we going to train them to transfer their settled mind from the silence of the meditation hall to the bustle of life in the world? Here was a chance to figure that out together.

Until these discussions, we had not given a whole lot of thought to disciple training, except to assume that it would be much like our own. But in most cases that was not really practical. We had done our residential training while relatively young and unencumbered in the rebellious and seeking cauldron of the '60s. In contrast, our own students were older—with partners, families, professions or careers, and the economic situation they faced was nothing like the abundance many of us had enjoyed fifty years ago. Long residential training at a Buddhist monastery like Tassajara was impractical for them. In most cases, their aspiration was to be like us, out in the world as hospice workers and chaplains, meditation teachers and sangha leaders, while still maintaining the ability to support their families and nurture their relationships. They needed focused and comprehensive preparation aimed at helping them teach Buddhism without the enhancements of Zen centers, altars, priest's robes, and residential schedules. In short, they needed to know how do the work of a Buddhist priest without depending on the trappings of formal practice.

From these peer group meetings, the S.P.O.T. training program was born in 2007, as a three-year program of residential training weekends. S.P.O.T. originally stood for Shogaku Priest Ongoing Training (Shogaku is one of Suzuki Roshi's Buddhist names), although today not everyone in the SPOT program are priests, and the term "SPOT" has come to stand on its own as the program title. By the time we began in Fall 2007, our program had six faculty and thirty trainees. At our first SPOT meeting in 2007, one of the trainees, recently ordained, began to tell of his new life as a priest. "As soon as people found out I was a priest, they began to share all their troubles with me. They began to ask me all sorts of questions. They poured their hearts out to me. I was overwhelmed. I didn't know what to say." Recounting his exposure and bewilderment in the company of his peers, he began to cry. We were all moved by his story, and we found it sobering to realize what we had all taken on. That emotional moment was, in a way, the birth cry of the baby SPOT. Now, as we write in 2011, SPOT has graduated thirty trainees and has started a second three-year program. Today most trainees are still priests or priests-to-be, but some are lay teachers.

ADDRESSING MISUNDERSTANDINGS AND CHALLENGES

Early on in our curriculum planning, SPOT faculty honed in on three common distortions of Zen practice in America: idealization of the exotic, imitation of Asian models, and repression of emotions. While some of these distortions may apply equally to other Buddhist traditions evolving in the West, we were keenly aware of how we had begun to idealize Japanese culture as superior, and to even imitate the understated way that Suzuki Roshi expressed himself as if this is what it meant to be "a Zen person."

"Idealization of the exotic" means the assumption that Asian teachers are naturally spiritually superior to us and that their mere otherness makes them wiser. In fact, Zen practitioners in America often have considerably more experience of meditation than Zen priests in Japan. Suzuki Roshi did not encourage our idealized notions of Japan, or even of him. Once when asked what honorific title we should call him after his death, he responded forcefully, "No! It is not a question of what I should be called, but what *you* should be called. You are the ones! Give me five or ten more years and you will be strong teachers yourselves!" Sadly, he made this remark only a year before his death.

In the last few decades we have learned—sometimes painfully—that Asian teachers come in all shapes, sizes, and levels of realization, just like human beings everywhere. Our idealized sense of their superiority may be partly due to our own lack of confidence and partly to a need for an idealized parent or authority figure in whom we can invest our trust. The best Asian teachers, like Suzuki Roshi, avoided taking on our unrealistic projections. He kept insisting on his own ordinariness. Actually, we try to model this role for our students; while we have some authority in teaching how to practice Zen, we don't know everything. And while the teacher-student relationship is important, the student must ultimately rely on his/her own relationship to the Dharma. As Dharma teachers, we are only a temporary but necessary bridge. We want our students to begin to learn to express their own Dharma.

"Imitation of Asian models" can be found frequently at Zen and other Buddhist practice centers. The robes, the rituals, the special way people move and hold their bodies—even the way they talk—can often convey a distorted picture of the essence of practice and of what really matters. We must remind ourselves that Buddhism and Zen are not just Japanese, Chinese, or Indian, for example, but universally human pursuits to relieve suffering. Of course, we need to honor the forms and rituals of our tradition, which have deep practice meaning. But we must stop believing that simply imitating the Asian way will automatically produce deep understanding. The essence of Buddhist practice will not come through imitating Asians but by finding our own way and truly becoming our Western selves.

"Repression of the emotions" means that Western practitioners can sometimes use the meditation experience to override their own emotional perceptions and needs. Meditation and practice can be used to calm turbulent emotions, but it can also be used to repress negative emotions and unwanted cravings. While we are taught not to cling to experience, we need explicit instruction in how *not* to avert unpleasant thoughts, sensations, and impulses. While we need peace and quiet to settle the mind, this settled concentration needs to be applied to studying difficult feelings and relationships. Too often, meditators believe that with enough meditation their problems should disappear. Instead we need more explicit teaching on working with emotions. In the absence of familiar interpersonal cues, the environment of the meditation hall—no eye contact, no talking, a constant effort to remain focused on our own inner state—can be used to create a sense of emotional disconnection. This can lead to repressed emotions in meditation and elsewhere in practice. The actual process of Buddhist meditation is the opposite of repression; true meditation is totally exposed, completely in touch with the arising moment and connected to the here and now. Indeed, we often joke that there should be a warning label attached to Buddhist practice: "Living and practicing in a Buddhist community could be harmful to your emotional health if improperly used. Avoid repression and mind-numbing."

THE SPOT METHODOLOGY

In explaining all of this to our trainees, we found it helpful to speak of three levels of training—personal, interpersonal, and transpersonal. Meditation experience opens us to the transpersonal core of Buddhism— the realization of the empty nature of our ego-selves and all phenomena. But the personal and interpersonal realm of relationships, afflictive emotions, group dynamics, projection, and idealization that arise in the authority role of priest, sangha leader, or teacher cannot be ignored. Belonging to a spiritual community, we cannot bypass or skip over our reactivity, the pain that arises in sangha relationships, and our longing for the teacher's approval. In other words, we have to reach the stage of a mature adult in the personal and interpersonal realm before we can fully internalize and integrate the transpersonal level of emptiness-awareness realization.

We took heart in the similar efforts being made at Spirit Rock in the Insight Meditation community. Jack Kornfield, Spirit Rock's founder, has pioneered a teacher training program that in the last twenty years has produced over a hundred vipassana teachers and practice leaders. Once, when asked what kind of people his training program was designed to produce, Jack answered, "Mature adults!" He meant "mature" in all senses of the word—emotionally, psychologically, and socially as well as spiritually. Author John Welwood has coined the term "spiritual bypassing" to describe the way meditators try to achieve spiritual maturity while ignoring, or "bypassing," their personal and emotional problems, because like all suffering beings, they want to leave the pain behind and get to the good part.

Welwood and Kornfield are saying much the same thing. Real spiritual maturity cannot happen on the superhighway of spiritual bypassing. Rather, it must wend its way through all the local roads of emotion and ego, transforming each obstacle as it goes. We cannot skip pain or conflict by spiritual workarounds that bump us to a higher plane while repressing or bypassing our human condition. We must instead use our carefully honed attention to honestly encounter our vulnerability and suffering, one breath at a time. Our liberation is grounded in accepting our suffering and remaining connected to it. We need to tenderly hold the suffering in clear awareness, a skill developed on the cushion, while we engage in the activities of our lives.

So we designed the curriculum of the SPOT training to address Westerners' tendencies to try to escape suffering by wrapping themselves in the exotic, imitating their naïve impressions of the Asian way, or repressing feelings through spiritual bypassing. Our curriculum and training methodologies continued to evolve as we completed the first three-year program and began the second course. Basically, rather than just sitting silently, we have designed exercises that gradually challenge the students' emotional reactivity in real time, and then we talk about how their reactivity might have tricked them—then we do some more meditation.

THE SPOT CURRICULUM: WHERE EAST MEETS WEST

Rather than refine the core skills of meditation and ritual (which trainees already study with their own teacher and within their sangha or residential community), SPOT focuses on the trainable and measurable skills that a Zen priest or teacher needs to minister to his/her group—the skills Western seminaries usually term "pastoral." These skills include: providing spiritual counseling in one-to-one situations; learning to give a Dharma talk or sermon that teaches laypeople the benefits of Zen practice in everyday life; and group leadership skills that enable priests or teachers-in-training to guide their sangha or group to become a cohesive whole. We use the SPOT group and its emotional challenges as the "test" sangha, so students can experience how to develop a cohesive group and how to navigate the inevitable emotional bumps in the life of a practice community. In addition, we include knowing how to prepare and lead effective Zen rituals and offer spiritual solace in times of human need, how to take care of our own emotional and physical needs in intimate relationships, and to share and teach those self-care skills to sangha members. This is particularly effective when we have the opportunity to face the SPOT community's losses as they arise. We are not just studying the suffering in the abstract, but we are living and practicing with the real thing.

The most basic skill of all is how to talk and listen to another human being; during SPOT training this is practiced in dyads to create the actual experience of the intimacy and tenderness that arises between two people. There is a saying in Zen: "You cannot eat a painted rice cake." To fully appreciate the vulnerability of being with another human being, balancing wisdom and compassion, we need to actually be present in the doing of it. The SPOT faculty aims to model this willingness to be present through frank discussions and interactions with each other—much of which is shared openly with trainees.

In teaching how to prepare and deliver a Dharma talk, we emphasize the importance of knowing the needs of an audience in a variety of settings, including prisons, hospitals, schools, and retreats for beginners—in other words, how to match a talk to the needs of an audience, and how to rely on one's own unique experience of practice as the basis for a talk.

Zen master Yunmen was once asked: "What is the teaching of the Buddha's entire lifetime?"

Yunmen answered "An appropriate response."

The Buddha himself always tried to offer the best medicine to his followers, discerning what was needed in each particular moment. We teach that effective Zen talks do not need to be inscrutable, clever, or full of Zen-speak. Zen talks most of all need to be helpful. Each SPOT teacher goes into some detail about how he/she prepares for a talk, and each trainee is required to give his/her own talk. Trainee Dharma talks are followed by audience participation and then by teacher feedback. It is a powerful experience for each trainee to hear feedback from his or her peers and then from each faculty member. Style, organization, delivery, and Dharma relevance are all grist for the mill in the feedback process, but most important is whether the student came across authentically teaching from his/her own understanding and life.

Perhaps the most complex task SPOT addresses is understanding the interpersonal, psychological, and spiritual aspects of the priest's role. We especially concentrate on issues of power, transference, projection, idealization, and conflict. Suzuki Roshi taught that sangha in and of itself is the full expression of Buddha nature, and in working with our own sanghas, we have found this to be so. Within the intimacy of sangha, our understanding or lack of it is fully exposed. Sangha relationships have the potential to reveal to us what we have aimed for, what the results have actually been, and everything in between. We can get caught up in our self-centered dream even as we struggle to articulate the Buddha Way. We note our preferences and aversions and trace them back to self-centeredness. We confront what we are afraid of, and what we are attached to. All of these things are clearly revealed in the healthy functioning of sangha. Our relationships in our sanghas may reveal our tendencies and habits so we can address old patterns from family of origin. When we belong to a group, our core issues surface. In our SPOT trainings, we bring this understanding of group dynamics into the center of the training and work on it explicitly.

For example, the lead-up to the graduation ritual of the SPOT 2007 class brought into focus our need to examine attachment and fear as a basis for our teaching and practice. In the last SPOT weekend before graduation, the faculty asked the trainees to design their own graduation ceremony, and as part of that process, challenged the students to select from their number a valedictorian to speak on behalf of the group. The faculty did this knowing full well that the Zen students had become bonded as a cohesive group, but the shadow of competition had not yet been exposed. This challenge, not unexpectedly, gave rise to significant conflict and disturbance among the trainees. The notion of a singular spokesperson—even one selected by the group—struck some trainees as somehow contrary to the "spirit" of SPOT. Of course each one secretly wanted to be the best, to be selected, but some of the students could not face their own desire to exceed their "beloved" peers. Facing competitiveness and fear of failure are a hallmark of the mature adult, and we did not wish to graduate students without encouraging them to face their own insecurity. Some students understood the exercise and found it to be the most fun of the whole three-year program. Others secretly campaigned for insurrection. The weekend was marked by controversy about the challenge, and about the selection process—should it be by majority vote, consensus, lot, or some combination? In the end the group decided to select not one but three valedictorians, thus defying the faculty's actual request. Issues of power, status, hierarchy, and competition all rose up and roiled the group. From the faculty's point of view, the valedictorian exercise ended up being one of the deepest trainings and the kind of difficulty that actual teachers would face in actual practice communities.

SPOT training is not a substitute for the one-on-one relationship of teacher and disciple. All participants must have their teacher's permission to join, and that relationship is honored. It is also not a replacement for monastic experience; trainees who can manage a training period are encouraged do so. Instead, our intention is to supplement and support those traditional training methods with new ones that embody Suzuki Roshi's vision for our practice in our own Western style.

PUTTING IT ALL TOGETHER:
A TYPICAL DAY OF SPOT TRAINING

During a recent day-long SPOT training, our theme was working with conflict in the sangha. Trainees had previously read a lecture by Suzuki Roshi in which he portrayed the three treasures of Buddha, Dharma, and Sangha as different aspects of one truth. Sangha, he said, was not just a group of people practicing together, it was itself an expression of ultimate reality—as much as zazen, sutras, and rituals. The thrust of the day's work was to connect our Western understanding of the power of group dynamics with this teaching of Suzuki Roshi's.

While Buddhism doesn't explicitly describe how groups work, Western specialists in group dynamics do. We believe that understanding group dynamics in Western terms is essential for sangha leaders so we created an exercise to allow trainees to feel the pull of the group in the context of conflict.

We constituted groups of six or seven trainees as a "practice committee" of a fictitious sangha. The committee's job was to deal with the following conflict: Most members of the sangha, including its teacher, wanted to start formal chanting practice (e.g. the Heart Sutra), but one member (who claimed to represent a constituency in the sangha) felt that chanting was too sectarian and would exclude potential new sangha members. The practice committee was to take up this issue and deal with it however they could.

Each trainee received a preassigned role; in most cases the role was secret. One was to be the dissenter, the member most resistant to the chanting idea. Another was to be someone who personally disliked the dissenter yet agreed with the dissenter's position about chanting. Another was to be someone who personally *liked* the dissenter but disagreed with the dissenter's position. One trainee was to play the public role of sangha president and meeting facilitator. A SPOT faculty member played the role of sangha teacher—though he/she was not to be involved in resolving the conflict. If the group members were faithful to their roles, it would be difficult to resolve the conflict without hurt feelings. The trainees' task was to concentrate mostly on what their feelings and body sensations were in the midst of conflict, rather than to resolve it.

Groups alternated between time "in role," acting out the conflict, and time "out of role," where they could reflect on their experience. In role, people got upset at each other, offended each other, and became impatient with one another. Out of role, people expressed surprise at how much their nervous systems had become engaged and reactive, even though the situation was "pretend." In the plenary session that followed, we discussed this at length. What is real, what is pretend?

The poet John Ashbery entitled one of his books, "Was that a real poem or did you just make it up?" Is our personality a real identity or is it just another role? Is there a difference? What is the difference? What is the relationship to that question and that experience to the core teaching of the Buddha about *anatman*—no abiding, continuously existing self? Who are we really? Who is the other person really? What is our role and responsibility as vow-takers and priest professionals to enact and express the Dharma in each circumstance? It is one thing to read Buddhist scripture on the topic of no fixed self; it's quite another to experience it in such a potent role-playing exercise. Our purpose in constructing the exercise was to make a vivid connection between the Buddhist teaching of no fixed self and our actual experience in the moment—in our emotions, in our bodies.

We believe that coming together as SPOT, we are on the way to embodying Suzuki Roshi's vision for Zen in America. But it is not just for Suzuki Roshi that we fulfill this vision—his vision is in fact what the Buddha had in mind for his teaching. Suzuki Roshi insisted we were not the Zen school, but just people who were following the Buddha's Way. The Buddha encouraged practitioners not to cling to his words, but to translate his teachings into their own native language, to illuminate their own lives. We need to remember this as our primary practice and not get caught in just following a formula or a recipe. Understanding ourselves intimately, we must become familiar with all of the ingredients and the intricacies of our specific kitchen, and then we must cook from our whole heart.

Beyond the Color Line:

CULTIVATING FEARLESSNESS IN CONTEMPLATIVE CARE

Cheryl Giles

M Y SEVENTY-FIVE-YEAR-OLD MOTHER lay dying in a Catholic hospital from complications arising from diabetes. My mother is black and working class, and she lived in an urban neighborhood. Throughout her life, my mother endured long bouts of debilitating depression related to untreated childhood sexual trauma, punctuated by good times that were too few and far between. She celebrated brief periods of joy—the birth of her grandchildren, graduations, weddings, and birthdays. But she spent most of her life hiding in the recesses of her mind—a tiny closet with a dim light—too fearful to come out.

There in the Catholic hospital, my mother tearfully apologized to me for not being a good enough mother. She reminded me yet again how much she had always loved me, something she never gave me reason to doubt, and assured me she would be fine now. Her words pierced my heart.

Somehow, I thought I was caring for my mother while she was dying, but she was caring for me. By accepting her suffering and gently guiding me to see her dying as another part of life, she was taking care of me. She

Cheryl A. Giles, PsyD, is a licensed clinical psychologist and the Francis Greenwood Peabody Professor of the Practice in Pastoral Care and Counseling at Harvard Divinity School. Professor Giles has extensive experience in the treatment of children, adolescents, and families with significant mental illness, high-risk behaviors, and traumatic stress. Her primary research interests are identifying the role of risk and resilience in developing healthy adolescents, health care disparities in African Americans, and contemplative care for the dying. She is a core faculty member of the Buddhist Ministry Program at Harvard Divinity School and a practitioner of Tibetan Buddhism.

was showing me how to go on without her and that she was not afraid of dying. It was a profound time.

On the other hand, I remember feeling alone and at sea with this experience. I longed for a "compassionate other" to sit with my mother and me—someone to help me process this deeply painful, gradual loss of the woman who gave me life and taught me to care about others, even while debilitated by her crippling depression. The hospital chaplain was a frequent visitor to many of the patients on the floor, but even though my mother was dying, he never found enough time to visit with my mother and me.

My mother was raised a devout Christian who long ago abandoned practicing any religious tradition, though her faith in God was strong. Days passed with no sign of the chaplain, not even a passing glance.

As my mother's vital organs began to fail and her body filled up with fluid, the doctor in charge recommended surgery to control the bleeding. Since every contact with a patient in a teaching hospital is an opportunity to learn, the doctor made a reasonable case for this procedure to his eager group of residents. But surely surgery on my dying mother would not save her and could not be reasonable. The doctor and I knew she was at the end of her life and even ready to let go. I wondered, did the fact that she was black, working class, and suffering from depression influence his standard of care? I cannot help wondering if having a "compassionate other" at my side, an understanding chaplain, for instance, would have made a difference.

Spiritual care practices are important to the decision-making and health of patients and their families by creating a space for them to express their thoughts and feelings about the pain and suffering they experience. Many studies now indicate that spiritual support is critical to our institutions. In one study, patients and their families reported they were more satisfied when a chaplain met with them. MJ Balboni and his colleagues reported in a recent article "It Depends: Viewpoints of Patients, Physicians, and Nurses on Patient-Practitioner Prayer in the setting of Advanced Cancer," which appeared in the *Journal of Symptom and Pain Management*, that most patients and practitioners view prayer between patient and practitioners "in some specific settings at least occasionally appropriate." And yet despite evidence supporting the need, most hospitals do not have enough spiritual support.

Even with all my training as a psychologist, one of the most difficult challenges of my life was being present to my mother while she was dying, and at the same time, witnessing the insidious racism that is so endemic to many of our institutions. While I wanted to simply be present to my mother during this profound rite of passage from living to dying—to focus on this loss—I was forced to cope with the additional pain of a doctor who saw my mother as a teaching opportunity and a chaplain who didn't see her at all. It was not difficult to recognize that she would have received better care if she was white and lived on the other side of the city.

After my mother died, the feeling of emptiness I struggled with left holes in my heart that refused to heal. As a black lesbian, I was trying to keep my life "on point" in the face of racism and homophobia. But the experience of my mother's death left me shaken and inconsolable. When my father died five years later, my depression and sense of loss deepened. I felt orphaned and bereft, with no grounding. Death shattered the reality I had created in my mind, believing I was content living my countercultural life and pursuing my own dreams, far removed by education and geography from the working-class neighborhood and racism I grew up with. The death of my parents caught me in an undertow, and I suddenly lacked the emotional resources and resiliency I had always taken for granted.

As a disaffected Catholic, I no longer believed in the theology that informed my faith for more than thirty years: that by being compassionate and loving to others, like Jesus, we are promised eternal life in heaven with God, free from suffering. Seeing me unhinged, a few close friends reached out to me and encouraged me to go on retreat, to "sit" with my anger, fear, and deep sadness. I desperately wanted to be free of suffering, so I followed their advice to attend a seven-day silent retreat at Insight Meditation Center in Barre, Massachusetts. That was my introduction to Buddhism.

WESTERN BUDDHISM

Our roles as caregivers do not always follow strict rules of engagement. What happens when patients, families, or even colleagues are different from us? How do we peel back the layers of race, culture, and social class that can cause our compassionate care to miss the mark, no matter how pure our intentions? What if the patient, whose race, culture, or social class is different from our own, perceives our compassionate effort as invasive or inauthentic?

The rapid spread of Western Buddhism has been an exciting development, but efforts to adapt Buddhist practice to Western culture have largely overlooked some of the most challenging issues. As more people of color practice Buddhism, one of the most significant among these issues is the importance of paying attention to race and diversity.

Several years ago, Hilda Gutiérrez Baldoquín, a Soto Zen priest and activist, published a provocative collection, *Dharma, Color, and Culture: New Voices in Western Buddhism*, about the dramatic impact of Buddhism in the US and the ensuing racial and cultural challenges that have developed:

> When we speak of Buddhism in the United States, we are speaking of a cultural movement that has brought to this continent ancient Indian, East and Southeast Asian, and Tibetan spiritual teachings and practices. For the first time in history, these teachings have arrived in a land that is racially heterogeneous. At the same time, they are taking root in a society that was founded by a white majority, on the unwholesome seeds of colonialism, genocide and slavery. In this meeting, the values of community, interdependence, and collaboration come face-to-face with the values of the pursuit of individualism, self-interest and competition. Deep bow meets handshake.

Gutiérrez Baldoquín tells us these "unwholesome seeds of colonialism, genocide and slavery" are rooted in our history, and they have become part of our identity as Americans, even though we'd rather not remember. To remember is to struggle with accepting blame and feeling a responsibility to do something to unburden ourselves of the guilt we feel.

We need to recognize that as the sangha meets with a teaching that professes equal access to enlightenment, it still wrestles with the fruits of "unwholesome seeds," a continuing legacy of power and oppression that infects our lives. It would be nice to think that we preclude power and oppression from entering our own Buddhist centers. But experience shows us that prejudices, discrimination, and racism held by the wider society does influence our own Buddhist communities, even while our members have the best intentions. Sangha is, after all, made up of individuals.

One of the challenges to American Buddhism is to acknowledge and bear witness that racism is real and dangerous, like the three poisons (grasping, hatred, and ignorance)—a toxin that creates suffering. Despite the long and sorrowful history of racism in the US, many of us would rather avoid dealing with it than be present to the ugliness that taints our capacity to be compassionate and caring. We have conditioned ourselves to deny the existence of racism, perhaps because when we experience it, fear overwhelms us—fear of our own racism and guilt, fear of our inadequacy to address it in others, and even fear of the offender.

We become hollow in the face of suffering and injustice, not realizing that through our silence, we stand with the offender. Rather than practicing being present with our fear, we react to what we are experiencing, working to free ourselves by whatever means necessary from what we imagine to be unbearable. In the end, our avoidance is strengthened by our inability to deal with our fear. But we simply do not want to be reminded.

The denial of racism is a major obstacle to cultivating compassion and reinforces our conditioned state of fear. It is an enormous psychological and spiritual burden to live a distracted life, caught up in our thoughts and feelings. By not choosing to see and acknowledge what we experience, we are choosing to live with blinders in a cozy conditioned state of ignorance. Gutiérrez Baldoquín's reflections urge us to recognize that the values that spring from the "unwholesome seeds" work to keep them rooted in place and foreclose on the opportunity for racial diversity and the richness of Buddhist practice. We can acknowledge the terrible suffering that comes from oppression and work to end it through our practice of cultivating a fully inclusive compassion and the diligent application of that practice to our work as caregivers.

LEARNING TO CULTIVATE
A FULLY INCLUSIVE COMPASSION

Pema Chodron, an American Buddhist nun and Dharma teacher in the lineage of Chogyam Trungpa, encourages us to work with strong emotions to cultivate compassion for ourselves and others. In *The Fearless Heart: The Practice of Living with Courage and Compassion*, Chodron reminds us that we all have a limitless capacity to be open and to love free of prejudice and bias, but we are only able to do this in small doses. Most of the time, we are stuck with holding on to strong emotions that distance us from ourselves, others, and the world around us. Our deepest longing is to be connected and free of the emotions that form barriers and limit our ability to be openhearted:

> Fear is the fundamental emotion. Fear manifest as prejudice. Fear manifest as aversion. Fear manifest as craving and addiction. We're afraid of something and therefore it starts to blossom in these various strong emotions of all kinds. Fear is the underlying thing. Fear obscures this open, clear quality of life. In order to free ourselves from being caught up in strong emotions, we need to work with our fear.

Chodron recalls the story of Machig Lapdronma, a twelfth-century Tibetan woman, who told her teacher Phadampa Sangye that after seeing so much suffering, she wanted to know how to wake up to help others and herself be free of suffering. In response to this request, Phadampa Sangye gave Machig instructions to work with five slogans to cultivate fearlessness:

- ▸ Reveal your hidden faults.
- ▸ Approach what you find repulsive.
- ▸ Help those you think you cannot help.
- ▸ Anything that you are attached to, give that away or let it go.
- ▸ Go to the places that scare you.

Let us explore these powerful teachings that can help us shift from living with fear to living with an open heart, beginning with our own

Buddhist practice and with our work as caregivers. Starting from a place of emotional distress (in this case, fear) should never be an obstacle to meditation. Adopting these teachings in our practice, both on and off the cushion, teaches us the skill of being present to our feelings about ourselves and to the compassion we feel for others. This is a doorway to enlightenment. Our challenge is to work with the ways that we close down and limit our capacity to cultivate compassion.

Reveal your hidden faults. To reveal our hidden faults is to uncover them, to bring them to light. That starts with noticing. When we perceive difference as negative, quite possibly we are unconsciously judging others for being different, and that can lead to shame. We may react to internal feelings that others who are not like us are not worthy of our compassion. Then we may feel guilty and ashamed of such thinking. After that, we decide we are unworthy for having these negative thoughts. When we become entrenched in this battle of pride, guilt, shame, and negativity, our world narrows and we get so distracted by the noise, we become mired in pettiness, leaving no room for compassion. Certainly, we are aware of the hidden faults of others—friends, neighbors, colleagues, and family. We see so clearly their blind spots, their ignorance and their messiness. We tolerate their hidden faults, and we try to accept them just as they are. But we cannot learn to cultivate compassion for others until we practice it on ourselves. By acknowledging our prejudice and racism and facing our fear of them with compassion, we learn to accept our own humanity. This means that we learn to work with the discomfort of the feelings that arise and carefully observe how they work on us. If we can tap into the power of this understanding we can open up and learn, heal, and grow from our experience rather than habitually react from conditioning.

Our memory of the stories and narratives that shape our lives is constantly changing. Beyond the memory of my grief when my mother was dying, it is surprising that I have no memory of why I did not reach out to the chaplain instead of waiting passively for him to come to us. Was he really ignoring us, or was he overwhelmed with more patients and families than he could attend? Maybe a dying child was consuming his efforts. Perhaps my own anger, resentment, or frustration became an obstacle to making the chaplain's acquaintance or even asking a nurse or doctor to send him to us. Perhaps my assumption of racism precluded me from looking at other possibilities. Or perhaps not. The point is that if I had been fully present to my experience and to the situation around me, I may have seen an opportunity to be open rather than shutting down.

Approach what you find repulsive. More than a hundred years ago, nearly forty years after the Civil War, W.E.B. Du Bois, an African American scholar and social activist, wrote *The Soul of Black Folks* to call attention to the heavy toll of slavery on blacks in America. In this treatise he recounts his deep concern for their well-being:

> Herein lie buried many things which if read with patience may show the strange meaning of being black here in the dawning of the twentieth century. This meaning is not without interest to you, gentle reader; for the problem of the twentieth century is the problem of the color-line.

These reflections were prescient comments on the enduring legacy of race in America. Today, the "folks" who find themselves behind the "color line" not only are black, but brown, yellow, red, gay, poor, very young and very old, and people with disabilities. When we participate in structural violence, e.g., systemic discrimination based on age, race, class, sexual difference, and ability, whether or not we are aware of it, our actions and attitudes prevent us from fully engaging and cultivating compassion. Can we engage with our practice to awaken and stay awake to the ways in which we foster racism by refusing to see what is in our midst? Or are we too repulsed by the notion of ourselves as racist and what we must do to change ourselves and, just as important, be willing to confront racism in others?

There are numerous examples of how race plays a major factor in how we relate to one another. Many difficult interactions exacerbated by racism, like my mother's death, are personal and remain private. Others involve public figures or large segments of the population and grab our attention when they become sound bites for the evening news.

Racist reactions in ourselves and in others deprive patients and their families of the fair and just treatment afforded to those who look and act like us. Our capacity for compassion suffers, and the care we give as a result is simply not good enough. Unless we remain present to our experience, refusing to let fear distract us from confronting our biases, we miss the most wonderful opportunities to be transparent and compassionate in our caregiving. Worse, we maintain the illusions that allow us to perpetuate racism, even when we do so unknowingly.

Help those you think you cannot help. When we give compassionate care, willingly and without reservation, we are helping, and the simple act of reaching out to another human being in need with kindness and love is a small step closer to healing the world. If a patient and her family do not welcome our best efforts, does this mean we are not helping? We might think so if we take her response personally. Indeed, it may be our own fear of failing that tells us we cannot help the person who rejects us when, in fact, she may be too frightened herself to allow us to connect with her. The Fourteenth Dalai Lama, teaching about compassion said:

> The more we care for the happiness of others, the greater our own sense of well-being becomes. Cultivating a close, warmhearted feeling for others automatically puts the mind at ease. This helps remove whatever fears or insecurities we may have and gives us the strength to cope with any obstacles we encounter. It is the ultimate source of success in life.

The Dalai Lama does not say that we have to make others happy, only that we have to care for the happiness of others, their well-being. When we sincerely try to help others by giving compassionate care, our success does not rest on whether or not we believe we can help. Success comes from the act of caring. We need not trouble ourselves deciding who we can or cannot help.

Our practice is to be of benefit to others and to give compassionate care freely and without judgment. When we question whether we can help someone or not, we get caught up in afflictive emotions that get in the way of compassionate care. We struggle with confronting our vulnerability and brokenness. When we lose touch with ourselves, we become overwhelmed, distant, and fearful. Imagine working with a patient like my mother, who was burdened with physical and emotional issues. This situation presents enormous turbulence for the patient (my mother) and the chaplain. Despite this, by being present in this moment there is an opportunity for the chaplain to establish trust and a deeper connection with the patient. Joan Halifax, a Zen priest and pioneer in the field of end-of-life care, reminds us in her book *Being with Dying: Cultivating Compassion and Fearlessness in the Presence of Death* that our caregiving requires us to have a "strong back, soft front." In this equation, a "strong back" means being in a place of equanimity or holding things in an equal way and a "soft front" means offering compassion. Both are necessary to cultivate compassion.

Anything that you are attached to, give that away or let it go. As the famous song from the Broadway musical South Pacific went, "You've got to be taught to hate and fear . . . You've got to be carefully taught." It was a song about learning "who to hate and who to love" and passing racism from generation to generation. We become attached to things. We also become attached to feelings, conceptions, and ideas. For many of us, conditioning to racism is so inbred, we have become attached to it. And yet, how many people who harbor racist feelings or biases against others, whether overt or covert, can articulate why they hold those biases? How many can justify their feelings, beyond citing stereotypes? And caregivers, in particular, are not supposed to have those biases. After all, aren't caregivers gentle, loving, and kind to everyone and anyone who needs them? Isn't it that kindness that motivates them to become caregivers and chaplains in the first place? How scary, then, to accept that we feel the way we do because of what we were taught to believe and because so often we are surrounded by others whose behaviors perpetuate and affirm those biases. Consider this: No one, no child, is born racist. They have to be "carefully taught." We do not have to accept that attachment. We can step across the color line.

Implicitly racist conditioning is a part of discontinuous arising of thought patterns that we picked up through growing up in this culture. As children, we did not choose to take this on. We merely absorbed from the environment, from our parents, peers, media, nursery rhymes, language, stereotypes, stories. This conditioning is how the white cultural ego defends itself against difference. Racism is not necessarily about believing in the stereotypes. It is being steeped in the cultural ego's fear of other, without even being aware how deeply it is in us.

Go to the places that scare you. For many of us, the challenge is not so much whether we go to places that scare us, but how we get there. When Machig Lapdronma received her instructions from Phadampa Sangye about how to live her life to benefit others, she had the willingness to train to see her blind spots, ignorance, and fears. Every day presents us with many opportunities to practice. But often we get trapped in our past by reacting in old, familiar ways. We latch on to the stories and judgments that we tell ourselves to find comfort, but in the end we find ourselves twisting in habitual patterns. Pema Chodron offers us insight into the practice of fearlessness:

> Through continual practice we find out how to cross over the boundary between stuckness and waking up. It depends on our willingness to experience directly feelings we've been avoiding for many years. This willingness to stay open to what scares us weakens our habits of avoidance. It's the way that ego clinging becomes ventilated and begins to fade. The Buddha taught us that suffering is the result of grasping and fixation. If we can sit with our uneasiness, discomfort, and uncertainty, rather than relying on tired old misconceptions that sustained us in the past, we can train to be open and relax in spaciousness. This is our natural state. But do we have the willingness? The story of Machig Lapdronma serves as a powerful example of what we can do if we make a commitment to our practice. Like many of us, she became weary being surrounded by suffering and could not see how to end it.

By training with her teacher, Machig was able to gain insight about the need to do her own work, before trying to help others. In this case, one of the critical challenges to American Buddhism is to encourage Dharma teachers to focus on antiracism work in their sanghas: By speaking out in Dharma teachings about the root causes of racism, encouraging sangha members to deal with strong emotions that come up in their practice, and providing space in the sangha to reflect on racism we can begin to alleviate suffering and oppression. Our practice becomes one of cultivating fearlessness in all that we do. We bring this attitude to our meditation, work, and interaction with others.

CONCLUSION

When I set out to write this chapter, my goal was to expose the ways in which we withhold compassion in caregiving out of fear, in particular, racism—arising from our fear of difference. Paying attention to our own fears can help us feel compassion for others.

My dear friend and mentor, Nancy Richardson, is a southern white woman, who for many years conducted antiracism workshops in her ministry and as professor at Harvard Divinity School. One of Nancy's most important teachings was that all white people are racist. The most one can ever hope to be is "antiracist racist." None of us will ever be perfect, nor can we expect to live without fear. But we can aspire to be open to the unfolding present moment. We can help in this small way to make a real impact: we can vow to practice fearlessness every day for ourselves and others to help alleviate suffering. We can stay true to a strong intention while opening to our own vulnerability and that of others: strong back, soft front.

PART II

Serving the Sick:
The Arts of Hospital Chaplaincy

The Four Noble Truths
as a Framework for Contemplative Care

Trudi Jinpu Hirsch

Do not close your eyes before suffering—find ways to be with those who are suffering by all means, including personal contacts and visits, images, and sounds. By such means, awaken yourself and others to the reality of suffering in the world.—THE BUDDHA

THE RELIGIOUS TRADITION we now call Buddhism evolved out of the Buddha's enlightenment and his realization that each of us is already "perfect and complete, lacking nothing." At the same time he understood that this was not something that could be taught. Each person must realize it for him- or herself. As one of the first people working as a Zen Buddhist chaplain and chaplain supervisor, I needed a way to introduce the Buddhist community to the practice of chaplaincy, which started out as a Judeo-Christian discipline. A little more than twelve years ago I discovered I was only the third Buddhist chaplain certified by the Association of Professional Chaplains (APC) and the first Buddhist supervisor to be certified by the Association for Clinical Pastoral Education (ACPE) in the world.

Rev. Trudi Jinpu Hirsch is an Association for Clinical Pastoral Education (ACPE)–certified chaplain supervisor and an Association of Professional Chaplains (APC)–certified chaplain. Rev. Hirsch is a Zen Buddhist priest with the White Plum Sangha. She trained under Roshi Daido Loori as a monastic at Zen Mountain Monastery for eleven years. Rev. Hirsch has been a faculty member and chaplain supervisor for the New York Zen Center for Contemplative Care, teaching Clinical Pastoral Education (CPE) groups and placing students at Beth Israel and at New York Presbyterian Hospital in New York City. She has worked for the HealthCare Chaplaincy for twelve years as a chaplain and supervisor at various hospitals.

A question I am constantly asked by others is: "Why would a Buddhist be at all interested in taking up chaplaincy, especially since Buddhism doesn't take up the question of whether there is a God?"

What I came to appreciate during my journey through clinical pastoral education (CPE) is that chaplaincy and Buddhism are a beautiful and perfect match. Buddhism abides in impermanence and points to the interconnectedness of all things. Its teachings and practice guide one toward being aware and awake in every moment. One awakens to the realization that there is nothing outside of this very moment. The past has already happened . . . it no longer exists; the future has yet to happen . . . it too doesn't exist. There is only "now," and this "now" is totally alive and filled with all possibility.

The practice of Zen Buddhism asks practitioners to take the path toward becoming a bodhisattva, living their lives imbued with compassion for all beings without exception. It demands that each one of us realize that the separation between oneself and others is an illusion and causes a great deal of suffering in the world. All of these facets of Buddhist thought are meaningful to and actively practiced in chaplaincy. Patients will ask each of us to see them, to hear them, and if possible to step into their suffering so that we might be able to feel them. They endlessly reveal to us how sickness, old age, and death have become a reality in their life. Their illness demands that we let go of our own fears and the places that we cling to that prevent us from embracing the suffering of others. As chaplains we are being given the opportunity to experience intimacy, empathy, and compassion. The cries of these patients touch our hearts and minds directly, and we realize these human voices as none other than our own.

The story of Buddhism begins with Shakyamuni's foray outside the protected walls of his kingdom, where he had been comfortable and removed from the world and its problems. He was shocked to discover "sickness, old age, and death" in the people he made contact with. This "face-to-face" teaching and his insight into the reality of suffering transformed his life. Starting with his first sermon on the Four Noble Truths, the Buddha spent the next forty years expounding on the realization he had experienced. He was referred to in his time as the "great doctor or healer." His healing pointed people to the present moment, and he used whatever means he could to guide students toward this "here and now" of their life.

These Four Noble Truths are:

1. Life is suffering.
2. There is a cause of suffering, and that cause is attachment or clinging.
3. If there is a cause, then there must also exist an end to suffering.
4. The guidelines to end this suffering were presented as the "Eightfold Path" . . . (following a path of "right" mindful thought and conduct).

The Buddha was creative in his pedagogy, and used a medical analogy to explain to his students how they should engage the Four Noble Truths. He likened the dysfunctional aspect of human attachment to a disease, and he likened the Dharma to medicine. With this analogy as a basis, he went on to pair the Four Noble Truths with the following process, defining how a spiritual seeker should engage these truths.

1. Diagnose the disease.

The chaplain or caregiver needs to be awake to whatever presents itself to him/her without needing to fix or to cure or change the patient in any way. The medical "disease" is just a part of the "dis-ease" of suffering. The chaplain will journey where the patient needs to go. This could be the fear of the unknown, the loss of independence, the worries around their diagnosis, the loss of hope or meaning, etc.

2. Identify its cause.

The chaplain or caregiver will be curious and wonder about what this patient might be clinging or attached to, which is producing suffering for him/her. This could be the "why me" question, or feeling abandoned by God or friends, or feeling lost or depressed, or possibly angry at the situation or diagnosis, etc.

3. Determine whether it is curable.

Is the patient able to touch, share, or sit in their suffering and reflect on or explore it, or is denial (clinging to an idea, for instance) or resistance to being present to their thoughts and feelings too difficult in this moment?

4. Outline a course of treatment to cure it.

The Buddha realized the uniqueness of each person and that even the Buddha could do no more than guide each person toward realizing that the answers or "healing cures" rested within each of them. He taught by many methods: story, verbatim, question and answers, as well as through meditation, contemplation, and modeling. He taught about compassion and wisdom, and employed these Four Noble Truths as the foundation of his teachings.

Let's look at these truths in relation to chaplaincy and caregiving.

The First Noble Truth: The Fact of Suffering. This truth states that the problems of life, especially the human experiences of birth, old age, and death, are inevitable. These experiences confront us with our transient nature. The desire to cling to what was or what might one day be has created great suffering. However, there is a difference between pain and suffering. The Buddha taught that pain is a specific response of the mind to the actual physical wound to the body in the present. Suffering, on the other hand, is past- or future-oriented, a response of the heart/mind to an imagined loss (whether it is a physical loss like "losing one's youth," or a mental loss like, "that belongs to me, and I am afraid to lose it"). Looking to a future of inevitable loss, we cling to what we are afraid of losing, and the result is suffering.

This first noble truth reminds me that life is constantly changing and I, too, will become sick, get old, and die. The realization of my own human condition helped open my eyes and heart to the suffering of others, inspired me toward chaplaincy, and continues to motivate me as a supervisor, teaching the art of chaplaincy to those who will come into contact with this first noble truth in their patients. These patients live and fully embody this first truth. Most patients are stripped of all that was once familiar and secure, and the core foundations of their lives are shaken. They become unveiled, raw, and vulnerable. As a matrix for learning this truth, there is no place more powerful, and no teacher more direct, than these patients. Chaplains and caregivers come face to face with this reality, and it holds the potential to deeply affect their life and practice.

The Second Noble Truth: The Cause of Suffering. In his presentation of the second noble truth, the Buddha taught that all suffering has its origins in cravings, also called attachments or desires. We crave and slavishly cling to a variety of things: there is craving for sensual pleasure, craving for existence, and craving for self-annihilation. Our desires also have a cause, and that cause is a basic, fundamental ignorance regarding our world and our place in it. These desires can be great motivating forces as well as great blocks along our path. In psychology, we label these blocks as resistance and then work to resolve them therapeutically. In Buddhism, we honor the resistance and aim to bring the student into greater awareness of it, exploring our part in its creation. CPE allows students to explore what they cling to and why they are attached. We explore whatever stops us from being authentic and we reflect on the layers of conditioning that have obscured our natural perfection and wholeness. In chaplaincy training, we teach students that caregivers can only be empathic with another to the degree that they have accessed all their thoughts and feelings within themselves.

The Third Noble Truth: The Cessation of Suffering. This truth says that there is always the possibility of putting an end to suffering. It teaches that as long as we cling to our attachments, hatred, and delusion, and are bound to the endless cycle of birth and death, we will continue to suffer. The Buddha said that the way to put an end to suffering is to realize our "true nature." To describe this "true nature" I will use the metaphor of the Ocean (God/Divine presence/Absolute). Let's say that the whole universe is a boundless ocean. Each of us can be seen as a distinct and unique wave arising from this ocean. When we take birth as this wave, we at first remember that we are none other than the ocean, and the ocean is us . . . we experience no difference. As we mature, we begin to invest in and believe our own individual waveness to be separate from the great ocean. This awareness of a separate self produces a longing to return, as well as a fear of what one might lose in this process. We feel alone and isolated from that which nourished and gave us birth. The more we believe in our separateness, the more we suffer. If we, just for a moment, can let go and experience or remember our "oceanness," then in that moment we are free to experience all waves as none other than ourselves . . . and ourselves as all beings.

As a Zen practitioner I have used meditation in helping to recognize and experience this "oceanness." Sitting for many years, I began to get a glimpse into the vast oceanness of each one of us. This is called "seeing clearly into your true nature." That nature is described as Shunyata or "emptiness" . . . empty of attachment, hatred and delusion . . . empty of a substantial self (this stateless state of nonbeing is described in the Heart Sutra as having no eye, ear, nose, tongue, body, mind . . . no realm of sight, no realm of consciousness, no beginning and no end). As a Zen student I struggled to awaken to this truth, and to not fall back into my patterns of conditioning, but to "let go" into the limitless possibilities within each moment.

I also strive to help my students develop awareness of their pastoral identities and how this affects others (patients). I aim at guiding them toward paying attention to the feelings and thoughts that are present in each moment, and to help them reflect on where and why they become stuck and experience suffering along their pastoral journey. We work together to step into the shoes of the "other" and reflect on where we separate ourselves or refuse to access certain feelings or thoughts that our patients might have. Buddha defined this as compassion (passion with) and taught us how to live our lives out of this realization.

The Fourth Noble Truth: The Way to End Suffering. This truth defines the Buddhist way of life and contains all the moral and ethical teachings and practices within Buddhism. It attempts to draw up a "how to relieve suffering" workbook, taking the student by the hand, yet allowing the student to lead. Basically, the fourth truth describes how one might live a compassionate life in community with others. It looks at how we separate ourselves from the present and shows us the way to return. It points to "right here, right now," and it shows us how to wake up to our lives, again and again. We learn to be aware, we learn to let go, and we learn to trust our "being-ness" (ministry of presence). This fourth truth puts a great emphasis on living actively and compassionately in the world and how to relate intimately with others.

Life and death appear in each moment; they appear instantly
and naturally, without thought. Every moment contains total reality.
—DOGEN ZENJI

In the hospital, CPE students come face to face with patient after patient.
That "life is suffering" is no longer a simple idea, something to dwell on
during seated meditation, but it is the actual nature of their lives. "There
is a cause of suffering," the second noble truth, takes on a fleshy meaning
as the student explores along with the patient the spiritual suffering that
comes from clinging to life and fearing death. "The cessation of suffering," the third noble truth, is an opportunity for the student to let go
of their separateness and to experience the possibility of being "at-one-
with" or intimate with each patient.

Looking at one's own mortality has always been an essential part of
Buddhist practice. We sit for many years looking directly at the nature of
death and what contemplating mortality brings up in each of us. "The
Path" is the fourth noble truth and was part of the inspiration behind the
creation of the New York Zen Center of Contemplative Care, where I
am on the core teaching team. The cofounders, Koshin Paley Ellison and
Robert Chodo Campbell (who are also included in this volume), and I
have helped to create a community of dedicated practitioners who also
practice as caregivers. The teaching staff are dedicated to be of service
to others and we guide our students toward realizing their authentic
and complete and perfect natures. We are building a community that is
founded upon compassion and service. Most of our students are being
trained in hospitals and within hospices. These students have courageously faced and embraced their patients' suffering and have allowed
these emotional and rich relationships to guide, teach, and transform
their own lives as well.

Clinical Pastoral Education for Buddhists first began around ten years
ago at Beth Israel in New York City when I responded to a need from
the Buddhist community. Students were asking for ways to make their
sitting practice real, and they were excited about having the opportunity
to engage their practice with the patients in the hospital. We explored
meditation, visualization, and relaxation as among the many tools chaplains can offer to particular patients. Students learned to listen with their

whole body and mind and to work with patients trying out ways to use breathing to alleviate pain and distress. We looked at ways to meet the energy level of the patient, expanded on the use of observation and mindfulness (awakening to the room as a whole), and emphasized that students be aware of their own feelings and those of their patients moment to moment. CPE emphasizes the action-reflection-action model of education, which works beautifully with the training that Buddhist students practice on the cushion.

In CPE, students begin to come face to face with suffering as they explore intimacy with their patients. This suffering puts students in touch with the questions of life and death and the impermanence of things. They learn to enlarge their sense of "self" and to understand themselves in relationship to others. As their defenses drop away they become more open to the myriad teachings that present themselves, moment after moment. They begin to see where they draw their boundaries and where they refuse to go. They have the chance to minister to the sick and dying and in so doing, minister to themselves as well. Quite a few students have continued in chaplaincy. Many have returned to their sitting practice with renewed energy and vigor as a result of the work they have done with their patients. I feel very grateful to be able to offer other Buddhist practitioners a way to make their practice come alive, a way to realize the Four Noble Truths as a living, breathing reality.

I would like to close this essay by citing a chant that is recited in the Zen meditation hall at the end of every day. I can remember the first time I heard this chant after a long period of quiet meditation. I was shaken by its haunting and urgent call to life. It asked me to wake up to the miracle of aliveness, right *now*, right *here*, not somewhere else, and not at some other time.

> Let me respectfully remind you
> life and death are of supreme importance
> time swiftly passes by and opportunity is lost
> each of us should strive to awaken. Awaken.
> Take heed . . . do not squander your life.

Buddhist Chaplaincy in a Christian Context:

A PERSONAL JOURNEY

Mark Power

THE DEATH of my Buddhist teacher was the impetus for me entering the profession of pastoral care. As I tended my teacher at the end of his life, the teachings on imperma- nence were palpable, vivid daily reminders of the fragility of life. After his death I felt a strong need to remain connected to that existential hon- esty. I wanted to be able to support others on their end-of-life journeys, integrating my own spiritual training while at the same time making a living. I had no idea what the options were; I hadn't any knowledge of chaplaincy from personal experience, so I explored the suggestions made by contacts in various healthcare settings. During this exploration I heard repeatedly that if I wanted to combine my spiritual intentions with livelihood I would need to attend a Clinical Pastoral Education (CPE) year-long residency. I was fortunate to learn there was a CPE center near my home.

I entered CPE at a Catholic hospital in Oxnard, California, in 1996. During my residency I found that very few of the people I met had any understanding of the Buddhist spiritual tradition. When I spoke about my faith background, my comments elicited a variety of responses; for

---

Mark Power is a board certified chaplain (BCC) and student of the Kagyu and Nyingma schools of Tibetan Buddhism; his primary affiliation is with Dzogchen Ponlop Rinpoche and the Nalandabodhi community. In his chaplaincy career he has worked mainly in end-of-life-care settings and currently works with a pediatric palliative care team at Seattle Children's Hospital. Mark serves the Nalandabodhi community as an administrator and member of the Mitra Council (council of West- ern teachers).

example, some people would refer to rubbing the belly of the "Happy Buddha" often seen in Chinese restaurants, or at times someone would comment " . . . but you don't look Buddhist." So, as a Buddhist chaplain working in interfaith settings, I found it convenient to defer to the common misconception that I am a Protestant minister. This provided an opportunity for building pastoral relationships. In the presence of pervasive misunderstanding and sometimes strong judgment, I often wondered what I was getting myself into. The experience of being regarded as an anomaly or generally misunderstood provided a lot of working material for the CPE residency and resulted in some surprising insights.

Walking into St. John's, the hospital in Oxnard, for my initial interview, I was ill at ease with the Catholic ambiance. In the main lobby were life-sized images of Christ and the Virgin Mary—every wall was decorated with symbols of the tradition. These images stimulated uncomfortable memories of a story my father used to tell of my Irish Catholic grandmother; she grieved that my family would burn in hell because my father married a Protestant. I anticipated that this bias was still prevalent and wondered what kind of reaction my Catholic supervisors would have to a Buddhist with a Protestant background. Not surprisingly, my preconceptions dissolved when I met the directors of the program, two of whom had been Roman Catholic Sisters. Rather than being standoffish about my background they were intrigued, open to what I would bring to the program, and curious about the effect my presence would have on my peer group. I was the first Buddhist that the program had hosted and that many of my peers and patients would meet.

Early on in the training, it became clear to me that while I was preoccupied about the influence these alien surroundings would have on me, I would also need to deal with my own baggage, which took the form of judgments toward the traditions, beliefs, and practices of my peers. If I was going to engage in this program with integrity I would need to open myself to the experience just as my supervisors demonstrated they were willing to do with me. When I had the courage to explore beyond my comfort level, I was met with encouragement, most notably from several Roman Catholic Sisters, some of whom were in the program with me and some of whom were chaplains in the hospital. Instead of finding my grandmother's fears of condemnation realized, I found allies.

The Sisters were sensitive and compassionate advocates whose kindness was a great support to me.

Our connection seemed at least in part due to shared experiences of marginalization. From my side, as a Buddhist chaplain in a Catholic setting, I often felt marginalized by patients and staff who viewed me with suspicion or expressed outright negativity. Some of the Sisters gave voice to feelings of marginalization as invisible members of the Church leadership, only nominally recognized by the male hierarchy. I was impressed with their persistence and skill. The Sisters expressed wise, compassionate leadership through quiet and sometimes mischievous means, and, when there was need for unrestrained advocacy, they were fearless. I learned a lot from them about the power of grace, humor, and humility.

Those who have been through CPE know it to be an arduous process. As a new intern, one is thrust into the role of "pastoring" a clinical unit in the hospital. You are expected to visit room-to-room "ministering" to patients and staff. The presumption of proactive visits was deeply challenging for me. It felt like proselytizing and I detested the notion, never mind being the proselytizer in-person. In practice, walking into hospital rooms uninvited, one quickly learns that the label "chaplain" conjures deep feelings for patients. Sometimes I would be welcomed with reverence and an expectation that my visit would invite an experience of grace, and sometimes I was met with derision and curtly dismissed. In other cases, my visit would inspire fear, "Why is a *chaplain* visiting; what's wrong?" So many feelings and projections arose in response to a single word, "chaplain."

I had a visceral reaction to these experiences; I did not want to be identified as a Christian because it was not who I was and I had spent much of my early life rebelling against Christianity. I did not want to be identified as a Buddhist because it caused confusion for patients, often followed by judgment, which in turn triggered my insecurity. This edge would be a potent point of reflection throughout my chaplaincy; it was for me a provocative koan. Was I willing to let go of my identity as a Buddhist in order to serve others? I wanted to say yes, but that ground became very shaky as I explored further.

The issue of identity was most challenging when families would quiz me about my faith. Patients and families often felt a need to know whether their chaplain was a safe emissary of "The Lord" or if, by contrast, they were in danger of being committed to hell by association with an unsaved soul. I would be peppered with questions like "What church do you belong to?" or "Do you take the Lord Jesus Christ as your personal Savior?" In these encounters I would experience deep internal conflict: Do I hold to my personal integrity by "outing" myself as a Buddhist, knowing that this often left the patient and family struggling with their preconceptions? Or, do I dodge the question and adopt the safe response of being a "nondenominational chaplain," a response which created an ambiguous but benign ground for relationship?

The latter approach at least allowed me to continue in my relationship with the patient. Over time I found this approach more satisfying and pastorally effective. The ambiguity caused by adopting such a generic label had its benefits; there was more opportunity for eye-level conversations in contrast to the highly charged dynamic that was more typical between "pastor" and "patient." When patients and families didn't know what category to put me in they tended to be more relaxed. Unfortunately for me, while this approach addressed one side of the question of identity, it did not address my internal conflict.

Within the pastoral relationship there is the potential for an exchange that allows for spiritual healing; in the current culture, defined mostly by Judeo-Christian beliefs and practices, prayer is the substance of that exchange. One could say that prayer is the currency of ministry. For that reason it was necessary for me to learn the language and etiquette of prayer; not surprisingly this added another layer of challenge to my training. My nontheistic beliefs were threatened and I felt deep resistance to calling on the Lord in prayer; I struggled with this daily.

What I noticed was that when I relaxed, there were times when prayer was effortless and inspired, and at other times, when I was fearful or uptight, my experience felt empty and hypocritical. I would swing back and forth from an effortless connection to painful resistance. This dynamic was persistent enough that I felt the need for some kind of clarification from my Buddhist teachers. In truth, what I wanted was not clarification but permission to stop the practice of prayer on "religious" grounds; I wanted my teachers to confirm my feelings of discomfort as intelligence directing me away from a theistic pitfall and to permit me to discontinue prayer.

When I talked with the masters of my Tibetan Buddhist tradition about this issue I hoped for a pass, "No, you shouldn't pray with Christians, after all you're Buddhist, we don't share their belief in God." However, that was not the response I received. I was surprised by the consistency of the message I received from each of the masters I consulted: "We pray, they (Christians) pray, there's not much difference." Huh? "When you pray to God, imagine Amitabha (the Buddha of Boundless Light) . . ." I wasn't given any support for my resistance.

As the CPE residency progressed, the process facilitated deeper insight into my hesitations about the relationship between Buddhist and Christian traditions. However, an unexpected challenge arose in relationship with my Buddhist community. My sangha friends found it curious and in some cases uncomfortable when I would share my experiences of leading prayer or conducting Christian memorials. Their reactions mirrored those of patients and families; they were incredulous, although for different reasons. A few friends exclaimed in disbelief, "You pray to Jesus?!" They seemed genuinely concerned for my well-being! Their reactions were unexpectedly encouraging: they actually helped me to see how concepts were a distraction from addressing hidden fears. This recognition prompted further exploration into the question of pastoral identity.

Over the years I thought my dilemma would clarify and I would simply exhaust the struggle and leave the uncertainty and the stress behind. That hasn't happened completely, but from the time of those formative CPE experiences to the present, the challenges raised in this livelihood path have consistently encouraged me to look deeper and to meet new discoveries with loving-kindness.

During CPE, the kindness of my supervisors, peers, patients, and patients' families encouraged me to recognize the importance of loving-kindness in my own journey—something that I had previously avoided in my Buddhist practice. I considered the need for loving-kindness an acknowledgment of weakness. It was too threatening to admit to myself I might need to develop self-empathy when there was so much need for compassion in the world. While I have some criticism of aspects of the CPE process, I found the rawness of the interpersonal exploration, which is such a powerful component of the training, to be a persuasive force for spiritual growth.

This growth happened in large part because of a common willingness on the part of my peer group to acknowledge our fears and humanity together. The openness of my peers and willing vulnerability across doctrinal boundaries nourished my own spiritual integrity. I didn't have to pretend to possess wisdom that I did not have. What I needed to do was come to terms with the underlying fears that distanced me from my own vulnerability and its strengths. CPE provided a safe ground on which I could explore these fears with kindness. Ironically, I found that the messy humanity of the CPE process was a catalyst for my Buddhist spirituality rather than a hindrance.

Having practiced as a chaplain for about fifteen years now, I see the path of chaplaincy as a potent one for deepening and strengthening one's Dharma understanding and experience. One of the benefits, surprisingly, is that it takes us quickly beyond the familiar to a place of ambiguity, a helpful though unsettling experience. It's helpful because the uncertainty we encounter in this work is a mirror of that which is often felt by the persons we serve. Entering this experience in the company of another creates opportunities for intimate connection, if we'll allow it. Within this vulnerable space, the qualities of compassion, mindfulness, and loving-kindness are naturally present and nurture spiritual healing.

As Buddhists, the promise of opportunities such as these is often the impetus that draws us to this work. The challenge for the Buddhist chaplain is to develop acceptance of the paradoxical nature of the chaplain's path. One needs to dissolve the barriers made by concepts of good and bad or acceptable and unacceptable spirituality. Then one can do the work of tending to the spiritual needs of a primarily non-Buddhist population—in "their" language and on "their" terms. The question for many of us is how not to lose one's sense of authenticity in this exchange.

One challenge for Buddhist practitioners encountering traditional CPE programs is the lack of insight on the part of CPE supervisors into the Buddhist understanding of selflessness and interdependence, an example being the importance placed on emotional expression in CPE. There is a tendency in CPE to treat feelings/emotions as having a special power to lead a person to a deeper truth and thus to regard them as gateways to healing the "self." CPE and Buddhist psychology would agree that relating to emotions directly and with respect one can better understand how they contribute to both disease and healing processes. Early on, a Buddhist chaplain may feel an inevitable conflict between the Buddhist teaching of no-self and the theistic teaching of the self and emotions as true and lasting. Yet, as mature Buddhist practitioners enter the CPE supervisory path, they will bring to the training an experiential language for skillfully broaching the topics of selflessness/interdependence and emptiness, which are widely misunderstood in Deistic traditions.

One of the areas I found most complementary to Buddhist spiritual practice was in tending to the bereaved. Like the Buddha's teachings, bereavement literature highlights the inevitability and universality of loss, the importance of journeying through and not around grief, the unique individual journey of grief, and the interconnectedness of humanity. Skillfully tending the bereaved most of all requires our unbiased compassionate presence, which is the basis of all our Buddhist practices. On the shared ground of loss and grief there is great potential for our Buddhist communities to be enriched by the beliefs, rituals, and practices of other traditions in their care of the dead. Chaplains are uniquely placed to serve as intermediaries bearing witness to other traditions and sharing their wisdom within our own communities as we care for one another, friends, and family.

An issue that continues to challenge Buddhists who wish to apply their spiritual training as livelihood is professional certification. In most healthcare institutions in the US and Canada, a chaplain must be professionally certified in order to be eligible for hire. Healthcare regulatory agencies, such as the Joint Commission for the Accreditation of Health Care Organizations (JCAHO), require that all professional caregivers must be certified according to consistent national standards. As Buddhists, many of us have journeyed for years on the Buddhist path and have perhaps undertaken the accumulated years of meditation and scholarship under the supervision of renowned masters and yet we lack credentials that are consistent with the standards of certifying organizations.

This is a significant impediment, but it is possible in some cases to surmount it by demonstrating an equivalency. To do so one must show in detail how one's experience of meditation and scholarship are equivalent with the training received in a three-year postgraduate seminary. This requires a great deal of work and there is no guarantee of its acceptance. However, the Association of Professional Chaplains (APC) has in fact generously granted equivalencies for the master of divinity degree (or portions thereof). I was successful in demonstrating an equivalency for an MDiv.

To apply for an equivalency one should get acquainted with the structure of the curricula from an accredited seminary. One needs to understand the overall requirements as well as the specific categories of courses (i.e. history and scripture; pastoral development, etc.), and how credit hours are tallied. With this understanding one then separates out the specifics of one's Buddhist education and experience, using the seminary matrix as a guide, and accounts for every detail of one's training. For instance, every academic class must include the hours spent in class with the instructor and the instructor's credentials; every meditation retreat must be quantified—number of hours per day; and qualified—what was the purpose or theme of the retreat and under whose direction was it conducted? (Ongoing daily meditation commitments are not considered appropriate for an equivalency.) There is a white paper on Theological Equivalency at the website for the Association of Professional Chaplains which will help those interested get a better understanding of the standards.

An issue connected to the process of certification is ordination. To become a chaplain it is expected that you are or will be ordained, or commissioned, within your tradition. There does not seem to be one agreed-upon definition for ordination, but a common conception is that it infers a monastic vow. Dzogchen Ponlop Rinpoche, my principal teacher, has worked closely with students wishing to become chaplains and regards this path as an important component in the transplantation of Buddhism in the West. In order to facilitate students' certification, Rinpoche offers the lay householder vows to his students. In these vows it is made clear that the student is empowered to represent Nalandabodhi (my teacher's Dharma organization in the West) in the Ministry of Healthcare Chaplaincy. The necessary letter of endorsement (another requirement of certification) was crafted by consulting with the documentation from a sampling of Judeo-Christian communities.

Finding a seat at the table of chaplaincy leadership with full rights and privileges will require ongoing advocacy and education with our multi-faith colleagues. We can take encouragement from the progress we've made in terms of the visibility of the Buddhist tradition in the last twenty years; for instance, Buddhist perspectives are imprinted on our culture through the visible presence of many respected masters (for example the Dalai Lama and Thich Nhat Hanh, as well as many others). Secular mindfulness practices inspired by the pioneering work of Jon Kabat-Zinn are widely used in mainstream healthcare institutions. Naropa University and the University of the West both offer Buddhist-based M.Div programs. The New York Village Zendo has established an ACPE accredited Buddhist CPE program—the first of its kind in North America. In addition there are other prominent programs that offer Buddhist contemplative training for anyone wishing to integrate these tools into their care of the dying: Frank Ostaseski and the Metta Institute and Joan Halifax and the Being with Dying programs are notable.

In summary, chaplaincy is a paradoxical path that can deepen our compassion and that constantly puts us in touch with the ever-changing ground of our being. It's not an easy path, and some will find the apparent contradictions with Buddhist practice untenable. For this reason whenever someone asks me how they can enter the profession, my first response is: "Why would you want to do such a thing?" Chaplaincy sounds like a perfect fit for budding bodhisattvas—spiritual care as livelihood, what could be better?

The Turning of the Dharma Wheel
in Its Many Forms

Robert Chodo Campbell

The fundamental delusion of humanity is to suppose
that I am here and you are out there.
—YASUTANI ROSHI

I N OCTOBER 2010 I traveled to Zimbabwe, Africa, as the
guest of a local hospice organization. While there I was
introduced not as Chodo, Soto Zen priest—the name and
title I go by at home—but as Robert Chodo, a friend and "Buddhist
pastor," in Africa to share my experience as a minister and teacher of
contemplative care in America. It was suggested I not wear my robes as
"robes might create distance." Even my basic black *samue*, the utilitarian
work outfit favored by Zen monks, was left behind in Manhattan. Outfit-
ted in a flannel shirt and khaki pants, I was eager to be of service.

Since my ordination I've worn only samue, and so to be again in
"civilian" clothes felt rather odd for me. Traveling and working in Africa

Rev. **Robert Chodo Campbell** cofounded the New York Zen Center for Contemplative Care, the first Buddhist organization to offer fully accredited chaplaincy training in America. In order to bring the work to a broader audience, he codeveloped
the Foundations in Buddhist Contemplative Care Training Program. Chodo is an
adjunct professor at the Institute of Buddhist Studies, and codirector of contemplative care services for the Department of Integrative Medicine at Beth Israel Medical
Center. His public programs have introduced thousands to the practices of mindful
and compassionate care of the living and dying. His groundbreaking work has been
widely featured in the media, including the *PBS Religion and Ethics Newsweekly*, and
in numerous print publications such as the *New York Times* and *Los Angeles Times*. He
is a senior Zen Buddhist monk and senior chaplain.

without my robes raised issues that surprised me. "Am I less a priest, less a chaplain? Who is arriving in Africa?"

I realized that in some important way, much of my identity over the past years has been tied up with how I dress and my shaved head. Do I need to "look" Buddhist in order to be one? Can I be seen as effective a caregiver in my civilian clothes? Am I just as much a Buddhist? Do I feel "less than," if I am blending in with the mainstream?

When training our chaplains and caregivers, we ask those who are Christian priests to experiment with their dress. If they wear a collar, we ask them to see how it would be to enter the hospital without it. So to be here without my own "collar," I begin to examine how important my priest identity really is. The truth: it's not the "priest" label that makes a good caregiver. I have seen the humblest of people provide care, from the janitor to the volunteer that brings library books to the bedside. Care is not about how one looks in the world, it's about how one is in the world.

On my first day I accompanied one of the veteran hospice nurses on her daily rounds. I could sense she was more than a little curious, and perhaps skeptical, of my reasons for being in Zimbabwe. "I've never heard of Buddhism; there is only one God and He is my Savior" were the first words she says as we set off. The first patient we visit is a pastor in his sixties with end-stage stomach cancer. From the outside, the cement and wood single-story house looks small and gloomy, with a jumble of pots, pans, and household appliances in the yard in various stages of repair. The requisite chickens scurry about pecking at the hard-packed dirt.

A woman I presume to be the pastor's wife answers the door and shows us into a surprisingly spacious living room. The pastor is sitting in the far corner in a rather grand, dark oak rocking chair. It seems oddly out of place next to the array of mismatched sofas and chairs. In this chair he looks like a very old farm hand sitting on the porch at the end of a long day. He is clearly happy to see the nurse and immediately courteous to me, standing to offer me this elegant seat. Up close I see he is probably in his fifties, but his stance and body weight are that of an eighty-year-old. I am formally introduced as a pastor from America. He then sits on the couch with the nurse.

What follows is one of the most exquisite instances of caregiving I have ever witnessed. We sit in silence while she gently holds his hand and gazes at him for five minutes, the room bathed in stillness, the nurse barely moving, breathing slowly and deliberately, looking into his eyes as if to say, "I am here with you, it's okay." She then asks, "How is your stomach today?" He replies, "Today I am blessed with some relief. The Lord has taken the pain away for an hour or two." His dark brown eyes, wide as saucers, fill with tears.

The nurse, gesturing to me, explains to the patient, "Chodo would like to talk with you, as a fellow pastor. Would you like that?" The pastor reaches out to hold my hand and the three of us sit together, again in silence, and then we begin to talk. The nurse tells me he needs another round of chemo but doesn't want to continue treatment, which would put further financial burden on his congregation. He tells the nurse that most of the time he is in great pain and cries when his wife is not around. Our conversation reveals his resilience, his absolute faith in God, and his resignation to what lies ahead for him. With no money, and only a brief window of time to enjoy his church and community, he tells me how much support his congregation has given him in recent months, including a collection that enabled him to fly to Johannesburg to see an oncologist and receive his first round of chemotherapy.

I ask him what gives him the strength to continue with his preaching. He begins to sob. "Up until last month I was able to walk to the church and give the sermon, but now I don't have the strength to walk more than half way. Then I have to rest and just return home." I ask, "Is there anyone who will come and fetch you in a car or taxi?" He replies, "I don't want to be a burden. I will stay home now and pray for God's help." I suggest, "Perhaps God would want you to give your congregation the opportunity to help you. Perhaps He would want someone to come here and take you to your church."

A very simple solution in a very ordinary situation, the great matter of life and death. A rush of tears follows as he looks directly into my eyes, "Thank you, thank you." The nurse squeezes his hand and mine, and with a nod signals it's time to leave. I ask if he would like a prayer, and he says "yes." As I try to do in my prayers with all my patients, I bring attention to whatever the current situation may be, and pray for healing for both him and his wife, as well as his two sons, who are living with an aunt since he and his wife can no longer afford to send them to school or feed them. I pray for him to continue to wonder what God's will is and to pray for the acceptance of God's will. As we ready to leave, he shakes my hand. Both of us know we won't see each other again. He holds my gaze and we both smile. He thanks me for the visit and the prayer.

As we leave the house, the nurse says, "I think your Buddha must have been one of God's children." I take this as acceptance and tell her, "Perhaps Jesus was a Buddha." She nods and laughs and we get into the car, under the watchful eye of the curious kids playing. I notice a boy with a stick rolling an old tire in the dirt street, and "thus the Dharma wheel turns" is the phrase running through my mind. We drive to the next house on the list.

That evening I am reminded of one of the first things I learned very early in my chaplaincy training. "One can only be as intimate with another person as one is with one's self." And to find intimacy with one's self there has to be a capacity for deep introspection and reflection. As a professional taking care of others, it's critically important to know who I am on a deep psychological, spiritual, and emotional level. Through contemplative practice we learn to realize that while there is separateness, there is no separation with the other. I believe that's what contemplative care is, caring for the other wholeheartedly, without getting lost in their journey. It is their journey, not mine—and yet we are companions for a time, guiding one another along our respective paths. I wondered how long I would hold the image of this brave man on his terrible, painful journey.

The following day I visit the HIV clinic located on the outskirts of the city. The social worker has set up an impromptu office outside, with chairs in a circle. I am introduced as a minister from New York who works with people who are HIV-infected, and she asks if they want to talk to me about their spiritual concerns. I meet the guardian of two sisters, aged five and seven, both HIV-infected by their father. Their mother had died, and they were now with their aunt looking for a place to live. The aunt was trying to make enough money to feed both her nieces and herself. I took a series of photographs that afternoon but don't need them, their faces are burned in my memory. I pray for them every day. It is easy to say they are just two victims in a huge epidemic of violence, but they are the two that *I* met.

And so I can't help but wonder and ask: what can *I* do?

My mind wanders to a day during my chaplaincy training in New York. I was assigned to the pediatric unit of a large hospital on the Upper East Side. It was there that I met Emma, four years old and a joy to behold. I was immediately struck by the number of "Get Well" wishes, cards, balloons, and handmade craft objects that filled the space. The windowsills were lined with flowers; there were streamers hanging from the ceiling. It looked almost as though a party were about to take place. Her mother, a very well-groomed woman in her late thirties, was playing with the little girl lying in the bed. Emma, unaware of her brain and spinal cancer, was giggling and kicking her feet in the air. This child was cherished and had the best modern medicine could offer, but even so she would not survive. Her father, a surgeon at another hospital in New York, looking bewildered and exhausted, asked me, "Where is God right now, chaplain? Huh? Why is this happening to my little girl, it makes no sense. You're the chaplain, tell me, where is God?" At that moment, Emma giggles and with outstretched arms calls, "Daddy." I look to the tiny bed, and then to him, saying gently, "There is God."

The family was deeply Catholic and so I offered this prayer for Emma:

> Father of tenderness and compassion
> you sent your son to share our human nature,
> to redeem all people and to heal the sick.
> Look with love on your children who are sick.
> Support them with your power,
> give them hope in times of suffering
> and keep them always in your care.
> We ask this through Christ our Lord.
> Amen

It is this same prayer I offer up for the two little girls in Zimbabwe.

Thinking of these children it is not so easy to say, "This is the Dharma, the way things are, karma, God's will." At times I want to scream, because it is all those things and it sucks.

I am brought back to the present moment here in Zimbabwe, by the voice, or rather the raspy whisper, of a seventeen-year-old boy (HIV-infected, perinatally). He recently suffered a stroke and was thrown out of his home by his father because he can no longer work. He had been working to raise money for the family practically his whole life. Now he appears before me, quiet, handicapped, abandoned . . . a handsome, lost boy of a man. There is something about this boy that reminds me of Danny.

Danny. I met him in 1988 at an AA meeting in New York City where we were both in our early days of sobriety. Danny was a street fighter, an Irish American kid from Hell's Kitchen. All the women were crazy for him; he was a very handsome guy. Almost twenty years later, during my training as a chaplain intern while working at an HIV/AIDS Residential Treatment Center in New York, I met Danny again. He was now HIV-positive and a crack addict. He had been in and out of prison and was once again battling his addictions. I didn't recognize him at first, but somewhere in the back of my mind I knew him. One day we got to talking about our respective paths and he mentioned the particular AA group where we first met. It was then that we realized our previous connection. Danny's decline was long and heartbreaking. He left the residence and returned twice more before finally giving up his life on the streets. When it was clear he was dying, I was with him almost every day.

One afternoon in early November 2008, I was sitting at Danny's bedside. He was barely conscious, and he was unrecognizable as that once oh-so-vibrant bad boy with a boxer's build that so many women (and men) had fallen in love with. I didn't want to leave him. It seemed clear it was just a matter of hours before he would die.

I had been asked to speak on a panel at the United Nations on AIDS education. I kissed his hand, told him I would be back in an hour or so. I hadn't needed to prepare a speech for the panel. I have talked many times on the topic of HIV/AIDS. I was infected with the virus in 1983, so I am quite adept on the issue. I would gather my thoughts in the cab on the way up town, and walk into the room as I walk into any patient's room—"not knowing."

The cornerstone of my spirituality is contained in the first three tenets of the Zen Peacemaker Order:

1. Not knowing; thereby giving up fixed ideas about myself and the universe
2. Bearing witness to the joy and suffering of the world
3. Taking loving action, doing no harm

When I am able to stay in a place of "not knowing," then every experience is fresh and new. Every time I walk into a patient's room, all preconceived notions and ideas are left at the door. I try to be in that moment, with the patient's needs, whatever his or her religion or background may be. Perhaps all the patient needs is someone to listen, to be present. Or maybe the patient will tell me to "get out." To actually "get out," when told to do so, is also an act of compassion—it can be empowering for the patient feeling vulnerable and powerless.

Just as I arrive at the U.N., my cell phone rings. It's the nurse from the residence, "Hi Chodo, Danny just passed away." I begin my speech: "I just got a phone call, and someone I have known for many years died ten minutes ago from AIDS-related complications."

In the midst of all this, how does my practice maintain me? Each morning I recite the gatha:

> Vast is the robe of liberation,
> A formless field of benefaction.
> I wear the Tatagatha's teachings,
> Saving all sentient beings.

My vow is to accept the turning of the Dharma wheel in all its many forms. I sit on the cushion. I meditate, internalize the teachings. And when I'm off the cushion (are we ever off the cushion?) I hope I can be *real* in the world, truly practice "not knowing" and bear witness to all that is good and all that is remarkably painful, in both others and myself. Because ultimately there is no separation, no one fixed "me" or "them."

We are not separate. And if I can't experience that, I am lost. It is all right there in the faces of those two little girls, in the boy with the stroke, in Danny, in Emma . . . it is all right here, and there is no separation between me and them, life and death, birth and suffering.

Compassion is the simple act of bearing witness in the face of this suffering.

It is all here right now.

Widening the Circle:

ENGAGED *BODHICHITTA* IN HOSPITAL CHAPLAINCY

Chris Berlin

AS THE FIELD of healthcare chaplaincy continues to evolve into a distinctly interfaith path of service, increasing numbers of Buddhists are discovering new opportunities to practice *bodhichitta*, the mind of awakening arising from true compassion, in action. Both traditional and nontraditional Dharma practitioners are seeking work as chaplains in hospitals and hospice centers as a way to bring the heart of Buddhist practice into their professional lives. I find it useful to view this work as a practice of "engaged bodhichitta," that is, cultivating bodhichitta by offering skillful, compassionate care for those directly experiencing suffering.

Given that the modern hospital environment is fundamentally interfaith and comprised of people from many cultures and spiritual traditions, providing support must involve widening our circle of care to include the experiences and cultures of those from all backgrounds and religions. A chaplain's work, therefore, becomes the work of meeting others where *they* are, rather than from within our own tradition or where we think

Chris Berlin has worked as a Buddhist chaplain in the Boston/Cambridge area. He has worked closely with cancer patients in Boston-area hospitals and with the AIDS population. He has extensive experience in teaching meditation and mindfulness to patients, clinicians, and to those in end-of-life care. He also seeks to develop clinical training for Buddhists in caregiving roles and presently offers workshops on meditation and yogic spiritual practice. Chris has a degree in Buddhist and Hindu religions from the University of California, Santa Barbara, and is a graduate of the Harvard Divinity School. He has studied and practiced both vipassana as well as the Tibetan Buddhist tradition.

they should be, and in this sense involves a willingness to become "self-less" as caregivers. Becoming self-less in this way entails balancing two essential aspects of bodhichitta practice: nonattachment and compassion. Understanding and balancing these two qualities allows us to cultivate engaged bodhichitta with a strong, wholesome foundation for the clinical setting in a way that can awaken our deepest aspiration for all beings to be free from suffering. Our approach to working with the sick, injured, or dying can then evolve into a more fully human and integrated practice of compassionate care.

When I first began working as a chaplain in a Boston cancer hospital, it was clear that my experiences of providing spiritual support to patients would mostly consist of interfaith encounters. A large majority of patients I encountered were Catholics and Protestants, but I soon found the hospital setting to be rich with those practicing various other faiths as well. This was well-illustrated one day upon entering the hospital chapel where a Muslim was engaged in his daily prayers while a Christian at the kneeler bowed his head in prayer and a young woman sat nearby on a cushion in quiet meditation. How unique to encounter this anywhere, this quiet, spiritual presence arising from a collective moment of peaceful, simultaneous connection with the sacred.

This scene mirrored the spirit of interfaith chaplaincy, a harmony between lived spiritual traditions only possible by coming together in mutual acceptance of the presence of the perceived "other." Given the richness of this pluralist atmosphere, a question invariably arose for me: "How do I bring a Buddhist background into this interfaith setting where few patients and staff are Buddhist?"

The wide range of issues, circumstances, and faith orientations I encountered with patients, families, and hospital staff meant leaving behind the Buddhist lens in order to be fully present with the lived experiences of others. As part of this process, I found myself increasingly relying on empathy and compassion as they arose naturally in the presence of suffering. Responding in this way toward others and their lived experiences and emotional responses holds the power to yield a sense of the "self-less" in such exchanges. The Buddhist notion of "no-self" expresses the wisdom that our true nature is inherently empty of any permanent, conceivable self enduring beyond that subtlest state of consciousness we might call Buddha nature, emptiness, or the clear light of *rigpa*. In this sense, we become "un-identifiable"—that is, without identity—as we discover the deeper truth of who we ultimately are when we are compassionate, nonjudgmental, and fully present beings. This self-less state unifies us with others as we enter into the practice of deep listening and we become fully present to them.

An instance of the importance of becoming self-less in this way arose one day in the presence of Ellen, an Evangelical Christian patient who expressed great concern for me upon learning I was Buddhist. She felt adamant that I was destined for hell and expressed the importance of my embracing Christ. My initial response to this was a subtle feeling of self-protection in the form of resistance, an inner impulse to disconnect, to back away from the encounter, and from Ellen, due to the force of her conviction. But, instead, I paused. I decided to stay with Ellen and experiment with being present with her where *she* was rather than responding in a protective way from within my own self-understanding. This meant shifting my focus onto Ellen's deep faith in Christ as we proceeded to talk about her genuine concern for others and her reliance on Christ during difficult times.

Although Ellen had originally expressed her concern for me, I reminded myself that the encounter need not be about me. I was thus better able to practice reflective listening with her and we could more freely explore her own deepest intentions springing from a heart strong in faith and deeply committed to Christ. By becoming self-less in that moment, and expressing genuine loving intent for her spiritual well-being, it was possible to lay a foundation for many rich conversations that would support her through the challenges of her illness that followed.

Another patient, Jane, was an accomplished artist and teacher who said wryly upon meeting me, "You're a chaplain? I don't know what you think you're going to do for me, I'm an atheist." I offered, "Let's find out together." Jane's dry wit belied a guarded personality when talking about herself. But she would candidly discuss her feelings about art, society, philosophy, and soon after, her own existential questioning. As our conversations deepened, we would explore together the meaning of her life and the prospect of dying. She also shared her feeling of "envy" for those comforted by a strong faith in God and the afterlife. By allowing her to be fully present in her religious disbelief and sit with the longing for something more, I could remain with Jane where she was and practice deep listening, rather than try to fill the emptiness with belief or problem-solve what she felt was missing in her life.

To do so, it was important for me to release any impulse I had to "fill-in" what initially felt like a lack in her spiritual life. Becoming self-less in this moment meant relinquishing my ideas, attachments, and perceptions about what I believed would have benefited Jane most. Instead, by cultivating a safe, uncluttered space, I could be wholeheartedly present to her and help her discover how she might experience a more genuine sense of love in her life and how to better cope with her fears and anxieties. It became important for Jane to experience the present moment more fully, learning the gentleness of accepting what is, while expanding the horizons of her understanding of that experience through the lens of mindfulness. This allowed her heart to soften and to receive and give love more freely. As time passed, she expressed gratitude that I was there, walking beside her as a close companion on her own path, a path she could walk freely and unconditionally. The freedom this sense of space made possible allowed her to experience her life in ever-more spiritual terms until her death two years later.

It was through encounters with people like Ellen and Jane that I learned the importance of releasing my attachments to what it means to be "spiritual" in order to become self-less in a meaningful way. This was necessary in order to fully embrace the essence of their own distinct spiritual lives. In fact, relinquishing the desire to approach them through a religious lens, or through an agenda of my own, better allowed for their own spiritual concerns to arise more freely and naturally. Being with them in a state of open acceptance of whatever concerned them most in the moment defined these relationships beyond the realm of faith and made room for deeper, more valuable exchanges that could include all aspects of their lives.

In my experience, what defines becoming self-less in this way is the ability to be fully and unconditionally present with others in a state of "not-knowing" without our own identifications, thoughts, or feelings getting in the way. Not-knowing means being spacious, not presuming to have the answers, or even an answer. When we approach others through a nonjudgmental "beginner's mind" in such situations, we are better able to genuinely seek answers together with that person where they are in a more helpful way. This opens the door to the spacious, common heart of bodhichitta as we actualize our aspiration for those we encounter to be free from suffering and its causes.

For a Buddhist caregiver, practicing self-lessness is equally important with those who identify themselves as Buddhists. Among the Buddhist patients encountered by hospital chaplains, we invariably discover wide-ranging differences in sects, traditions, practices, and cultures. What it means to be Buddhist for some is interwoven into the traditions of their homeland, be it Cambodia, Vietnam, Thailand, Korea, or China. For others, it might be defined by a particular Theravadan or Tibetan lineage or teacher who emigrated west. In light of such differences, the spirit that characterizes our work with those of other faiths (or none at all) can also apply to those who share our own.

In one instance early in my career, I somewhat naively asked a Cambodian patient I had just met, Samnang, what form of Buddhism he practiced. He responded with a quizzical expression implying, "What do you mean?" and then stated plainly, "I am Buddhist." For Samnang, there was no distinction between Buddhists, just a belonging to the universal community of the Buddha. As a child, he would visit the local temple with his family, and as he grew older, Buddhism provided him with an important outlook on life. More recently, prayers to the Buddha had become important to him as his illness and the anxiety of uncertainty loomed over him.

What was most meaningful between us now, though, was not our mutual faith, but rather a heart-connection imbued with mutual positive regard. What Samnang most needed when he came to the hospital for treatment or tests was a friend to share the experience with, someone to show genuine concern, balanced with a steady, nonanxious presence. Although we occasionally discussed Buddhism and the meaning of his own faith, our visits were based in empathy and basic human kindness, qualities not only valued by Buddhists but by anyone coping with suffering regardless of his or her faith. Usually alone, Samnang would welcome me in the spirit of friendship and hope during anxious times.

On the surface, this was a different kind of relationship than one I shared with another patient, Thomas, a devoted Theravadan practitioner originally from the Midwest. Thomas had little interest in relating to "eclectic" Buddhists or to those who profess a *buddhayana* approach (the overall, unified vehicle of Buddhism). He had rightly summed me up as one of these—at least, in principle—after carefully interviewing me to find out what sect I belonged to. An AIDS patient with cancer, Thomas was without family and lived alone. He struggled with many health complications that would frequently cause him to be hospitalized for several days at a time.

Although we discussed vipassana practice and his Theravadan orientation, our brief relationship was similarly based on companionship and presence. He would summon me on occasion when admitted to the hospital and we would discuss his coping, explore a passage from his favorite book on Buddhism, or talk about his life history. Thomas was careful to disclose both his personal life and his Dharma practice, but developed a trust in our relationship based on sharing the simple heart of being human and being genuine. These qualities, authentically shared, were the essence of trust for Thomas, qualities that took he and I deeper than our perceived differences in traditions. I like to think our respective views converged at the deepest source of the shared Dharma, but it was nevertheless clear that, like Samnang, Thomas benefited most by having a compassionate friend and an attentive presence during the more fearful moments of his illness. Buddhism itself served as an entry point for our relationship and provided a bridge between the two of us so we could explore the deeper realms of his emotional and spiritual life together.

To become self-less is to connect with others, not through the lens of belief or preconception, but through basic human experiences. This is the key to interfaith chaplaincy and the skillful means behind putting bodhichitta into action with those from other traditions. When we approach someone experiencing the vulnerability that comes with suffering, kindness and compassion allow for an expansion of the mutual heart through basic human experiences we may all share at one point or another, whether it be vulnerability, fear, resistance, loneliness, anger, loss, sorrow, love, connectedness, gratitude, or peacefulness.

As we seek to cultivate "no-self" in such ways, however, it is also necessary to point out that becoming self-less does not mean abandoning a strong sense of our own practice, faith tradition, or spiritual outlook. It is essential, in fact, to remain confident in the foundations that ground our spiritual lives so that we may remain resilient in this work and rely on those foundations as we encounter the more intense levels of suffering we come across in clinical chaplaincy. Becoming self-less is instead all about *how* we are present with one another. When we locate ourselves with the one in our care right where they are, and do so with nonjudgment and unconditional openness, the empathy we practice offers us deeper insights into their own lived experiences and allows us to willingly share the burden of the suffering they carry. As we become self-less in this way, the heart of wisdom expands and we too can be transformed, especially when our spiritual tradition supports us in the process.

As an engaged practice, becoming self-less by fully locating ourselves in another person's lived experience relies on our balancing two central qualities of cultivating bodhichitta: detachment and compassion. Understanding these through the lens of Buddhist wisdom, and keeping them in equilibrium, allows us a strong, wholesome foundation for effectively encountering suffering in the clinical setting. A good example illustrating the importance of this balance occurred in the Intensive Care Unit where I was summoned to visit Richard, a young man in his late thirties from China with lung cancer.

Richard had been given less than twelve hours to live and now lay intubated and under heavy sedation. The ICU is a place where the frenetic energy of loudly beeping infusion pumps and life-support monitors combine with nurses hurrying here and there, doing all they can to keep critical patients stabilized. I watched as the muscles of Richard's body tensed while he struggled to raise himself up onto his arms only to release again, causing him to fall helplessly back onto the mattress. The thought occurred to me, how often we expend so much effort in our lives with such minimal outcomes. The mystery of suffering entered my mind as I sat with him, wondering, *How far beneath the surface of his body does his suffering reach?* I had often returned to the Buddha's assertion that pain and the body's decay are inevitable to those of us fortunate enough to have been born human but that we also hold the potential to become liberated from the anguish of suffering through right effort, right mindfulness, right concentration, and all that the Buddhadharma has to offer us. *But for this man,* I thought, *here and now, where is the boundary between bodily suffering and mental anguish?*

After Richard's diagnosis, his primary worry had been what would happen to his wife, Jenny, if he died. His strong belief in the Buddha and accepting life as it is, combined with the prospect of a short-lived future, provided him with the wisdom that every moment of the here and now is supremely precious. As I contemplated what mattered most to Richard now, the noisy distractions of the ICU quickly faded, dissolving into the background as I entered into being with him in undistracted presence. Nonattachment was the only vehicle to enter into this level of connection: nonattachment to all outward-directed senses, including hearing and all perception related to my surroundings; nonattachment to the running commentary that questioned the nature of suffering; nonattachment to anticipating the ominous silence that would suddenly appear if the monitor for Richard's vital signs were to stop. Completely releasing these attachments became essential to clear the way for compassion to arise more freely from the space of a still, nonreactive heart. Chanting helped to focus my mind and imbue the moment with intention.

Then, I used a Vajrayana practice I'd learned to release my remaining distractions and settle into an unbroken attention. This gave me the space needed to visualize the light of Amitabha above Richard reaching down through the crown of his head to gather the luminous drop in his heart and show it the pathway back up to Amitabha's pure and blessed realm. By maintaining a steady focus on the essence of Richard's heart-consciousness in a nonattached way, it was possible to be present with this practice without disturbing the subtle flow of consciousness this meditation seeks to awaken. Nonattachment here allowed a genuine intent for Richard's awakening to become imbued with the deep aspiration that all suffering be released from his mind and body.

When leading discussions or workshops on mindfulness, I encounter people who express concern about the meaning of nonattachment. For some, it is associated with a cold, unfeeling state empty of interest or passion for anything or anyone else. But nonattachment in the Buddhist sense is not an absence of feeling or connection but rather a mindfulness of our own reactive impulses and an ability to refrain from being carried away by them. It is the practice of not fighting, feeding, or projecting onto ourselves or others our attachments, fears, or aversions as we willfully enter those places of suffering from which others seek to flee.

As was the case with Ellen and Jane, becoming self-less depends on being nonattached while also remaining mindful of one's own internal responses. Although it is important to be present with these responses, to take note of them and not merely push them aside (out of sight does not necessarily mean out of mind!), being mindful of one's reactions needs to be balanced with an awareness of what the other's needs are in the moment. In many ways, this process is a natural one and somewhat effortless once we gain experience and practice. Similarly, with Richard, nonattachment from both my internal tendencies and external distractions was necessary to provide adequate spiritual support in the triage atmosphere of the ICU. With nonattachment and mindfulness laying the foundation of our practice, the aspiration for all beings to be free from suffering can more freely become the momentum we need to cultivate the essence of awakening that is bodhichitta in action.

Every aspect of chaplaincy work benefits from valuing mindfulness and nonattachment as allies to compassion, including the self-care we need to make part of our lives when engaging in this work. As a self-care practice, nonattachment allows us to be present with suffering without contracting around our own reactions to what others say or experience, and it is detachment that keeps us from merely intellectualizing what we witness in order to gain some distance from the discomfort it might cause us. To be deeply engaged with others means to enter the space of the common heart without being thrown off by fear or our own reactions to circumstances. This is the central task for spiritual caregivers to remain effective and to preserve energy, resilience, and an overall sense of well-being.

Whereas nonattachment keeps us steady, compassion connects us deeply. Whether practicing *metta*, *tonglen*, or simply being fully present to another in a self-less way, the effects of developing the essence of awakening through bodhichitta practice are never generated without deep connection to others. Bodhichitta cultivation is not a solitary practice, but it depends on accepting the suffering of another person fearlessly, without judgment, and offering compassion in return. This entails recognizing the unity we share both within the common heart and within the experience of suffering itself, and this defines compassion in a deeper way.

Compassion, as the aspiration for all beings to be free from suffering, embraces the journey, allows us to be fully present, and freely offers the heart's own deepest wisdom. It allows us to manifest a still, spacious heart. The stillness arises out of nonattachment, and the spaciousness grows from compassion. This is the source of a courageous presence that is able to provide genuine comfort to the sick, injured, or dying.

Even for those who are ill or dying, practicing compassion for others opens the gate to bodhichitta and can be transformative. Lama Yeshe taught that cultivating bodhichitta when one's life is about to end holds the greatest benefit and offers the most merit of all practices, beyond that of any death meditation or ritual practice. Whether one is facing the end of his or her life, or one is in a caregiving role, the essence of awakening that compassion for others provides has the potential to heal and enlighten us at the source of our deepest wisdom and the wellspring of our consciousness: the heart. In this way, what we offer can become immeasurable, widening the circle of those to whom we offer our deepest kindness during fearful and challenging times.

Healthcare chaplaincy offers us a unique opportunity to allow our work to become an active spiritual practice. If we approach this work in a heart-centered way, the hospital setting can evoke in us a reflective process as we are touched daily by human suffering. And we may be compelled to make sense of the reality of impermanence we witness in terms of our own lives. But whereas we may at times feel challenged by what we experience, we are given an opportunity to explore more deeply how to bring balance to the relationship between the compassion we make available to others and the detachment we need to remain in the midst of it all. As *upaya*, skillful means, this balance allows us to practice self-lessness without fear in our work as we encounter people carrying the burden of suffering that often comes with illness, injury, or dying. Encountering them through the common heart of oneness is the essence of compassion and the transformative power in bodhichitta.

Buddhist caregivers committed to an interfaith path of service will discover their own unique ways to widen the circle and make the practice of bodhichitta available to those of all traditions in an engaged way, in a lived way. When we are able to trust this process, we can then respond to the challenge of crisis by placing ourselves fully with others in the midst of their own experiences. For the short time we are in human form, we have this great opportunity to benefit others and cultivate the mind of awakening through compassion in action. And, in so doing, we may find that what is Buddhist is the experience at hand, the reality of what is before us, and what is fully human within us all.

The Jeweled Net:

WHAT DOGEN AND THE AVATAMSAKA SUTRA
CAN OFFER US AS SPIRITUAL CAREGIVERS

Koshin Paley Ellison

WHEN I WAS eight years old, my grandfather showed me a photograph taken in Tokyo, Japan. In the center of the photograph stood a monk with his begging bowl: still, smiling, and energized. For me the monk was the image of someone dedicated to being fully alive. In my imagination, he invoked what I felt as a child lying down in the grass beneath the great oak tree swaying in the wind in my backyard. I felt full of wonder, fully alive. This experience is one of the first Dharma teachings I received. It evoked a feeling that surfaced again when I first saw the serene Buddhist statues in the New York Metropolitan Museum of Art—there is a Way, a lineage, a religion of being fully engaged amid the suffering of the world.

Looking at that photograph, I noticed all around the monk were blurred people running, their faces looking strained. This was a scene from the Vietnam War, one of the many that became an iconic symbol of

Rev. Koshin Paley Ellison is a founder of the New York Zen Center for Contemplative Care, the first Buddhist organization to offer fully accredited Buddhist chaplaincy training in America. Koshin is an adjunct professor at the Institute of Buddhist Studies. He is the codirector of contemplative care services for the Department of Integrative Medicine at Beth Israel Medical Center, where he also serves on the medical ethics committee. His public programs have introduced thousands to the practices of mindful and compassionate care of the living and dying. His work has been widely featured in the media, including the *PBS Religion and Ethics Newsweekly*, and in numerous print publications such as the *New York Times* and *Los Angeles Times*. He is a senior Zen Buddhist priest, chaplaincy supervisor, and Jungian psychotherapist.

that era. As a child raised in a chaotic home life, this image offered me a new way of being in the world. Much later, during stressful periods of my own life, I began to reflect on the use of the wrathful and serene images of the Buddhist statues that expressed the spiritual possibilities available to me when suffering in my life seemed unbearable. By day, amid the natural beauty of my suburban neighborhood, neighbors chatted over picket fences and shared barbeques.

But, underneath this seemingly benevolent environment, I sensed the shadowy terror—domestic violence, incest, and alcoholism. Our family was one of these locations of the shadow of suburban life. After encountering Buddhism in my late teens, I would ask myself, *If enlightenment is possible everywhere, then how is enlightenment in the shadows?* Then in my twenties, the contradicting beauty and the harshness of this world weaved together with all the layers of my reality and my developing cultural and religious life. In the photograph of the monk I saw the possibility of integrating the inner and outer. I saw these interpenetrating patterns coexisting. There was the net holding us, the path differentiating and uniting us, and the shadows shaking and training us. Now in my forties, I contemplate these experiences of body and mind, along with the stories of monks and the Buddha, in all of their seeming contradictions, and internalize them into my being, the known and unknown. Contemplation is the function that continues to allow me to look deeply into my actions.

When I teach and supervise chaplain interns I use the metaphors of the net, the path, and the shadows as a frame for my supervision of people doing Clinical Pastoral Eduction (CPE), and I draw upon the teachings of Zen Master Dogen and the Avatamsaka Sutra.

THE NET: INTERCONNECTEDNESS

Anton Boisen, the founder of CPE, saw the people he ministered to in the psychiatric hospital as living human documents. He understood that a lived spirituality involves more than reading books and writing papers; it requires engaged intimacy with the experiences and stories of people and our connections with them.

The Avatamsaka Sutra resonates with Boisen's classic phrase, affirming the experience that existence and relationships are deeply valuable, in the words of the sutra: "a vast net of jewels." According to the Avatamsaka Sutra, everything in this world, imagined and experienced, is a jewel in the vast net of the universe. When one jewel is touched, the whole net trembles. Every jewel also reflects in its surface all the other jewels. This image of a net of interconnected jewels is a powerful symbol of the intra-personal, interpersonal, social, religious, and cultural networks that con-nect us. We all belong to the net, an inner and vast collection of images and relational experiences that reverberates throughout our unfolding lives. Through the lens of the net, we can look both up close, from the point of view of one or more intersections, and from far away, from the point of view of the entire net. We see the finer threads of interconnec-tion, and as we take a wider view, we see the whole. The ideas of whole-ness and interconnection are deeply interrelated. As Dogen writes, "to study the way is to forget the separate self, to forget the separate self is to allow the universe to advance." Opening to a larger sense of self allows intimacy and interconnection.

I have a piece of calligraphy hanging in my office that says, "One moment, one chance." This is a Zen expression reminding me that each moment is completely unique, and we just have this one chance, this one instant, to encounter it. From this point of view, everything has the potential to be experienced as fresh and new. An emphasis on freshness and newness has become one of the mainstays of my work as a CPE supervisor at the New York Zen Center for Contemplative Care. In that role, I train chaplain interns in the role and art of hospital chaplaincy. Students are invited to explore with each other and me their jeweled nature, cracks and all, as well as the whole net of our social, cultural, and spiritual experiences. This exploration of intrapersonal, interpersonal, and cultural contexts is an expression of what is alive in the present moment for each student. As their Dharma practice comes alive in the moment through their chaplaincy work, students connect with contemplation in a continuing process of discovery of themselves as a jewel in the net. There are aspects of chaplaincy training that are important for contemplation: contemplation on experience, awareness of social reality, inquiry into spiritual or theological traditions, and searching for clues to intimacy. These aspects of focus can be points of intimacy, and in CPE, a way to reveal interdependence. I try to bring my attention to four modalities: how students are relating as chaplains in themselves and with each other; how students are separating and connecting; how students are exploring, challenging, and embodying spiritual texts; and how the group as a whole is making separation and interconnection. The Avatamsaka Sutra's jeweled net becomes a place of active reflection, a place for learning, where the net is vast and difference can be explored and reflected in each person. Within the net I reflect with my students on their differences and sameness so that those points can be places of connection within themselves and with their patients.

The jeweled net analogy has not only been deeply valuable for my work with interns, it has also been valuable for my own inner work as I navigate the landscape of acting in a supervisory role. Working with an awareness of interdependence has heightened my awareness of how I relate to others. For example, my personal history of experiencing bigotry as a gay man and as a Jewish Buddhist priest has led to a pattern of pushing away my vulnerability because I fear judgment or have questions about trusting. I use my awareness of going through this process of vulnerability to model facing my fears to students who are training in spiritual caregiving. I believe that our unconscious and my students' unconscious are in communication. So I am consciously aware of how my process affects my students. This is modeling the concept that we can only be as intimate with another as we are with ourselves.

These are facets of my jewel I can attempt to hide. Yet the analogy of the net helps me see that hiding is not always the best choice. I can discern times when it is right to disclose these facets of myself because the act of disclosure models the possibility for others who might be struggling to bring their shadows to the light of consciousness, knowing the net holds together, cracks and all. This dynamic came up in a CPE unit with a Episcopal student. I learned, after accepting her into the program, that she was struggling to reclaim her Episcopal religious practice. She had left her religious practice due to challenges of doctrine and had begun a Zen Buddhist practice. At first I was annoyed with myself for not exploring this sensitivity in her interview, but I then realized this was a perfect lesson unfolding for my own growth as a supervisor.

When the Buddha encountered difference and separation, he said something that we might take to mean, "Treat others as if they were you, because they are." Reflected in the eyes of this woman, I saw my own struggles with my early religious life. I can use my full self and use this experience to connect. A growing edge for me is to use more of my story in moments of learning. So I decided to use my connection within myself to hold the space for her to explore her relationships with her church, patients, the group, and me. As she felt seen, she saw the cracked jewels within herself and allowed her to integrate her own connection to her faith and community. She began to question her theological positions and decisions. She has since reconnected with the Episcopal Church and taken on a liturgical position. Having reclaimed her faith, she expressed gratitude for having a safe space to reflect on her alienation from the church. This process, though difficult, helped to increase her compassion toward herself and others. Without tapping into my own spiritual formation, we would not have known the vastness of the net.

THE PATH: SELF, NO-SELF, INTERPENETRATION

In the wake of the challenges of my early life, how do I integrate my spiritual practice with my being in the world? That picture of the monk takes on new meaning. He is not stoically serene, but he is a man like me who struggles each day with how to keep returning to the present. Using all the ingredients of his life, including being in relationship with the people fleeing around him, he becomes who he is. Monks since the time of the Buddha have gone to their community every day for nourishment and engagement. The community offers nourishment and the monk offers prayers in return. There is mutuality, an interdependence of relationship. At this phase of my life, the photo symbolizes a path, a way of being with my students of interdependence. When I set myself apart from them, the way I first saw the monk in the photograph, this doesn't serve relationship. In Buddhism and in popular culture, there is an expression: If you see the Buddha on the road, kill him. If I see myself acting like a stoic Buddha, I know I am hiding out in an idea of enlightenment that is not the real thing. I need to kill that idea of "Buddha" and become intimate with the relationship.

The parable of Suddhana in the Avatamsaka Sutra exemplifies the net through his path or spiritual journey. Suddhana wanted to know how to function in the world. He meets a wise old man who exemplifies the quality of wisdom and sets him on a journey to meet fifty-two teachers, and after he meets them he is told he will know how to compassionately function in the world. On his journey he encounters a drunken man, a ghost, a little girl, a wise woman, an ascetic, and many others who might not be seen as they are, teachers. Through his study and raising questions, he finds himself in all his diversity. It is the classic religious and mythological tale of realizing that he is a unique jewel in the net.

What I love about this tale from the Avatamsaka Sutra is the message that everyone you encounter is a teacher. I grew up in a secular Jewish home where identity had to do with humor, culture, and passion for questions. My stepmother was on the board of the local Zen center, and she was my first connection to Zen and the inner experience that bloomed forth from the photograph. I suppose that makes me a "Jew-Bu," a Jewish Buddhist who practices Buddhism with a strong Jewish cultural identity. It has been my path to realize the net within myself and all those I encounter as reflecting jewels. When I was twenty-seven, my Grandma Mimi began to decline physically and I became her primary caregiver, and this was a moment when I began to see the integration of my spiritual practice with caregiving, as one practice. Caring for another jewel, being intimate with her suffering and joy, became the living manifestation of the photo of the monk on the street. Out of those moments with Mimi came a calling that led me on this path. My life has been a path of continuous integration, continuous practice. The path has been at times winding, a mandala, a spiral, but never an even one-dimensional course. And my own path makes me curious about how students' paths have unfolded and helps me guide them in their own forms of integration.

Zen Master Eihei Dogen, the thirteenth-century Japanese monk who founded the Japanese Soto Zen School, provides a threefold framework that I use with students for understanding our calling, and our paths to livelihood and intimacy. Dogen takes the traditional Buddhist understanding of deep inquiry into the true nature of the self through a contemplation process of (1) studying the self, (2) forgetting the self, and (3) allowing the world to interpenetrate. This threefold inquiry is a process that students and supervisors can explore together and can use to understand a parallel process in patients' lives. CPE offers a space to be curious about the personal, intrapersonal, interpersonal, and cultural in our lives. As a supervisor, I work to show the way into the experience of interpenetration and dependent coarising in the world of birth and death, joys and sorrows, questions and answers, mourning and celebration. I teach my students how to become intimate with their experiences using these three stages.

Studying the Self. To study the self means to study who we are psychologically, spiritually, and physically. In my CPE units, we do this through meditation, interpersonal group work, experiential learning, and individual supervision. We start with the essential question: Who am I? Together we explore this question from various views from the net. Another way we explore this is in Interpersonal Relationship Group (IPR), where we also learn about who we are in relationship. In a recent class, a male Zen student began to see that by being open about his anxiety he was able to connect with others. He shared his anxiety, and the other group members were able to connect with him through their own experiences of anxiety. Before this, he thought he was a person isolated by his anxiety. After that class he felt both freed by the potential for it to be a place of connection as well as a new sense of himself as less isolated. Then our learning goals for the unit are developed from this question.

Forgetting the Self. This is Dogen's second aspect of development. In CPE, I see this as what we experience when we have a self-concept and then allow something new. This is a key aspect of manifesting the awakened mind. In the beginning of a training group, we talk about this in terms of entering a patient's room. First, we must reflect on what is happening inside and outside of us—studying the self. Then the students are encouraged to develop rituals of "forgetting the self" and letting go into the moment fresh. Some students develop rituals of taking a breath, putting their hand on the wall or feeling their feet on the ground. In IPR a Zen woman experienced this "forgetting the self" when her peers asked her to share more of herself. She had thought she was too afraid to be vulnerable. When asked by a peer to be the person she thinks she is not, she stepped forward into a new moment. She found that she was able to talk more freely than she ever knew.

Allowing the World to Interpenetrate. Allowing intimacy with the fresh moment is the key aspiration in Zen. When we can study ourselves, and then forget ourselves, we can allow the world to interpenetrate. I would also translate this last aspect as allowing ourselves to be intimate with the world. Supervisors and students work together to allow the world to be a part of their lives. In my last CPE group, a Jewish male student was a part of the palliative care team. He knew that he had difficulty embodying the pastoral authority of his role as a chaplain on the team. After feedback from his peers and supervisor, he began to explore his self-concept as a shy person. He discovered that he actually felt excited about being on the palliative care team and had spiritual assessments he wished to offer. He returned to the group two weeks later reporting that he had two team rounds where he participated fully. He felt empowered to provide spiritual care to patients. The group relished this moment of witnessing their peer's newfound confidence in his pastoral authority. Dogen's three stages are linked directly to how the vast net of jewels functions operationally. When we choose to live with a larger sense of self, do we choose what is always available to us: intimacy and change? It is like a foot before and a foot behind in walking. Totally natural. Our aliveness is experienced flowing freely from inside to outside, true boundlessness, true freedom. This is the freedom from patterned ways of being. This is both the promise of Zen practice and how I understand chaplaincy.

Dissatisfaction, suffering, and unwelcome change are also our teachers. They teach us where we can lean in. We grow through our awareness of these emotional states and learning to function with them in a new way. This is vital to a true sense of spiritual maturity, to prevent spiritual bypassing. With contemplation of our direct experience, we can practice the courage of turning toward what is difficult. A good spiritual friend points out to us where we are stuck, hiding, or even abusing. I run my groups in the model of good spiritual friends who can risk intimacy with each other. They don't stay silent. They take risks. This is something I work to foster within the student-teacher relationship and within the peer group.

This is particularly present in mid-unit evaluations. Mid-unit is a time where each chaplain intern wholeheartedly reflects on his or her intrapersonal and interpersonal relationships, and then this reflection is shared. Each intern connects with his peers and teacher about what is specifically connecting and what is disconnecting in his relationships. This is a kind of inner work rarely encountered in our society and in most religious communities.

There is a student in her forties, and she is transitioning from a community she has belonged to for nearly a decade. Together we looked at her intrapersonal feelings, how her awareness affected how she functioned with her peers, teacher, and patients and staff. At the mid-unit, her peers reflected that they all experienced her as a wonderfully charismatic, gifted chaplain and leader, and this was not familiar feedback for her in her spiritual community where she was appreciated as long as she wasn't seen too much. This feedback allowed her to experience the world as full of new possibilities. She allowed the world to be interpenetrating with her experience. New identities were available to her. She visibly changed and became enlivened and the entire group noticed and celebrated this. Through this experience, I have a much broader relationship with this student as I can now explore more of her. We also discovered together that her challenge is to trust herself, that she is perfect and complete just as she is. Rather than creating a place of trying to change a student, we create together a place of becoming more deeply ourselves, which then becomes a parallel process that students discover in their spiritual care to patients.

SHADOW AND CRITICAL PURCHASE

What about the people we can't reach?

The Avatamsaka Sutra speaks of a person who has fallen so deep into the dark, he or she can't be touched by the teachings of awakening and the path. Students meet these patients who have abandoned all hope and have been so traumatized that it seems that they have fallen into this deep dark. What then? How to sit with our hopeless and helpless feelings in the moment and in relationship? Those who live in the deep dark reflect to the students their own experiences of losing control, hopelessness, and past hurts. When the practices of awakening or intimacy seem to fall short, what then? Sometimes all there is to be with is the deep sorrow or the encounter and to ask the painful questions about how that person lives in us.

After repeated exposure to the tragedy and trauma both in my personal life and in the lives of my patients, I have come back to the net of jewels. Great sorrow and great darkness are also jewels interconnected and interpenetrated with all things. Black holes are part of the dynamic universe. The awakened Buddha mind is only complete with the suffering of the world. Scripturally, I connect to this through the story of the Jizo Bodhisattva. Jizo is the mythological Buddhist figure who can go down into the hell realms and see a "mote of dust of goodness" in each person. Jizo points to an aspect of us that can go into the dark and not be consumed by it. Jizo reveals that mercy is among us. Jizo is a figure that we can both petition for help and embody. Jizo calls us to pay attention to all beings in the world. No one is left out of Jizo's net.

I often view darkness, sin, evil, and shadow as symbolic of jewels in the net, but I need to be aware of how Dogen and the sutras in my tradition are all about nonseparation. I need to widen my view to allow for the majority of the world who believe in dualism in very real and important ways. I have to kill the idea of "nondual" to be present to my students and patients. I need to keep expanding my limited views of the net. I sometimes think that everyone can expand their view to encompass all that I see. But this is not seeing: it is just plain old assumption. Students will become the path that they are, and in doing so they will help their patients become the path *they* are.

With Zen and Buddhism itself, change is the truth of life. Buddhism grounds itself in constant change. Everything is constantly changing— even if we don't notice it. So in working skillfully with religiously conservative students and/or deeply wounded students, this view may not be the most helpful. Some students need solidity, stability, good and bad. Some will appear stuck in a deep dark place. I would like to continue to remember the image of the net, the night sky in the country of vast star fields—and not assume I know the movement or inner life of any of them.

When my life felt like it was spinning too fast, I encountered that image of the monk, and now I have experienced him as a dynamic person with ten thousand joys and sorrows who is in direct relationship and interdependence with those running around him. He depends on all those around him in the net. From stillness and intimacy, the spring bubbles forth out into the world. The stillness brought me out of difficulty enough to encounter myself directly as the whole spectrum.

In the evening in Zen centers all over the world, the day ends with this chant: "Let me respectfully remind you. Life and death are of supreme importance. Time swiftly passes by and opportunity is lost. Each of us must strive to awaken. Awaken! Take heed. Do not squander your life." This is also the message that my Grandma Mimi said to me in the hospice, when she said, "It goes so fast. Drink every moment." Darkness and light are all a part of this great drink.

As I walk the many paths with my students, I listen with my whole body and mind for how their uniqueness is expressed, and this allows intimacy. In this way I can care for their jeweled webs, with the whole range of possibilities and experiences. I often find myself in awe of their jewels and threads.

Dogen says, "Every moment of practice is complete." In the educational process of chaplains, at the table, we practice intimacy. Each person is completely unique and deserves our awe just because they are. CPE invites this attitude and practice. When we share our raggedness and beauty moment by moment, we reveal our true nature, which allows authentic intimacy. Traversing heaven and earth, there is nothing not part of the jeweled net.

The Way of the Chaplain:

A MODEL BASED ON A BUDDHIST PARADIGM

Mikel Ryuho Monnett

The Tathagata has come into the world to befriend the poor,
to succor the unprotected, to nourish those in bodily affliction, both
the followers of the Dharma and unbelievers, to give sight to the blind
and enlighten the mind of the deluded, to stand up for the rights
of orphans as well as the aged, and in doing so to set an example for others.
—PAUL CARUS, *The Gospel of Buddha*

THE CURRENT MODEL of healthcare involves a relationship between a patient and a team of healthcare providers. These may include not only medical doctors but nurses, respiratory therapists, laboratory specialists, x-ray technicians, and of course, professional chaplains. In the context of providing care to the patient, the chaplain's job is unique in that he or she is required to help patients make use of their own spiritual resources to deal with the suffering they experience. A chaplain needs many skills to be able to this.

Mikel Ryuho Monnett is a member of the Zen Peacemaker Order and the Karma Kagyu lineage of Tibetan Buddhism. A longtime student of Ven. Khenpo Karthar Rinpoche and Joan Jiko Halifax Roshi, Chaplain Monnett received his bachelor's degrees from the Ohio State University in 1987 and his master's degree from Naropa University in 1999. A writer, lecturer, and ardent advocate of Buddhist chaplaincy, he is a member of the Buddhist Chaplains Network of the ACPE and previously served as the Heart Services Anchor Chaplain at Barnes-Jewish Hospital at Washington University Medical Center in St. Louis, Missouri. A specialist in disaster chaplaincy, he was twice deployed to major catastrophes in the US as part of a spiritual care team. He currently lives in Ohio with his wife, Tara Gidwani.

In what follows, I'll use several key Buddhist concepts as a frame for understanding what is required for a chaplain to truly be of service.

COMPASSION

At the heart of the Buddha's teachings is *karuna* or compassion for ourselves and others. The Buddha taught that karuna should act as the foundation of any action that we undertake, for we come to embody helpfulness and authentic presence with others only when we can put aside our own selfishness and work for the benefit of sentient beings. The Buddha said we should continually evaluate our motivation, to ensure we are acting from a compassionate place. Without karuna, our actions are tainted by our own sense of self and the distortions that brings, and thus our actions can at most accomplish a temporary good. As the great indigenous Australian activist Lilla Watson wrote, "If you have come here to help me, you are wasting your time. But if you have come because your liberation is tied up with mine, let us work together."

As chaplains, we must ask ourselves if we are doing this job just because we need a paycheck or perhaps because of prestige? Those of us in the field know this is emotionally difficult work and most chaplains are not paid that well or accorded a lot of respect.

We would like to think that those who do this work are motivated by a genuine compassion, a desire to help others. Most of the chaplains that patients and families comment on as being the best are those that they feel have a genuine empathy for them and are able to stand with them in their moment of grief or fear. And this can only happen through the development of a genuine sense of compassion.

UPAYA (SKILLFUL MEANS)

Secondly, what kind of *training* is needed, what are the skillful means a chaplain needs to be effective—what are a chaplain's *upaya*? Chaplaincy is a skill like any other, and a person needs to be trained to be able to do it. In fact, a whole industry has evolved around the training of chaplains, not only from the perspective of spiritual traditions, but from a Western psychological view as well. And before many traditions would consider certifying a person to represent them as a chaplain, they would want to make sure that person had a solid grounding in their faith tradition by virtue of ministerial credentialing and advanced study, usually represented by a degree or its equivalent.

Recently, there has been a lot of discussion about what is the proper amount of training and whether there should be a set of standards. My own view is the more training and education I have, the more tools I have to help others. But you can have all the training in the world and still not be able to apply it in actual practice. In the end, like in many things, there is a natural skill involved in making that human-to-human connection that some people have and others don't. Supervised training often helps to reveal whether or not a person is able to do this type of work.

One of the best examples of where expanded training can help is demonstrated in two of our most recent national tragedies: Ground Zero and Hurricane Katrina. In both cases, there were many local clergy that did a fantastic job, especially in helping their communities get back to a new normal *after* the disaster. But before that came to pass, there were a number of disaster chaplains that helped the community to get to that point.

Disaster chaplaincy is a specialized area of pastoral care that can augment the skills of spiritual caregivers and make their reach more extensive. Disaster chaplains must perform under hardship conditions, sometimes without the conveniences of phones, power, food, and even water. The chaplain deals with a population that may have lost its definition of self and community. The hours are normally long and irregular and the stress overwhelming: there's just *so much* to cope with. This makes the strains and pressures on caregivers extremely intense and can quickly lead to that bane of chaplains: compassion fatigue, which can sometimes even escalate into PTSD. But with skillful means developed through proper training and self-discipline, these pitfalls can be avoided or dealt with skillfully.

PRAJNA (WISDOM)

Buddhism makes a distinction between hearers (those who have heard the teachings but lack understanding), learners (those who are striving to understand the teachings), disciples (those who have learned and are striving to master the teachings), and masters (those who truly understand the teachings).

So the third assessment we need to ask of chaplains is what *experience* do we have, where do we stand with regard to our direct experience of the teachings? You can have all the motivation and training in the world and still not be able to apply it effectively to the problem at hand. The difference is between *learning*—knowledge or skill acquired by instruction or study—and *wisdom*—the ability to apply what has been learned in an effective way.

One of the hardest things to impart to students in a supervised clinical setting is that learning happens when we are given the opportunity to make mistakes. By giving students the opportunity to make mistakes, they are able to try out what they have learned and to see what works for them and what doesn't. In this way, the student learns to come from a place of authenticity rather than modeling themselves after a conception or merely aping the actions of a mentor. This authenticity can only be gained by real world experience and is one of the chaplain's most powerful tools.

SHILA (MORAL DISCIPLINE)

Fourthly, we should ask what is their *discipline*? What code of conduct do they adhere to? Chaplains are often called upon to help people deal with situations when they are most vulnerable. Devastating illnesses force people to reevaluate their sense of self-identity, of who they are. If the chaplain utilizes his or her skills properly, they can often help people to achieve a new level of spiritual understanding. But because such people are so open and vulnerable in that moment, they can also be exploited by a person lacking self-control.

We've all heard stories about clergy abuse, where clerics have used the access and trust given to them by others to satisfy their own needs and desires. The Buddhist community is not any more immune to this than are any others. The role of chaplain can be an especially troubling one in this respect because we deal with people seeking the answers to the most fundamental of life's questions: Why are we here? What is life about? How can I find meaning in my life? During the time people are asking such questions, they are in a vulnerable place, where they can be taken advantage of. Therefore, it is vital that chaplains adhere to a code of moral conduct that would prohibit them from doing so.

Furthermore, it is vital that when a person is seeking spiritual direction the chaplain refrain from proselytizing. As stated before, the chaplain's job is to help the patient utilize the patient's *own* spiritual resources to deal with the situation in which the patient finds him- or herself, not to take advantage of the situation by converting the patient. For a chaplain, the ability to avoid this temptation (and to resist others) comes through the development of *shila* or moral discipline.

VOWS AND LINEAGE

It is said that in the time of the Buddha a sage in the next town was teaching what the sage called "Buddhadharma." The monks surrounding the Blessed One went to the Buddha and said, "This sage is not a member of our order—he should not call what he teaches 'Buddhadharma' for he is not one of us!" The Blessed One listened patiently and then asked, "Does what the noble sage teaches lead to the attainment of enlightenment or away from it?" The monks thought carefully and then admitted that the path the sage laid out in his teachings would indeed lead a practitioner to liberation. Then the Blessed One said, that being the case, "Whatever is well-spoken are the words of the Buddha," and the matter ended there.

Every school of Buddhism eventually traces its lineage in some way back to Shakyamuni Buddha. As one famous Zen teaching poem says "To encounter the Absolute is not yet enlightenment"; it is merely a glimpse of emptiness and much work still needs to be done before true enlightenment is obtained. This is why all Buddhist traditions place emphasis on working with a qualified teacher who has tread the path and knows the way.

There is another reason for this emphasis. The teacher will often proscribe precepts or vows of conduct for individuals in order to help them to realize the Way. These vows are taken voluntarily and serve to help students to discipline their mind; they are only given when both student and teacher agree the student is ready. These vows—whether householder or monastic—are a sign that the teacher believes the student to have achieved a certain level of understanding and is ready to take on the more difficult parts of the path, which entail a self-discipline that is challenging to keep. Yet it is the effort and desire to keep these vows that differentiates the disciples from the hearers or the learners (to use the taxonomy introduced above) and eventually leads to liberation.

This brings us to the questions of authority. By what *authority* is a Buddhist chaplain acting in his or her role? In the chaplain's case, the connection to teacher and a lineage of ethics ensures that the person providing pastoral care in the name of a spiritual tradition is faithfully and accurately representing that tradition and its values. The chaplain should epitomize the tradition and be recognized by an endorsing body as embodying its beliefs and creed.

In sum, these characteristics frame what is required for a chaplain to be effective at relieving the suffering of others. And with these traits, a chaplain can make bad situations a bit better, simply with his or her presence.

PART III

Dharma Behind Bars:
The Arts of Prison Ministry

Gary's Story

Dean Sluyter

FOR THE PAST six years I've been the volunteer Buddhist chaplain at Northern State Prison, considered the roughest maximum-security institution in New Jersey. Our sangha of about fifteen men—officially termed Buddhist Studies class—meets every Thursday night in a bleak, gray-green cinderblock chapel that's freezing in winter, sweltering in summer. My supervisor, a rock-ribbed conservative Southern Baptist minister, conducts a Bible Studies class in the adjoining room.

During our meditations, we frequently hear the muffled voice of "The Rev" coming through the wall, rising and falling in the cadences of fire-and-brimstone preachment, answered at regular intervals by the murmured assent of his congregation. There's a P.A. speaker directly above our heads, and the sound is painfully, bone-rattlingly loud. Perhaps a dozen times during a two-hour session, we have to suspend our discussion in midsentence as the P.A. blares, "ATTENTION ALL AREAS, ATTENTION ALL UNITS: OFFICER MORALES, PLEASE PICK UP LANDLINE 17," or, "ATTENTION ALL AREAS, ATTENTION ALL UNITS: LAST CALL FOR MEDICATION. LAST CALL FOR

Dean Sluyter has practiced various forms of nondual contemplation and devotion since 1967. He is the author of *Why the Chicken Crossed the Road and Other Hidden Enlightenment Teachings*, *The Zen Commandments*, and *Cinema Nirvana: Enlightenment Lessons from the Movies*. He cofounded the New Jersey Sangha and pioneered the Buddhist Studies program at Northern State Prison in Newark. As an English teacher at the Pingry School in New Jersey, he developed the Literature of Enlightenment and Mindful Awareness programs, which introduced meditative practice and insight to several thousand students. In 2010 Dean moved to California, where he is currently at work on a book about his experiences at Northern State.

MEDICATION." In my Dharma teaching on the outside, we talk about things like surrendering your expectation of what the next moment will bring, but the idea can seem a bit abstract; here, where you can't even expect to get through a sentence, it's for real.

Gary is the longest-serving guy in the sangha: he has been locked up for twenty-eight years. He's also our most astute, earnest, conscientious member. In our little circle of blue plastic chairs, he always places himself just to the left of the little table where I set my meditation bell and sits up very straight, alert, physically tuned to every word that's said. He's usually the first to master a new prayer or practice and to politely but firmly correct me if I get something wrong or leave something out. When others have trouble with the teachings, he's quick to gently help them find the right page and line or pronounce a Tibetan mantra correctly. A slim man of perhaps English and German blood, with a few tattoos on his arms and a tiny blue stud in his left ear, he's pushing fifty, his thin mustache and close-cropped hair starting to gray.

One Thursday night I arrive in the chapel and find Gary in a state that I've never seen him in before. Clearly agitated, he can't stay in his chair. He strides straight up to me, takes both of my hands tight in his, and, close up, looks intently into my eyes. "A few days ago," he says, "I found out that I'm coming up to the parole board again." That sounds like good news to me, but he goes on. "In twenty-eight years, I've come up six times, and I've taken six hits." This means he's been denied parole six times. "The thought of taking another hit was just"—he shakes his head—"unbearable."

He stares even deeper into my eyes. "It was making me suffer so much, I couldn't take it. There was so much pain that there was just no place to put it. Finally, there was nothing else to do . . . so I opened myself to the suffering of all sentient beings. And my suffering dissolved in their suffering."

For a moment, everything else—the cinderblock chapel, the other men, the prison, time and space—everything else falls away. There's nothing but my hands in Gary's hands, my eyes in his eyes, and some raw space in which both of our hearts are blown open. Finally I stammer, "Gary, it's a miracle. It's the miracle of Dharma."

We take our seats, I ring the bell, we chant our dedication prayers, and we hold our practice session.

A few days later I'm in a New York studio, being interviewed by Dr. Mehmet Oz on Oprah & Friends Radio. The interview is supposed to center on my books, and it does for a little while, but as soon as I mention my prison work, Dr. Oz becomes fascinated, and that's all we talk about for the rest of the hour. Early in the session, when Dr. Oz asks if I'm a Buddhist, I talk about the difference between Buddhist and buddha, and explain that I'm interested not in spreading Buddhist doctrine but in helping people to become buddhas, to wake up to their liberated essence. Then I tell him Gary's story, and when I get to the end Dr. Oz says, under his breath, "Wow—he's a buddha."

Then Dr. Oz's wife Lisa, who is also participating in the show, asks, "What's he in for?" I tell her I don't know, and explain that, unlike what you see in movies, part of the ethic of prison life is that you never ask a guy about his crimes.

On my way out of the studio, Dr. Oz's people give me a CD of the session. The following Thursday night I bring it with me to our Buddhist Studies session, pop it into the cheap little boom box which is our sole approved audio equipment, put a piece of Scotch tape over the lid to hold it closed, and have the guys pull their chairs in close so they can hear the show over the tinny speakers. Gary listens with even more than his usual intentness, his eyes closed the whole time, his chin resting cupped in one hand. He doesn't say a word. But at the end of the session, as guys are filing out, a few of them joshing about Gary the buddha, he walks up to me, stands tall, looks me in the eye without blinking, and says, in a quiet, even voice, "Felony murder. I was seventeen. Now I'm forty-nine. I was so stupid."

I'm speechless. Finally I murmur, "Gary, everyone's stupid when they're seventeen." But I feel how utterly unhelpful my comment is. I think of the stupid things my buddies and I did in high school, which, if they'd gone just a little differently—if we'd, say, hit the brakes a half second later—might have destroyed our lives and those of others; but which, as it happened, we had the privilege of leaving behind, half forgotten in a haze of intoxication and adolescent hormone-madness. I realize that, when I met Maggy and got married, Gary was already locked up. When my daughter was born, Gary was locked up. While I enjoyed my long and fulfilling teaching career, raised my kids, went through the twists and turns of a twenty-five-year marriage, met great spiritual teachers, went on pilgrimages and silent retreats, gained confidence in my ability to transmit Dharma to others, wrote books, led workshops—Gary was locked up.

Still standing tall, Gary walks out of the chapel. His session with the parole board has not yet taken place. Part of the system is that a guy is never given a firm hearing date. He just knows that sometime in the coming weeks he'll be summoned from his cell without warning and made to wait outside a door with several other nervous men. I try to imagine what it's like to know that your chance for freedom will depend on how you present yourself to three strangers in a twenty-minute conversation that might take place anytime, within the next hour or the next month. Excruciating, I think, but also—like everything else in this place—an opportunity for intense Dharma practice.

At subsequent weekly sessions, I naturally ask Gary whether he has had his hearing, and the answer is always no. Eventually he is called to wait outside the door, but that's as far as he gets. Apparently, someone in the institution has it in for him, and he keeps being moved to the back of the line, so that the board runs out of time before they get to him, and he is forced to wait a few more agonizing weeks.

Then, one Thursday night, perhaps two months into this process, I come into the chapel and take my usual seat to Gary's right. Immediately he says, "I had my hearing." His expression is impenetrably neutral, but I can see that he's straining to control some strong emotion—though *which* emotion I can't tell. "They kept pushing me to the end of the line again. I had to wait three hours. The whole time, I meditated my butt off. When I finally got inside, they started asking me the same questions, pushing the same buttons they'd pushed the other six times." Tears start to well up in Gary's eyes, and my heart sinks. "But the buttons weren't there. They couldn't find a reason to keep me locked up. They're letting me go."

Now I'm starting to cry too. Quickly I glance around the room at the other guys and realize from their quiet smiles that they've already heard the news and have been waiting to let Gary spring it on me. In any other setting, I'd rush across the five or six feet between us and hug him, but ever since "The Rev" busted me and another prisoner for unauthorized hugging, I'm more careful. I stretch my arms straight out toward Gary, and, laughing, he air-hugs me back.

More weeks pass before Gary actually leaves us. Then, because he hasn't maxed out his time, he doesn't go straight to the street but first spends six months in a halfway house in Newark, working a janitorial job downtown during the day and signing in at night. Occasionally Duffy, another prison sangha member, gets a letter from him and reads it to the group. Gary writes about what a strange sensation it is, after twenty-eight years without touching money, to have a little cash in his pocket: how, when he walks, he can feel the folded-up packet of bills rubbing against the front of his thigh.

The months pass. One night I'm about to lead the Wednesday-night Dharma session that meets in my home when the doorbell rings. That's unusual, as our local sangha members all know they can just walk in. Someone goes to the door, I hear a familiar voice ask whether it's Dean Sluyter's house, and Gary walks into the room, his khaki uniform replaced by a polo shirt neatly tucked into a pair of slacks. Now we do some serious hugging. I introduce him to the group—vaguely but accurately—as an old, very dear friend, and I lead the meditation with an idiotic grin on my face. Afterward, during dessert hour, Gary and I go off into a corner and speak quietly. "I went to visit a buddy," Gary says. "He got out last year after being locked up twenty-*nine* years. We just sat in his backyard and looked at the sky. After a while, he said, 'Gary, let's get up, walk to the corner, and get ice cream. And we *got up. Walked to the corner. And got ice cream.* Dean," he says, "people have no idea." He doesn't elaborate, but I understand. Most of us have no idea how precious these ordinary things are and how casually we take them for granted.

Gary and I keep in touch. He moves home and enrolls at a vocational college, intent on getting his degree as fast as possible, which will be difficult because he's supporting himself with a day job at a fast food place. His elderly father has been in poor health for years but has hung on to see Gary's freedom. Now that Gary is out, his father goes into a steep decline and dies within a few months. Shortly after, I call Gary to meet for breakfast at a local diner; I have some news for him. Over bacon and eggs, he tells me about the funeral. "My family still lives in the same town where I grew up, and people I hadn't seen since high school turned out. But after the service, as they realized who I was, I could see them whispering and just quietly edging back, avoiding me."

Then my news. I happened to tell Gary's story to a wealthy acquaintance, and now he wants to help by paying Gary's college tuition, as long as he maintains a B+ average. Stunned, Gary puts down his fork. "I—I really don't know what to say. No one has ever done anything like that for me."

"Okay. Now, my friend wants to remain anonymous, so we'd have to set up some way to get the money straight to the school. Maybe I could call the registrar and—"

"Wait. I think I have to think this over. Would that be okay?"

I'm surprised, but of course I say, "Sure." A few days later Gary calls and asks me to tell my friend he's very grateful but he thinks he can put together enough grants and scholarship money to make it on his own. He'd rather do it that way.

And he does. Two years later, Gary graduates with a straight-A average and a degree in information technology. He gets a job as an I.T. manager for a local company; the boss hires him over several other applicants who are younger and, on paper, better qualified, explaining how impressed he is to see a man of Gary's age with the courage to take a leap into something new.

And one day, while Gary is still working his fast food job, a woman walks in and orders a cup of coffee. They start to talk, something clicks, and he knows he can't let her leave before he gets her phone number. The last I hear from him, they are at the beginning of what promises to be a lovely romance.

I don't know how things will work out for Gary . . . or for me, or you, or anyone else. Probably no one understands this better than Gary does; he graduated from Northern State with a doctoral degree in surrendering expectations.

But a Buddhist sage once said, "If you want to know your future situation, look at your present actions." To me, Gary's story is proof that no one has to be defined for a lifetime by the single worst moment of his past. Present moment by present moment, we continually create and re-create the future. And if we keep acting in each moment from a space of integrity and openheartedness—as I know Gary is—the future is a clear horizon.

Compassion Radiates through Rock

Margot Neuman, with Gary Allen

Whatever joy there is in this world
All comes from desiring others to be happy,
And whatever suffering there is in this world
All comes from desiring myself to be happy.
—SHANTIDEVA, *The Way of the Bodhisattva*

NE AFTERNOON many years ago, I was chatting with a colleague. I mentioned to him that I would soon be going to see my family in Florida—a simple statement, but one which would change the course of my entire career. "You're going to Florida?" he asked with a great deal of interest. He'd been writing to an inmate incarcerated in the Florida Department of Corrections and knew

Margot Neuman is executive director/founder of Ratna Peace Initiative and Veterans Peace of Mind Project. She grew up riding horses in Central Florida. She graduated from Central Florida University in 1980. In 1973, she became a student of Tibetan meditation master Chogyam Trungpa and has practiced and studied Tibetan and Shambhala Buddhism for the past thirty-eight years. She has been a meditation instructor and teacher for twenty-five years and has taught meditation in prisons eighteen years. She fulfilled a longtime desire to teach mindfulness practices to veterans as a means of coping with posttraumatic stress in 2009. As part of her veterans program, she is collaborating with "Medicine Horse," a mindfulness-based equine-assisted therapy for youth-at-risk, troubled teens, and victims of trauma.

Gary Allen grew up in Vermont, studying English at the University of Vermont, and subsequently receiving BA and MFA degrees in writing and poetics from Naropa University. He has lived in Boulder, Colorado, all his adult life, except for five years spent teaching English in South Korea, as well as traveling around Asia. He's the author of two books of poetry, *The Missionary Who Forgot His Name* and *Love Strolls Among Its Own Fires*, as well as the editor for *Walking the Tiger's Path:* *(continued overleaf)* that I had extensive experience with meditation. "There is an inmate there who would really benefit from seeing a meditation instructor," he hinted with a slight question in his voice. "This man was originally given the death penalty, but his sentence was later reduced to life in prison. Would you be willing to go visit him in the prison and give him instruction? Is that too scary?" he wondered. For some reason, this simple, straightforward request over the phone set my heart pounding. Apparently, my heart knew that I had every intention of visiting this prisoner. I was a trained instructor, and I'd taken the bodhisattva vow. It took two weeks for my head to reach this conclusion, but before long I found myself driving down desolate back roads of Florida, using the two hour drive time to rouse my courage. Once I arrived and made my way through security, I was okay. I was at the point-of-no-return anyway, so I could relax and enjoy a sense of adventure.

The chaplain was a very kind, elderly gentleman who had previously been chaplain for a prison in Korea—an extraordinary stroke of luck for me as this was my first prison visit, and he was completely respectful of other religions. I was hesitant to begin with, so I'd hoped not to be greeted by a scowling chaplain who thought of Buddhism as heretical. He met me at the gate and spent quite a while with me, explaining what to expect as well as the rules and why they are important. He spoke kindly of the difficulties prisoners must endure. He had succeeded in assuaging my fears, but it didn't last long. I was turned over to a prison guard who escorted me to the cell block housing the inmate.

"Now pay attention to the route we're taking to the cell block," he instructed as we navigated a rather long walk with numerous turns, "because you are going to have to find your way back on your own when you are finished with your visit." *Ummmmm, excuse me?* I thought to myself. "In that case, I wish I had paid closer attention," I said out loud.

A *Soldier's Spiritual Journey in Iraq* by Paul M. Kendel. He has studied and practiced Vajrayana Buddhism for thirty-three years under the guidance of Chögyam Trungpa Rinpoche, and he directs Shambhala Training meditation programs around the US. The education director for the Ratna Peace Initiative, he's taught meditation to prison inmates since 1990, and teaches mindfulness in Ratna's "Veterans Peace of Mind Project."

Also alarming to me, the path to the cell block led through the prison yard, with inmates walking back and forth, greeting us with cheerful calls of "Good morning." (I had not as yet learned that prisoners aren't lurking in corners, waiting for an opportunity to ambush volunteers.) I was sure he would relent and offer an escort for me, but to my utter astonishment, he did not. What could I do but carry on and begin my visit?

The cell block, housing prisoners regarded as dangerous, consisted of a guard station located behind bulletproof glass, with cell blocks extending out like spokes of a wheel. The spokes contained rows of cells, and inmates were screaming and yelling back and forth to each other. It was a very loud atmosphere and altogether harsh. I waited in a small room which functions as a meeting room for inmates and attorneys. The guard returned about five minutes later with Geof, the inmate.

"Are you nervous?" he smiled kindly, his hands cuffed in front of him.

"A little," I responded. "But more importantly, I'm very happy to be here with you." At that moment, I was indeed happy to be there, and he was very grateful, honored even, that I would visit him. He spoke to me of his crime, admitted his guilt, talked about his extreme regret and sorrow. We talked of his discovery of Buddhism; we talked about his life, the reality of his life sentence; I gave him meditation instructions, and we practiced together; all this occurred with deafening, chaotic cursing and yelling in the background by perhaps a hundred inmates. It was all right there; that's what it's like in a maximum-security prison in semi-lockdown conditions. The feeling of it oozed into my bones, and while, strangely, it did not really distress me, it completely opened my heart to the kind of life prisoners lead.

For Geof, my visit must have seemed something from another planet. I witnessed how much it meant to him, how much it spoke to his humanity. One of the most fulfilling rewards of prison ministry is to see the appreciation, and yes, relaxation, on the faces of the incarcerated when they realize that there is a set of sensibilities and beliefs in the world which cares about them and has not forgotten them. A visit from a volunteer is a rare opportunity for prisoners to relate with someone who does not speak to him as a prisoner but rather as a worthy human being. It's an extremely refreshing contrast to that of society at large, which typically reviles them, and, as Sister Helen Prejean said, regards them as "disposable human trash." How is it possible for offenders or society to accomplish any healing whatsoever when this basic human need is heartlessly disregarded?

When I left the prison two hours later, I was stunned by the enormity of the meaningful interaction that had just occurred. I reflected on the Buddha's enlightenment in India 2,500 years ago, and 1,200 years after that, Padmasambhava took the teachings to Tibet. My teacher, Trungpa Rinpoche, escaped the Chinese Communist takeover of Tibet in 1959 and brought the teachings to the West. It felt somehow meaningful to travel down the desolate back roads of Florida to a high security penitentiary, with these same teachings entrusted in my novice care. "Compassion," I thought, "is an unstoppable force—without obstruction, it radiates through rock."

This was the beginning eighteen years ago of what is now the Ratna Peace Initiative, a nonprofit organization associated with Shambhala Buddhism that, among other activities, serves prisoners through visits and correspondence in all fifty states. In the years of our forays into the prison world, we have met a population of decent human beings living through the darkest hours of their lives.

Prisoners constitute a diverse group of people. Society at large harbors a blanket interpretation of what is in fact a population of individuals who have made terrible mistakes, or have been in the wrong place at the wrong time. Some have been lost in a haze of drug addiction. Some have caused great harm—others, not so much. Many have been "victims" of politicians representing an overly puritanical set of ideological beliefs, eager to demonize prisoners in order to win election on a tide of citizen fear. Ratna's teachers have met individuals in all categories and, in most cases, have been with them long enough to witness positive changes. It is a joy, not to mention a sense of fruition, to witness the transformation of a heavily burdened mind grow lighter and more at ease.

A case in point is Taylor, a man who attended our weekly Buddhist meditation group over a period of several years. His background had been very violent, I learned, and each time he arrived for the class, I rather wondered why he wanted to be there. Arrogant and contemptuous, he openly stated that he didn't like people and didn't care what happened to them. He found them to be "annoying and stupid idiots." His violent history didn't seem to trouble him. Yet I was surprised to see that he appeared in the door of the small chapel, ready to meditate and participate in the talk and discussion every week without fail. "This will be the acid test," I mused, "of the efficacy of meditation and Buddhist teachings."

I don't know what the turning point was—perhaps it occurred slowly, over a period of time, but it became apparent that his heart was opening, and he began to hear the teachings with less doubt and cynicism. Past violent actions began to weigh on his conscience, and worry about his own karma mushroomed. He became impassioned with the desire to uncover the "real Taylor" underneath the rage. He began to understand how blind his conclusions had been. I had provided audiotapes of Pema Chodron's commentary on Shantideva's "Patience" verses, which expound in great detail the inaccuracy and ineffectiveness of anger in any situation whatsoever. Over the next few months, he could be found in the chapel in his free time, listening to all five recorded talks over and over.

One evening he announced that he'd decided to follow Pema's advice to practice generosity one day per week. "Normally when I go to the commissary and someone asks me to pick something up for them, I say, 'Get it for your own damn self.' But on Generosity Day," he continued, his face looking tortured, "I groan, grit my teeth, and say, 'Fine, okay!'"

I had to smile to myself, because he was clearly exerting a staggering level of discipline to reverse his usual response. As further evidence to Taylor's determination, that same evening, I asked another inmate, Tony, if he had also been listening to the tapes.

"I can't," he replied. "I don't have any earphones, and chapel rules won't allow you to listen to anything unless you have them."

As Tony was speaking, I noticed that Taylor, who was sitting behind him, grimaced and struggled as though tearing a New York phone book in half. Suddenly he blurted out, with something of a scowl on his face, "Okay, Okay! You can borrow my earphones. But don't mess 'em up, man!"

Soon thereafter, we began the study of *lojong* and *tonglen*, the Mahayana teachings of compassion, which instantly struck a chord with Taylor. As each week progressed he seemed to be softer in his attitudes, more kind in his demeanor, and happier in his smile.

"I don't know what's happened to me, Mama," he said, addressing me by the nickname the inmates used for me. "I can't bear to see any-one suffering! If I even see a little kid on a TV commercial get hurt, for God's sake, I have to turn away so the guys won't see the tears in my eyes. It's embarrassing!"

Just before he was released from the prison, he wrote a thank-you letter:

> I have gotten over so much of what I was holding inside myself: rage, anger, hatred, everything you would think about a pris-oner. They oozed out of me at all times. So I could not have explained what they were as I was so lost inside of them that they seemed normal . . . they seemed to be helpful to me, which is about as perverse as a man can get, thinking that all of this hatred and rage is helpful, but they seemed to be my defense; a way for me to deal with this world without getting hurt. I know now what I was really feeling, but how do you give up even the most perverse belief system when you have been brainwashed by its seeming successes?
>
> This is where I was when I started meditating, which is why I must thank you for myself, and for all of us that you have devoted so much time and energy to. It is simply astounding to me to think about all the endless good you have done in so many prison communities, and I am humbled and heartened that you would go into prison and show us, the lost of the lost, a better way. I have seen you change each one of us, one by one, with such patience and courage . . . and I know that it is little more than a miracle that I was blessed, to be brought to a situation where I could be separated from the world that was killing me in order to hear the Dharma with my heart, and be shown a perfect love by my instructor.
>
> How is it so easy for you to come in contact with us, most of the worst the world has to offer? But there is something in your eyes that tells the truth of the matter, that you are doing something pure and that you see us as we may become, the golden buddha covered over by mud. You have taken the

ideal that we are worthy of these jewels and that has not gone unnoticed by us. There is nothing so beautiful as a pure heart and an exertion that extends from its purity, and I am amazed, astounded, by the purity and the compassion that it takes to do what you do.

Lastly, I would like to thank you for something that you may not have seen, but was given to me by you. I would like to thank you for my future and my life that would have been, otherwise, a recurring nightmare of violence and death and realms of endless lives gone awry. I cannot thank you enough.

I had tears in my eyes as I read the letter. One can live a lifetime without receiving such appreciation. If I had *ever* needed motivation to continue on (which I don't), this letter would have done it.

As much as I appreciated the gratitude (he gave me too much credit), the more significant point here is that his letter is a precise articulation of how much can be contributed to the welfare of others by sharing what has been given to us. I'm not a martyr; this is not self-sacrifice. I love what I do, and it brings me joy, and the same is true for all the devoted members of Ratna.

When Taylor was released, he was a changed man. He secured a job and enrolled in college where he earned a 4.0 average. He married and became a doting father to his young stepson. He continued with his Buddhist path and was even able to meet and personally receive blessings from Khenchen Thrangu Rinpoche. He had brought his family to the children's blessing that day, so I took the opportunity to introduce him to Rinpoche. As Taylor and his family were leaving, his wife commented to me, "Thanks for fixing him."

"You're welcome, but I didn't fix him—he fixed himself."

And that is the teaching in Buddhism. No one can do it for you and you can't do it for anyone else. The Buddha showed us which way to walk, but the walking is up to us. Taylor was a strong walker.

This is a key point regarding prisons. While prison tends to be difficult at best for Dharma practice, with some help, determined inmates can turn its irritations and obstacles into a potent path. However, relating to prisons from the outside is regularly fraught with problems. For example, while probably 99.9% of the US mail reaches its destination, mail to prisons simply disappears and never finds its addressee with remarkable frequency.

One may go as a religious volunteer to a meeting at a prison one night a week for seven years and then show up as usual and be told there's no record of who you are and be refused entrance. One might drive two hours one way, go through the whole process of identification, passing through the metal detector, removing your belt, shoes, etc., then get through the process of the inner gates, only to have the place go on lock-down and have to leave—or make the whole trip simply because the prison didn't warn you that a lockdown had already occurred. Perhaps you make the trip and no one shows up because the prison stopped advertising your program for some unknown reason. There are many such issues.

The complexity, inefficiency, and institutional paranoia of prisons require—not just of the inmates but anyone who relates to them—a quality of equanimity and patience, which we as Buddhist "ministers" must apply regularly as part of our path.

One of the most difficult obstacles that crops up is the uncooperative administrator because nothing can get done, particularly for Buddhist inmate groups, without administrative assistance.

A good percentage of prison chapels are run by chaplains who are very helpful and dedicated to facilitating the religious life of all faiths. Prisoners have few rights, but one that is guaranteed to them by the Constitution of the United States is the freedom of religion. As a prison chaplain, the major duty of the post is to ensure that prisoners of all faiths receive what they need to practice their faith.

However, chaplains with Christian fundamentalist religious beliefs can cause a great deal of difficulty for Buddhist practitioners. I hear of it constantly in letters from inmates who are struggling to practice in an entirely hostile environment. Inmates sometimes write that when Bud-dhist materials arrive from organizations such as ours, the chaplain qui-etly slips them into a drawer, where they remain indefinitely. A chaplain will insist that an inmate does not need a meditation cushion or mala. Shockingly frequent is the report that Buddhists aren't allowed to meet in the chapel.

I personally encounter discrimination when I visit such a chapel—the chaplain will do what he can to discourage me, knowing that ultimately he cannot keep me out because I have the credentials and that is the law. I visited one such prison—the chaplain begrudgingly let me in, but then failed to notify the inmates that I was there. Only one inmate with whom I'd been communicating knew about my visit and showed up. As Buddhists, we were not allowed in the main chapel (an illegal denial), assigned instead a small, cold, rather dark room. We waited and waited and no one came.

I walked to the chaplain's office. "Why aren't the inmates here?"

"Well, I don't know," he responded with undisguised contempt. "Maybe they couldn't be found. I'll send a clerk out to look for them." This was so obviously a stalling tactic; it was laughable. We were required to leave the institution after two hours; one had already elapsed.

"This has happened before," Zach said. "When Bo Lozoff [a very famous prison teacher] came to speak to us, a lot of inmates were interested in attending. Same as now, Bo was waiting for the rest of the inmates to arrive."

"When is this going to get started?" Bo inquired of the chaplain.

"Well, I can't tell ya' when it's gonna get started, but I can sure as heck tell ya' when it's going to end," was the appalling reply.

At such times, as a pastoral counselor I am tempted to report the unmitigated illegal behavior of the chaplain, however, there is a substantial risk that the inmate will suffer retaliation in some form (which is why inmates themselves seldom report various kinds of abuses to the administration). As Buddhists volunteers, like the inmates, we also have to take the insults in such situations as these.

I treasure these experiences, surprisingly, because I learn firsthand the helplessness and lack of control that is the life of a prisoner. When I see how angry some of the inmates become because of this, I can't help but conclude that a chaplain is not doing a good job for his charges if he creates rage in them. I don't ever have to doubt that they are telling me the truth when they complain, and I also know firsthand the importance of not allowing such treatment to escalate to anger. It would be self-defeating in most cases. It doesn't help; it only aggravates the suffering.

Anger and aggression play a central role in prison life and mark the experience of prison from all sides—society, family, the courts, the institution, the inmates, and the prison staff. It's often a state of aggression and violence that turns people into criminals and lands them in prison. "That's my whole problem," some will say. "I wouldn't be here if I weren't so angry." An angry upbringing or environment leads to acting it out, and often enough, society contends with that behavior by locking it up.

Even if this is not the case, nonviolent inmates often liken their arrest, trial, and sentencing to a situation full of predators, sociopaths, and sometimes brutal guards, where they're branded by society as its "filth," and often abandoned by family, such that it leads them to stew in a hellish cauldron of rage toward themselves and toward the world. This can easily seal them into lifelong sociopathology. On the other hand, if they realize that they can't go on trapped in their own hatred, in conflict within themselves and everyone around them (and prison has all kinds of quick punishments for hot heads), it could finally wake them up to look for a different way.

It was both revelatory and completely sensible to us, then, when Tibetan master Khenpo Tsultrim Gyamtso advised us to teach inmates the "Patience Chapter" in *The Way of the Bodhisattva*, a classic, extremely detailed exploration of the causes of anger and the cultivation of its antidotes, patience and compassion. It's the Mahayana vision of compassion that brought us into this work to begin with, and it has certainly required (ourselves included) the cultivation of patience in working regularly with all the irritations of prisons. But for inmates, the ability to let go of their raging states of mind through meditation and through contemplating the issues of anger and discipline allows them to see their situation more clearly. They begin to look beyond their own needs to discover the suffering around them, including that of the prison staff and guards, as well as their fellow inmates. It is a watershed insight that turns their lives around. Men and women, very battered by their life experiences, begin to actually find their way out of their emotional hell realm maze, an inner prison constantly reinforced by the outer one, and into the fresh air of their own humanity. Once they make the connection between the cause and effect of rage, they begin to restrain their temper and treat others with decency and empathy, thereby curing the fundamental affliction of prison itself: self-absorbed aggression.

We have seen lives turn around in remarkable ways when they come to this crucial understanding. We know many examples of even good lives with happy marriages, children, high-paying jobs, the backyard barbeque—the American dream—completely destroyed. We have seen people finally come to terms with themselves, their actions, and their conduct in the world, and transform their desolate lives in prison into fertile ground for service to others. Instead of just "killing time," which could encompass one's entire lifespan, they become motivated to work with the prison environment—its bureaucrats, onerous rules, capricious punishments, endless convict games and dramas—to improve conditions for other inmates. From negotiating for a yoga class or more inmate privileges to helping indigent prisoners obtain some basic toiletry items or a little more food, they manage to make something of value out of what was lost and wasted.

They begin to envision ways to help others upon their release from prison.

Over the years of doing this work and developing Ratna Peace Initiative as an organization, we've accumulated and evolved our materials, from the most helpful kinds of Dharma books for inmates, files on everything from vegetarianism to advice on dying, even a through-the-mail refuge vow ceremony given to us by Sakyong Mipham so that inmates can take the refuge vow in their cells. Our correspondence courses are very popular, studying respectively sitting meditation and contemplation practices, the whole path of Dharma, and Shantideva's "Patience Chapter," as we were advised by the Khenpo. Above all, we've tried to remain focused on giving inmates personal interaction and guidance through our correspondence, abundant commentary on their course work, and prison visitation, feeling that, based on long experience, this is a crucial element in transmitting the Dharma and helping them make a connection to their own humanity.

Ratna has also evolved into additional projects. We counseled Sgt. Paul M. Kendel in the discovery of his spiritual journey while he was deployed to Iraq. His book, *Walking the Tiger's Path: A Soldier's Spiritual Journey in Iraq*, chronicles his experience of applying Buddhist principles of nonaggression and compassion in the midst of a war zone. In 2009, we instituted a program teaching a more secular mindfulness meditation practice as a psychological tool for military veterans suffering from posttraumatic stress disorder, called "Veterans Peace of Mind Project." As part of our program, we have collaborated with "Medicine Horse," an equine-assisted psychotherapy treatment also based on mindfulness techniques.

Throughout all our work, we've witnessed the power of the Dharma to uplift and transform lives, from the trauma of combat and military service to the harsh, antithetical prison environment. Our conviction in its virtue and efficacy sustains us through the many obstacles of trying to run a small nonprofit and work with the vast morass of the prison system, growing green shoots among the concrete and razor wire.

We Belong to One Another

Penny Alsop

T HE FEDERAL CORRECTIONAL INSTITUTION in Tallahassee, Florida, sits atop rolling hills on acres of bright green pastures where ancient oak trees dot the landscape and others cluster near a tiny halfhearted stream. Summer blooming crepe myrtles line the driveway leading to the entrance, dropping pink, white, and lavender snowflake blossoms in August when the air is thick with hot humidity. Flocks of Canadian geese forage in the grass, pecking at bugs and rounding up their babies when they wander from the bucolic pasture onto the searing asphalt parking lot.

From the highway, one can see the red tile roof of the prison, the old brick of its facade, and the tall palm trees hugging the front doors and mistake it perhaps for a grand hotel. Preoccupied and moving swiftly from a distance, it's easy to miss the three rows of razor wire surrounding the perimeter of the yard.

Locals are often surprised to hear that there's a federal prison in our neighborhood. And few who know of its existence realize that it houses women—mothers, wives, daughters, grandmothers, and sisters. Rarer

A native Floridian, proud Southerner, and single mother, **Penny Alsop** has had incarnations in this lifetime as an Appalachian Trail hiker, ski instructor, llama wrangler, farmer, small business owner, nonprofit founder, and introvert all the while. Penny's interest in Buddhism was piqued at age twelve. Upon reading Herman Hesse's novel *Siddhartha*, she recalls tapping the blue cover of the paperback book, saying, "That's what I want." She took refuge with Pema Chodron and bodhisattva vows with Khandro Rinpoche. In 2009, Penny began chaplaincy studies with Roshi Joan Halifax and Sensei Beate Stolte at Upaya Zen Center. She was ordained as a Buddhist chaplain in 2011. Penny has served as a meditation instructor at a women's federal prison for the past ten years and is a volunteer chaplain for hospice.

still is the individual who knows that over *one thousand* women live there. This is one of the painful realities of incarceration. Once an inmate, *you* are easily forgotten. From the outside, no one knows you're there. From the inside, relentless scrutiny tinged with suspicion is unabated. This combination of invisibility and hyperconspicuousness is a potentially toxic mixture leaving many feeling as if they no longer exist fully as human beings or that their lives matter.

Nonetheless, there are many people—chaplains, wardens, officers, and volunteers alike—who are devoted to bringing as much kindness as possible into a system that is hard on everyone.

While this short account may offer a glimpse of what it's like to live or work inside, as a weekly volunteer, I cannot know much, truly, about what it is like. Instead, my hope is that my account of the past ten years serves as a reminder that things, and in particular people, are rarely only as they seem at a distant first glance. It's also a call to everyone to reconsider where one stands within the world of the forgotten; those who, for one painful reason or another, are reluctant members of a population who are easily discarded, shunned, overlooked, and otherwise made invisible—the ones who are left to fend for themselves in the dark shadows of some grand hotel.

I began volunteering in response to a request made by an inmate who had contacted the Shambhala Prison Community (SPC) for help in finding someone to lead Buddhist services. The prison's head chaplain was enthusiastic and supportive at the prospect of introducing Buddhism to the institution. When my meditation instructor called to ask if I'd lend a hand, I agreed to go inside to get a feel for the situation. I attended a very short program that the SPC's executive director, Bill Karelis, led. By the time we left the compound and before making it to the parking lot, I'd made my decision.

Since that visit in the early spring of 2001, I have returned to the prison every week, with few exceptions. With others' help, we've also led several weekend retreats, day-long practice periods, and shorter writing and poetry workshops. Once a month I meet with meditation students individually, to talk about their practice. The size and makeup of the group morphs for no apparent reason, as new inmates find the group and as others are released. Virtually all of those who attend the meditation sessions have a religion or spiritual path other than Buddhism; to date, predominantly Catholicism. I've met a total of five Buddhists inside in all this time.

I've led groups of thirty, and on occasion only a single person will be in attendance. Many sessions have included me as the only English speaker with no translator. The size of the group is of no concern. I've promised that I will continue coming every week as long as at least one person wants me there. In ten years, there's been just one instance where only a single person showed up and never has there been a time when no one showed up for meditation.

While the original impetus to go inside came as a result of a specific request, what keeps me coming back is primarily the unspoken entreaty of the prisoners. It's the same one that we all share: to be seen as worthy in our own right. It's this, and an ever-deepening understanding that we belong to one another, that brings me back.

Mother Teresa said, "If we have no peace, it's because we've forgotten that we belong to each other." I think that we could spend the rest our lives contemplating the meaning of what it means to belong to each other and just as long allowing the natural arising of a response to the embodiment of this belonging to unfold. "Belonging to one to another" patiently waits for us to show up.

It's Mother's Day, 2002. Hundreds of women crowd into the small, sparsely decorated chapel. Hard plastic chairs line the wall at a right angle to the center of room, squeezed in to make room for as many people as possible and still many stand. At the podium the chaplain stands waiting as more people file in. He has stayed several hours late to conduct a special service. "It's the hardest day of the year for them," he whispers to me. "Much harder than Christmas," he adds emphatically.

Everything runs according to a definitive schedule in prison. Running twenty minutes behind as we are now doesn't mean the program will go beyond the specified end time—it means we've lost twenty minutes of our time together. With people still coming in, the chaplain begins. "Who here is a mother? Raise your hand if you are a mother," he says. Almost every hand in the chapel goes up.

I make myself look at as many faces as I can see from where I've taken a seat against the wall. It's almost unbearable as I push myself to imagine what it would be like to be separated from my daughter—unable to talk to her when I want to, unable to receive a text message that she's arrived safely at her destination on a rainy night, unable to hold her in my arms when she's sad or take care of her when she's sick, unable to look into her eyes.

The ache in my heart is palpable, made more intense as the chaplain tries to determine who is the youngest mother in the room. "Raise your hand if you are a mother and under twenty-five," he says. Many hands go up. "Under twenty-one. Under twenty." It's finally narrowed down to a single nineteen-year-old. She's the youngest mother in the group, who desperately needs parenting of her own, I suspect. His investigation continues for the oldest mother. The mother with the most children. The mother whose home is farthest away. His intentions are good.

He wants to celebrate motherhood, yet excruciatingly deep rivers of pain etch the faces in the crowd, few are dry-eyed. The recognition of their motherhood is appreciated and simultaneously gut-wrenching.

Later, when the service finishes, many linger even as time is running out to get across the compound before it closes. Failure to do so is an infraction that could land one in the special housing unit. Still, M., who has sat with the meditation group every week without fail for the past year, approaches with her inextinguishable smile to hand me bright yellow flowers she's taken from the small patch outside. She's not permitted to give me anything nor am I allowed to receive anything, not even a piece of paper. The exasperated chaplain says, "I wish you would stop doing this," as he reaches between us for the now wilting flowers, handing them to me with a sigh. His intervention makes the gift acceptable, though later he instructs me to throw them away.

M. hasn't seen her youngest child in over ten years. She beams brightly when I ask his name. She asks me if I have children. I'm new here. I don't know the unwritten rules and am not sure how to answer until the ache in my heart intervenes, erasing the doubt of what's acceptable. "Yes, I have a daughter," I reply. M.'s smile is a wide as the sky. "Que linda!" she exclaims. M. regularly asks about my daughter from that day forward.

Many years later, M. is finally released. Having served over fifteen years for crimes she never revealed to me, I see tears in her eyes for the first time in the nine years we've known one another. I've bent over to touch my forehead to hers as a farewell, a wish for her happiness and a gesture of the tremendous respect that I have for her; this woman, far and long from home, with an indomitable spirit, unshakable kindness, courage, gratitude, and insatiable curiosity. M. has been responsible for spreading the word of the group's existence and encouraging dozens of women to attend. With her release, our biggest and most vocal cheerleader will be gone.

I've been through this parting as sentences are completed, many times. It's a separation that's both joyous and oftentimes tremendously sad. M. has told me that meditation saved her life by helping her to not be afraid. She repeats that now with the help of a translator. Her tears spill over then as I unsuccessfully attempt to choke back my own. What comes out instead is something akin to a stifled wail.

Given other circumstances, we'd be friends. This is the moment of saying goodbye, but it has qualities of death, too. Because prison rules do not allow contact between volunteers and ex-offenders, it's likely that we'll never see or hear from each other again. "Thank you, Miss Penny," she says in English as clearly and articulately as any native speaker. It's the first full English sentence she's ever spoken to me. It is almost certainly the last.

This is a system that relies on rules and standard operating procedures. It's much too easy to rely solely on them and there is precious little room for much else. Every now and then, there's a break from the rigidity and intensity. It's the weekend of the longest meditation retreat we've held in the prison. Forty-five women are in attendance. Miraculously we've been permitted to bring in flowers, a large gong, extra cushions, incense. Everyone is vibrating with anticipation and excitement. A gathering like this simply doesn't happen, and what's more, permission has been granted to hold "the count" right in the chapel that's been emptied and scheduled just for us for the entire weekend.

Every day, several times per day, each inmate must return to her housing unit to be counted. Failure to be in the right place at the designated time is another major infraction. The warden, however, agreed to allow the participants to stay in the chapel to be counted, allowing the program to continue with only a brief interruption.

When it's time to conduct the count, the volunteers are asked to step far back from the group of inmates seated on the burgundy meditation cushions and straight back chairs at the center of the room. We make our way over to the dais to wait while each name is called and checked off a preprinted list of names and numbers. This is not roll call. The purpose of the count is to make certain that everyone is where they should be; much more than a matter of determining whether one is present or not. Failure to be present and accounted for could result in a lockdown of the entire facility.

As names are called, women stand up, echo their number. Again, I force myself to watch as mature women stand up when their name is called and remain standing until they are told to sit down. One after the other, women who have birthed children, run businesses, completed graduate degrees, traveled far and wide, survived abuse and addiction, stand and sit on command. The recitation of their numbers chills and embarrasses me.

Recollecting other instances where humans have been reduced to numbers is so shocking I'm first numb, then outraged, then humiliated for them and all of us who stop noticing, long before we remember our shared humanity. Desperate to make a place for some dignity to remain, I cast my eyes downward to wait it out.

Later that weekend, we're granted yet another unheard-of allowance. We're permitted to join the inmates in the dining hall for lunch. I'm eager to spend this more relaxed time with women I've come to know quite well. The meal is plain, almost pitiful, but the delight of being able to share a semblance of normalcy, such as sharing food, is delicious.

We belong to each other. Our belonging is made evident in the most mundane ways. When these exchanges aren't possible or when they are taken away, it's so easy to forget our mutuality, our intimate bond with one another and who we are.

One of the reasons for going inside is to foster the practice of remembering.

Remembering our ineffable and inextricable connection to one another.

Remembering our own fundamental goodness. Remembering the fundamental goodness of others.

Just as inmates are told that they can choose to use the time in prison to lead them to more freedom or more restriction, we too have a choice to make. We can choose to stand on the razor's edge of connection to all sentient beings, or we can let a particularly difficult story trick us into believing that one is more deserving of love than another.

I sense that the inmates I serve deeply appreciate my presence in the prison. There is appreciation for meditation instruction, for a quiet place to practice, for retreats and workshops, yet the resounding refrain I hear is that they appreciate being "treated like a human being." I understand that I am in the position to show love and gratitude for their existence without being required to run it through a filter of hesitation, rules, regulations, assessments, adjudications, and security. When it is possible to respond to such a call, our shared humanity implores us to do so. When it is not possible to respond to such a call, our shared humanity implores us to look elsewhere.

I do not view my presence in the prison as anything special or noble. I feel at home there and that needs no scrutiny. I am acutely aware of how we all are teetering much closer than we realize to choices that may end up in our own incarceration, in one form or another. As a mother, I have a particular sensitivity for what it means to be unwillingly separated from those whom we love. Roll this all up together and you simply have someone who is willing and able to go into this difficult situation. It's quite ordinary, this belonging to one another.

The chances are exceedingly rare to hear firsthand someone's story of incarceration: what led up to it, what life is like inside, what was missed, and how it's changed someone. We won't know of the aftershocks upon release and attempted reentry; the bravery, the sheer force of will and the depths to which one must reach to get up and try again. We run the risk that a subtle form of not caring can slip in as we're shielded from these painful details. What we do know is that life in prison is difficult beyond imagining.

Standing at the edge of a world that is largely good enough and one that is decidedly not, the call is to be a bridge for one other. When we can, we must set in motion the words, gestures, deeds, and aspirations that make a resounding echo for freedom from suffering for everyone, without exception; rekindling the ancient memory of our intimate connection to one another, our fundamental good heart and the things that we love that make us fully human.

I was asked by a fellow chaplaincy student if I thought my presence in the prison is helpful to the women with whom I study and practice. "I don't know," I answered. "It doesn't matter whether it is or not," I said as I silently recalled how in the deep South where I am from, when someone dies, friends, family, acquaintances, everyone, gathers at their side. Nothing much happens except the delivery of massive amounts of food. There are endless hours of just sitting there.

I go because that's what we, in our belonging to one another, do for each other. We show up and we stay.

All My Relations

Richard Torres

E ACH MORNING as I walk toward the entrance of the Oregon State Penitentiary, I watch and listen for the calls of birds. The *eek-eek* of blue-grey scrub jays and the *caw-caw* of crows. I enjoy watching the crows float over the thirty-foot concrete walls, barbed wire spirals, and electric fencing to find their perch in an enormous oak tree that stands just outside of "the institution." Sometimes, a hawk defies the scolding crows to perch atop an antennae extending from the roof of the visitor's building. The birds are an excellent barometer of what's going on inside on any given day. Their behavior transmits the weather as well as the mood of the institution. On more than one occasion, the birds have alerted me to unseen dangers behind the prisons walls.

One morning as I walked toward the institution a scrub jay gave out an especially loud alarm call. There were no predators in sight. The weather was clear and calm. I knew the jay's call was a warning for me. Since being

Richard Torres is a chaplain at Oregon State Penitentiary. He received his master of divinity degree from Naropa University and practiced Zen Buddhism under the instruction of Gerry Shishin Wick, Roshi at the Great Mountain Zen Center in Boulder, Colorado. Richard completed a residency in clinical pastoral education at Aspirus Hospital in Wausau, Wisconsin, and served as a hospice chaplain before being called into prison ministry. While serving as a prison chaplain, a deep sense of kinship was awakened between Richard and members of the Northwest Native community. Richard's advocacy for the spiritual practices of incarcerated Natives led to his being welcomed into the healing ceremonies of Northwest Natives. This prompted him to reconnect with his own Native heritage and to be initiated by Taino elder Miguel Sague. Richard lives in Oregon with his wife, two children, and German shepherd and is currently developing rites of passage for young men.

initiated into the ways of my Taino ancestors I've developed immense respect for what the birds communicate—and I've learned that there are times when the birds carry messages from our relatives in the spirit world. I slowed my pace, heeding the jay's call, and stood outside of the institution for a few minutes, feeling a bit awkward as I wasn't certain of the reason for my hesitation. When I reached the chapel my colleague Sister Bean asked if I was okay, and went on to explain that a gang fight had taken place in the stairwell that leads to my office just minutes before I arrived.

This simple ritual of paying attention to the sight and sounds of birds helps me to remember that I am supported by my relatives, before entering an environment that's hellbent on maintaining the illusion that we're all alone.

Once inside the visiting lobby the physical reminders of separation are everywhere.

I greet Sgt. Matson standing in the dimly lit master control room behind bulletproof glass.

"Morning, Dennis."

"Morning, Richard."

Dennis passes a set of keys for me through a small opening in exchange for my identification card: fifteen keys in all, plus a whistle that I can blow if I'm in danger. The enormous key that opens the 10 x 6 steel door to the chapel floor looks like a key to a medieval dungeon. I pass four steel gates, two steel doors, and two wooden doors on the way to my office. The men dressed in blue and denim are called inmates, the men and women dressed in grey or black military fatigues are called officers, those in civilian clothes are called "security plus staff." I belong to the latter category, and I am prohibited from wearing blue lest I be mistaken for an inmate.

The first time I walked into the prison my heart was racing and I felt like I was going to vomit. I noticed how much energy was invested in maintaining control. The environment heightened my awareness of how fear of the worst possible outcome is capable of conditioning our actions. Simple tasks like keeping track of my keys and locking every door behind me took a while to get used to. Losing track of my keys produced a feeling of shame and panic akin to not having my homework in grade school.

I could feel the tremendous pressure within prison culture designed to make newcomers conform to the rules and had to remind myself that this was not normal. These days keeping track of my keys has become routine. I understand that all the barriers and vigilance on the verge of paranoia are intended to maintain safety. I've learned how a lack of awareness of the rules in this environment can have grave consequences on the safety of my fellow human beings.

In the five years that I've been a prison chaplain, there have been gang fights too numerous to count. I've met men with black eyes and missing teeth who tell me they "fell," afraid to reveal the truth for fear of greater reprisal. Three men have committed suicide, a mentally disturbed man was stabbed to death shortly before his release, and an officer was stabbed in the face with a pen. A few days ago, just across the border in Washington State, a female correctional officer was strangled to death in the chapel. As a chaplain, I've only caught a glimpse of the reality that prisoners and correctional officers live with on a daily basis. In fact, much of the violence is hidden from my sight.

In my office, my day begins by running through emails, gang activity updates, security threat updates, and voicemails with requests from religious volunteers or emergency notifications. Kosal, the inmate chapel clerk, brings in a stack of "kytes" or inmate communications with requests to be added to religious services, requests for authorizations of religious property or religious diets, pastoral counseling, a call home to speak with a relative or a girlfriend, or threats to sue the department for infringing on their religious rights.

Sometimes, along with the kytes, Kosal brings in a paper cup filled with hot water and sets it on my desk.

"Man, you didn't have to do that. Thank you."

Kosal beams a smile, bowing as he backs gracefully out of the office. I pull a tea bag from the box on my desk and sink it into the steaming hot water.

The box of tea was given to me as a gift from Kosal. I hesitated to accept it at first, as accepting gifts from inmates is against institutional policy—strictly prohibited as it might encourage inappropriate relationships between staff and inmates. I know the reason: that gifts can lead to manipulation and bribes. It's all for safety and security, and yet, I knew from Kosal's body language and the feeling in my chest that my hesitation was dehumanizing. Kosal is not just an inmate, Kosal is my friend—and the crazy thing is that I can get fired for expressing that.

The prison environment puts its staff in these double-binds all the time—having to choose between keeping economic security or humanity. Although such binds permeate our culture, prisons make these double binds starkly obvious. I don't break rules for the sake of being rebellious, but if you simply go along to get along, obeying the rules without looking at the context—the context of a culture that prioritizes economic profit over people, a culture that incarcerates 2.3 million people who are disproportionately poor and of color—it's easy to forget who you are and that we're all interrelated.

Of course, I wouldn't accept gifts from anyone just as I might not accept candy from a stranger, but Kosal's no stranger to me. We've developed a relationship built on trust and respect.

I've known Kosal for three years. We've shared a lot of stories about our lives and what we've learned about life. Some of Kosal's stories are tattooed in a mural of black ink on his muscled 5'1" 130 lb. frame. On his right pectoral, a soldier boy armed with an AK-47, telling the story of war, the brutal regime of Pol Pot and the Khmer Rouge supported by the United States government, telling the story of his families' flight from his Cambodian homeland to America. On his left pectoral, a Long Beach gangbanger holding yet another AK-47, on his arms with scenes of gang warfare amid lotus flowers, buddhas amid assault helicopters and American B-52 bombers. On his back is the red-faced prince battling the monkey king, detailing his own struggles between dark and light.

"I try to escape the gang life," says Kosal. "I manage to elude them 'til I was fifteen . . . and I'm small so I was good at hiding." Kosal gets animated, grinning as he bobs and weaves like a boxer. "I could hide, hide over here, hide over there . . . duck into a doughnut shop once. One time I got caught by one of the gangs and reminded them that they already beat me up that day so they left me alone that time. I got tired of running, tired of getting beat up by the Mexican gangs, by the black gangs. I got tired of getting beat up by everybody. One day I just cracked, so I finally joined a gang." Kosal hikes up his pant leg to point out the bullet wound just above his right knee cap and counts himself fortunate. "Kosal," he says, "my name, it means 'fortunate.' My parents gave me that name because my four older siblings died in the killing fields. I was fortunate to escape to Thailand. My parents carried me across the border on foot, avoiding land mines, pirates, and the Khmer Rouge."

Kosal is doing seventy years for aggravated murder. He's become a gifted poet, writing of the joys of adolescent fondling, his father's physical and verbal abuse of his mother, his regret for not being able to be present to care for his son or massage the feet of his mother in her old age as is custom for the eldest child in his native culture. He regrets the life he has taken from another family. Kosal heads the Asian cultural club at Oregon State Penitentiary, organizing fundraisers, one of which resulted in the proceeds being used to construct a school in Vietnam. He does his best to keep the peace between rival gangs, still hustles on the card table, and generously takes care of his friends with his winnings, usually envelopes, which are hard currency within inmate culture. "I'm a winner," he boasts. Kosal *is* a winner, in a real way. Despite the institution's attempt to define him by the single worst moment of his life, to erase acknowledgment of the neglect that contributed to why he is here, and to isolate him from friends and family, he hasn't forgotten that he's related, that his life and actions are intertwined with others.

My daily practice as a chaplain, and as a human being, is to question the institutional values and roles, to question myself, and to speak up when those values and roles are dehumanizing. It's a constant challenge to see the context behind the social roles maintained by the institution, to see beyond the labels of officer, staff, inmate, or my own role of chaplain or Buddhist chaplain.

Often the first question that religious volunteers ask me when they find out that I am a chaplain is "What kind of chaplain are you?" Meaning. which denomination do I identify with? I have a hard time answering that question and usually sidestep it by telling them that I serve people of all faiths or no faith at all. I've been fortunate in life to receive teachings from people of many different traditions; I was raised Catholic, practiced Zen with Shishin Wick Roshi, attended retreats with Franciscan and Trappist monks, worked alongside Evangelical Baptists and Pentacostal pastors, participated in sundance and tepee ceremonies, and was intiated into the shamanic practices of my own Taino roots. But perhaps the most significant teachings that I received were the reverence and humility that were modeled to me by my grandparents.

My experience of these different traditions wasn't just spiritual shopping—each seemed to provide a greater context of meaning that no one tradition could have provided for me alone. We can all learn something from everyone; no religion, no person holds the truth exclusively— and yet institutionalized religions tend to lean away from this reality.

Perhaps what I enjoy most about being a prison chaplain is that I'm not confined to interacting with people of one denomination. I'm challenged to speak plainly, simply, and humbly from own my experience so that the truth of my words can be felt rather than relying heavily on religious doctrine. I have always been more interested in religious experience and its practical application to the difficulties we face in life. These difficulties that we face are the same for all human beings—greed, hatred, indifference, and the institutionalization of these values through various -*isms* such as racism, classism, sexism, or anthropocentrism. How each tradition deals with these human difficulties, or avoids dealing with them, can be helpful in discerning how best to resolve the difficulties we face. Like plants, I believe that's it difficult for human beings to grow in a monoculture; I value diversity and believe that learning about our differences has the potential to steer humanity in the direction of greater unity.

People that I meet have all sorts of ideas about Buddhists and chaplains. If they fixate on the "Buddhist" identity, they expect an Asian monk in robes, or if they fixate on the "chaplain" identity, they expect a balding older white man carrying a Bible and wearing a suit and a tie. I'm just not either of those guys. I do not try to be Asian or a church pastor. I do not bow all the time with palms-together in *gassho* or quote religious scripture. I get comments like "I never would have thought you were a chaplain" and "You don't act like a chaplain." They tell me that I'm awful colorful or passionate to be a chaplain. I don't meet the stereotypes. Most often, I'm referred to by staff and inmates simply and affectionately as "Torres."

My teacher Shishin Roshi always encouraged me to apply the teachings to the context of my life, to my own experience. And I can relate to that. I can only be who I am and apply the Dharma to what my life has taught me. So I'm more apt to give a shoulder bump and a handshake than a bow. I'm more likely to quote KRS-One, Bob Dylan, Jimi Hendrix, or Utah Phillips than Shantideva. I've studied Malcolm X and Martin King, Noam Chomsky, Howard Zinn, the Young Lords and the Black Panthers as much as I've studied Dogen Zenji or Trungpa Rinpoche. I know my own Nuyorican culture and American culture better than I know Japanese or Tibetan culture. My father always told me, "Love your culture son, but never let it limit you." So I've tried to honor and absorb wisdom and kindness where I find it, in whomever I find it. I don't confine myself to Buddhist dogma.

I don't talk much about Buddhism, though the practice of meditation has opened up so many opportunities to hear people's stories and recognize just how hungry we all are for someone to listen. I never cease to be amazed by the power of listening to people's stories with nonjudgmental presence. This presence is cultivated through the practice of meditation and creates a space for people to heal or gain clarity over issues that have troubled and confused them for years. Through emulating the kindness that so many of my teachers have extended to me, I take the time to get to know the men, the women, the officers, and the inmates, and their stories become a part of who I am.

When I ask inmates about their families, about their grandmothers especially, I have noticed their eyes light up. I make an effort to remember the names of their children, parents, and spouses and recall those stories so that when they think they're going to crack maybe I can remind them they're not alone. Shishin Roshi always told me, "The other side of alone is all one"—and I've experienced this myself. I remind the men that if they can touch their suffering, lean into their aloneness, they can find out what it means to be a human being. I remind them that this insight is the one thing that no one can ever take away from them.

In the end, I feel that the most sincere offering I can make is my practice. I try to extend common courtesies that are not so commonplace, like an apology when I'm insensitive or disrespectful, something that inmates are not used to hearing. I ask people how they're feeling, rather than how they're doing, which I learned was a stupid question after receiving the response, "How am I doing? I'm doing shitty; I live in a bathroom with another man!"

As a chaplain, I feel I have succeeded in my work when men come to my office because "Torres" is someone they can be "real" with, when men sit in front of my desk and feel like they're sitting behind it, or when I'm standing in front of the bars and they can forget that they are behind them. When they drop whatever baggage they're holding to be vulnerable, to grieve, to laugh, to forget for a moment that they're an inmate.

When the poets, artists, and musicians come to my office to show me their artwork or share their latest rhyme or song, I know that I am the one who is privileged. When one of the officers seeks me out to share his difficulty at home or to ask my help consoling an inmate who has just lost a relative, I know that I am privileged, as when the inmates tell me that it's like I'm one of them, the ultimate taboo. The truth is I have no idea what it's like to be an inmate. I mean, I go home at night to hug my wife and son. But I do know what it's like to be in prison. I know what it's like to internalize a culture that treats you as less than a human being: I know that a culture that teaches us to minimize our suffering and the suffering of our relatives for the sake of economic security or convenience compromises our dignity and leads to self-hatred and unhappiness. The most poignant lesson that I have learned repeatedly from prisoners, like my friend Kosal, is that freedom resides in realizing that we are all in this boat together and shaping our lives in accord with that realization.

When I first told Kosal that I had been given the opportunity to write about prison and wanted to include a portion of his story, he felt honored but was also adamant that I did not give readers the impression that he was sad. "Don't let them think that we are feeling sorry for ourselves in here. Tell them that we are happy, that there is happiness even in here."

At the end of the week as I leave the office, as I thank him for his presence and his friendship, Kosal conveys the secret to happiness when he smiles and says . . . "At your service."

Caring for Each Other Behind Prison Walls

Nealy Zimmermann

W E DROVE to the prison together—Mary Lou, George, Frank, Lewis, and myself. I had invited them to meet with a group of inmate bereavement volunteers at a maximum-security male correctional facility in Connecticut. Mary Lou runs an arts program for veterans at a VA hospital. George, Frank, and Lewis were in Mary Lou's program, having suffered from PTSD for many years since the Vietnam War.

After going through security we entered the facility and arrived at the "multipurpose" room where the bereavement volunteers had gathered. There was a general sense of the veterans and the inmates greeting each other with respect. We sat in a circle. An inmate commented on how honored he was to be visited by the veterans. One of the veterans commented on how impressed he was by the bereavement work these men were doing. Mary Lou asked if any of the inmates was a veteran. No one responded. We talked more. Lewis described his difficulties after the war—family members having to walk on eggs around him due to bursts

Nealy Zimmermann, MA, is currently the director of the Connecticut Coalition to Improve End-of-Life care. She helped develop a prison hospice program in Connecticut to train inmates to provide end-of-life patient care and bereavement services for their fellow inmates. She has coordinated or co-coordinated most of the program's fourteen hospice and bereavement trainings since 2000, worked on curriculum development, and has given a number of presentations during the trainings. She was a student of the late Chogyam Trungpa Rinpoche and is currently a student of his successor, Sakyong Mipham Rinpoche. She is a meditation instructor and teacher in the Shambhala Buddhist tradition as well as an active member of the New Haven Shambhala Center. She is currently working with a group of Buddhist practitioners to organize a series of "A Day of Mindfulness" retreats at various prisons in Connecticut.

of anger, how he couldn't hold down a job, how he ended up selling cardboard on the streets, how he didn't understand what was wrong with him . . . Suddenly one of the inmates started talking about his experience in Vietnam. The veterans exclaimed their joy in discovering a fellow veteran and immediately went over and, one by one, gave the inmate, who had become emotional, a big hug.

The bereavement volunteer program began with the recognition of the unique difficulties inmates face while trying to deal with loss while incarcerated. These unique difficulties became evident to me through my volunteer work helping to train male and female inmates to become hospice volunteers. My observations were corroborated by the research of Ginette Ferszt on grief in a women's prison in Rhode Island. The following is a quote from her study, "Grief Experiences of Women in Prison following the Death of a Loved One":

> Women in prison have limited opportunity to grieve and have their grief openly acknowledged, publicly mourned, or socially supported. Therefore, it can be described as disenfranchised. Disenfranchised grief can create additional problems for the griever, leading to a more complicated bereavement. When a mourner's perceived needs for support are not met, a more difficult bereavement can be expected.

Ferszt's research strongly resonated with my experience of observing the grieving process in the three prisons in Connecticut where I helped with the hospice and bereavement training.

A few examples of obstacles to normal grieving that I have noticed in the correctional environment include powerlessness, lack of privacy, issues of trust, the need to "behave" or else being sent to to the mental health section of the prison, and separation from family members. I have also heard several stories of unresolved grief due to the avoidance of the pain of loss leading eventually to crime and incarceration. Avoiding the pain of loss was expressed in answers by female inmates to a bereavement training homework assignment question in which they were asked to write about emotional avoidance:

"I avoided the pain of my mother's death by being very violent . . . I was a raging bull, mad at the world."

"I avoided all of my pain about my father's death by staying drunk most of the time."

"I avoided the pain I felt about not having a father by acting as if it didn't bother me. Then I started lashing out and having anger issues."

"I never avoided the pain of losing my son until I arrived at jail. I am scared to reveal my pain because I do not want to be vulnerable. I have to put on a mask to others."

"Wearing a mask. I have done this damn near all of my adult life. Dealing and using drugs made me feel like I owned the world . . . But no one would ever see me down and out because . . . the way I talked mask(ed) my pain of loneliness and fear."

These poignant words from female prisoners show us the internal feelings and conflicts that result from suppressing and avoiding the pain of loss. That suppression seeks to express itself over time. In the correctional environment where addressing grief and loss is difficult, the internal conflicts and the pain of suppressed loss can be heightened, possibly leading to more intense suffering and acting out.

Based on the evident need to address grief in prison and the model of the hospice program that had been in place in the Connecticut correctional system since 2001, I collaborated with correctional staff to develop and implement the Bereavement Volunteer Program in 2005. During bereavement training, inmates are guided through their own grief process and learn how to listen to fellow inmates experiencing a loss, any kind of loss.

It all started several years before in 1995. At that time, I and others heard about the prison hospice program, the first in the country, that Fleet Maull had helped start in a federal prison in Missouri as an inmate. I had known Fleet before his incarceration as a fellow practitioner and student of the late Tibetan teacher Chogyam Trungpa Rinpoche. In the early '90s Fleet founded the National Prison Hospice Association to help other prisons around the country integrate the philosophy and care of hospice into their facilities.

At that time I was living in Connecticut, where I met and got to know Florence Wald through her daughter, who was also a fellow practitioner. Florence was one of the founders of hospice in this country. When she heard about Fleet's work, she was interested in helping to start a prison hospice program in Connecticut. This was quite a few years after she helped spearhead the hospice movement in this country and had learned some lessons from that experience. It was now 1995 and she was seventy-eight years old. Thus began a new project for her, to which she devoted the last years of her life.

I learned a lot working with Florence. A small team of us started out by doing a literature search to become informed about the many big changes that had taken place in the correctional system over the last few decades including the increase in prison mortality rates due to AIDS and drug use. We received funding to do a feasibility study and met with many people around the state, visiting a number of prisons and hospices. Early on, a hospice nurse presented a proposal to start a hospice program at one of the prisons. Florence felt the proposal was premature. She went on to say that there was a need for a sense of the ground before going forward, a sense of the reality of the situation. She said that if we were to go in as saviors, we could undermine their self-respect, and expressed the need to go slowly and thoroughly since we are talking about changing a medical model within a system—action should be the last step in such a process. She mentioned that this same tension occurred in the early stages of the hospice movement.

I thus found myself in the fortunate position of having met and studied with Chogyam Trungpa Rinpoche and then being mentored and working closely with Florence Wald, who, although she was not a Buddhist, understood how to work with people and systems to make change. We were bringing together two divergent entities—one whose mission is to protect society from those who have caused harm and suffering to others, and the other, to provide compassionate care to those who are suffering from loss or terminal illnesses. And who better to provide that care than the inmates themselves, who have a deep common bond with their fellow inmates of having lost their freedom, a bond an outside volunteer would not have. Florence understood that. She had confidence that the inmates were capable of being good caregivers. The inmates felt that and were drawn to her.

One inmate wrote a condolence note to her family after she passed away in 2008, saying, "I will not ever be what I used to be because she was willing to see the good in me even before I could. What she passed on to me I am only too willing to pass on to others. Thanks Flo, from the heart."

TRAINING INMATES IN HOSPICE

The degree of civilization in a society can be judged by entering its prisons.
—FYODOR DOSTOEVSKY

The essential job of working with inmates is not to "save" them but to actually see them as potentially compassionate, confident, and wise human beings and to help them see that for themselves.

With this view, we perceive prisoners as having the same longings and potential to be decent human beings as everyone else. There is also a recognition that we are all capable of causing harm to others and that whatever harm is done is usually due to bad judgment, confusion, and suffering. Prisoners find themselves in a situation that is difficult to deal with in that they are likely suffering due to actions carried out due to confusion; metaphorically it is what we all experience, only in a more heightened way. It is easy to mentally set them apart, and see them as "bad." Often their behavior makes it easy for us to do so. To open one's heart after hurting others is very difficult, especially in a prison environment. As one inmate said: "It is easy to be hard but hard to be easy."

Living on the outside of prison, we have many choices, so it is easy to avoid our predicament through endless distractions and denial. Inmates, on the other hand, have their backs to the wall, literally and figuratively. If and when they start to see their reality and to deal with it, as opposed to trying to distract themselves or denying it, they are open to transformation. Furthermore, I have heard several of them say that because they have taken from society, they wish to give back. Such compassion longs for an opportunity to manifest. There are many excellent self-help programs in prisons these days that are indeed very helpful, but few opportunities exist for prisoners to give to others.

The Hospice and Bereavement Program is one program that gives them that opportunity.

THE TRAINING FOR BEREAVEMENT VOLUNTEERS

Over the last ten years we have trained one hundred and thirty men and women to become hospice volunteers, twenty-five to become bereavement volunteers, and forty-four to become both hospice and bereavement volunteers. We integrated the bereavement training into the last two hospice trainings. The hospice aspect of the training focuses on training the participants to provide companionship and hands-on care for chronically ill or dying patients. The bereavement training prepares the participants to listen to another person who is experiencing grief without trying to fix the pain of the loss but acting simply as a sounding board, thus allowing the griever to find his or her own way to cope.

During the trainings, we brought in outside instructors, knowledgeable in the various aspects of hospice and bereavement training. Like most hospice volunteer trainings, we include presentations on hospice and its history, clinical aspects, spirituality, effective communication, grief and bereavement, hands-on care, and advanced directives. The training is a combination of lectures, experiential exercises (including role-plays), homework assignments, and sharing. Unlike most traditional hospice trainings, we also introduce meditation or mindfulness practice. We teach meditation in a session we have called "Care for the Caregiver" as a way to cope with caregiver burnout. Meditation is a foundational practice of Buddhism but in and of itself need not be framed in a Buddhist way. So although the introduction of meditation practice is in line with Buddhist practices and values, it is presented simply as a tool to relax, settle the mind, and train ourselves to be present with whatever arises in ourselves, which in turn prepares us to be present with others.

During the bereavement training, we use a workbook specifically written for inmates, one of which was written for females called "Picking Up the Pieces" and the other of which was written for males called "Life Beyond Loss." They are both published by the American Correctional Association. The workbooks are similar but have slight differences related to the divergent ways men and women grieve. Chapter 1 of the work-

books is particularly powerful: it identifies the many losses we all experience throughout our lives. This chapter is often an eye-opener for many
of them. In addition, there is a chapter devoted to the loss of freedom due
to incarceration. The inmates read the workbook and answer questions
related to the content as homework assignments. At the sessions, we go
over the "ground rules," emphasizing confidentiality so that they feel safe
to share whatever grief issue they may have which they have started to
contemplate with their workbook questions. They take turns sharing and
listening in small groups, dyads, and in role-plays. They have the opportunity to feel heard, which they appreciate as a need that is frequently
unmet during incarceration. They learn to listen deeply. By listening to
someone expressing something from deep within, compassion naturally
arises, a connection takes place, and superficial judgments melt away.
These are learning skills that they can use the rest of their lives.

The bereavement volunteer training is always powerful. One trainee
summed it up beautifully in his graduation speech:

> How could I help other men see loss and grief as an explora-
> tion of opportunities instead of the often felt limitations of
> hopelessness? It seemed like a daunting task because as a man,
> I know we are often denied the opportunity to express our
> pain openly. Men are encouraged to hide pain by being strong,
> being in control, or covering it with anger. Prison environment
> further complicates things because of the fear that expression
> of sadness will make them appear weak and out of control.
>
> To my relief, the training in this program not only addressed
> my concerns and taught me how to be an effective bereavement
> volunteer; it also deepened my understanding of myself. It was
> great that throughout the training the counselors constantly
> addressed our personal grief. They understood the importance
> that care for oneself allows one to be able to provide care for
> others.
>
> I also learned that I didn't need to have the answers. I need
> to provide guidance that will help someone see that he has the
> answers: that he has the hope and power within himself because
> empowering someone is one of the greatest gifts you can give.

Ultimately, our goal as bereavement volunteers is to help someone acknowledge his loss and grief, and have his grief validated so with time he can reinvest in life. We have the privilege to journey with those in sorrow and let them know that they are not alone in this hard process regardless of who they are.

CARING FOR OTHERS

The traditional list of transcendental virtues in Buddhism include generosity, patience, discipline, diligence, and meditation, all of which are infused with prajna-wisdom. I have found that the inmates are able to manifest all these virtues in their hospice and bereavement work. I've seen these virtues through their generosity in being willing to care for and listen to another inmate, by being patient with an environment that by its very nature is frustrating, by maintaining the discipline of not giving in to the pressure of old habits and friends, and by finding joy through the diligence of their work. At one of our meetings with the male bereavement volunteers, we had a discussion about how as bereavement volunteers they need to manifest as trustworthy—or else why would anyone open up to them?

They also have to be available at any time—to be sensitive to another's state of mind and ready to listen. Here is how one of them described this:

> I had recently finished my bereavement volunteer training . . . I was headed toward the laundry room to continue doing my job when I was approached by another inmate. He wasn't someone I would normally talk to so I was getting ready to brush him off, but then I thought to myself, "Oh yeah, I am a bereavement volunteer now," so I used my training and listened as he told me how he was denied for parole. I ended up speaking with him for forty-five minutes.
>
> Being a part of the bereavement volunteer program has truly made me a better person. I actually find myself watching people to see if they may need someone to listen to them. I

know I will be able to apply the skills I have learned in my everyday life. Being a part of this program has been one of the best decisions I have made.

I've heard and seen this kind of thing often. In some cases, an inmate may start out as seemingly selfish and unconcerned about others, but through his understanding of the truth of suffering and then being given the opportunity to help fellow inmates, he changes. This work provides the insight that even in the worst places and in the so-called worst people, transformation and compassion can take place.

THE DEATH OF AN INMATE

In our first hospice training, which began in December of 2000, Mike was one of eighteen participants. It became evident early on that he was very talented, both with art and with words. He won the contest to design the logo that all Connecticut inmate hospice volunteers still wear to this day when they go to the infirmary to be with a patient. In 2007, I learned one inmate expressed deep appreciation for the support and care he received from Mike when he entered the chronic phase of hepatitis C. Mike helped him emotionally, physically, and spiritually during this difficult and scary time by spending many hours with him encouraging him to take care of himself but mostly listening. Because of Mike he made the decision to become a hospice volunteer himself.

Below is Mike's description of tending to the death of a fellow inmate and his contemplation of that experience. He was in the next room finishing up with another hospice patient, when . . .

> I first noticed, rather heard, the loud nature of someone in distress, knowing it was the patient, and also thinking it unusual if he had recently been sedated . . . I went to his room, seeing two of the hospice volunteers trying to calm him down, as he struggled to suffer through each breath, hearing the gurgling of fluid, the "sigh" of discomfort upon exhaling, and it just came upon me that he was in dire straits; sort of instinctively, two more hospice volunteers showed up. We knew that the

nurse was on her way in, so we took out the chairs, placed him in the center of the room, got some coffee started. The nurse showed up, and I just figured I would try and be some help, just stay back and let his "team" handle things. I held the patient's head in my hands, hummed/sung his country music in his ear, talked with him, wiped down his forehead/hair, talked with the fellows, shared some laughs, some quiet, tried to help keep his mouth clean. He was breathing up blood, the congestion effecting every breath, received shots every hour, the nurse saw to that . . . he started to ebb, 4:15–4:45, nails turned color, breathing was less labored, shorter . . . as we all realized it wasn't long . . . we just sat with him, as he slowly passed, each breath coming further and further apart, hardly any chest movement . . . Approx. 4:58 A.M., he was gone.

As his family was notified, his sister thanked all of us, saying how he would not have received this care at a nursing home. We all sat for some time afterward, at various areas of the day area, looking, at the open door to his room, everyone dealing with the enormity of the hard experience of a life passing, in different ways.

I can't help but think that if not for hospice, he would have died a far different death, as I try to understand what his sister meant by her statement, the view of the family, having experienced this program firsthand, seeing the care given, I attempt to contemplate motivation, what drives us volunteers to give, as prisoners?

The common qualities abound—compassion, concern, love, all of the reasons people volunteer to do this—but, again, from a prisoner's perspective, it just seems there is more, a more intense awareness of every little nuance of his care, everyone person paid such attention to everything, as we changed him, as we watched him as staff came and went, this was "our" death, "we" were given the gift to be here, this was each and every one of us, as seen through our own vision, in the patient's eyes, I think every man present to some degree, saw himself in that bed, being thankful to take care of the smallest detail, making J. as comfortable as possible in these parameters.

Just facing mortality is only part of our issue, it's facing it under these circumstances that heightens our awareness, our desire to be vigilant, the inability to control your own destiny behind these walls, having to rely fully on other people for everything, knowing that in prison, out of sight, out of mind, I personally find great comfort in knowing that some of my brothers will not let that happen, as I fully believe that unless you have experienced the isolation, desolation of prison, the helplessness, that only a fraction of that perspective can be comprehended.

In some ways, the weight of these prisoners' crimes and the intensity of their incarceration experience makes them go deeper to find a resolution to their predicament, and this in turn creates a deeper understanding of other people's suffering. Observing these transformations inspires me beyond words, and I hope that by sharing these stories others will likewise be inspired.

Buddhists Behind Bars

Terry Conrad

EVERY WEDNESDAY, I get up a little after 4:00 a.m. to catch the 5:00 ferry from Galveston to the Bolivar Peninsula and then drive for another hour and a half to the Mark Stiles Unit in Beaumont, Texas. I'll spend the next eight hours working with inmates as a Buddhist volunteer chaplain. This work is the most satisfying thing I've ever done.

Thirty years ago I was living and working as an artist in the mountains south of Santa Fe, New Mexico. The highway into town passes the state penitentiary, and I can remember feeling drawn to working with the men inside. At the time I was doing work with the New Mexico Artists in Education program and felt the sense that if inmates were able to express themselves through art, maybe they would be less inclined to act out in ways that are harmful to them and the community.

Years later, living in Texas, I became the student of a Buddhist teacher who asked if I would be willing to answer his "jail mail," the letters he got from inmates that read his best-selling book on Buddhism. I thought it was interesting that he picked up on this and agreed. This was a challenge for me due to a lack of confidence in my own Dharma practice.

Terry Conrad is a certified volunteer chaplain in the Texas Department of Criminal Justice. For the past eight years he has worked at the Mark Stiles Unit sponsoring a Buddhist meditation group and an ethics class based on the book *Ethics for the New Millennium*, by H.H. Dalai Lama. As director of Project Clear Light, a nonprofit prison outreach organization, he offers a free correspondence course for inmates on the lojong teachings. He heads up a contemplative practices program in a faith-based dorm on the TDCJ Ramsey Unit.

Initially I developed what amounted to a form letter response to the numerous requests that came in for information on how to get more Dharma books. Occasionally there was a letter with deeper questions about how to practice, to work with difficult emotions and issues that came up being in prison.

One letter in particular came from an inmate in a maximum-security unit in Beaumont, Texas, asking if there was any possibility that someone might come onto the unit to sponsor a Buddhist meditation group. I was drawn by this request so I responded that if my teacher gave me permission I would see what I could do. The inmate wrote me back the name of the unit chaplain to talk with about arranging to come into the prison.

In Texas this begins by filling out a chaplaincy volunteer application form, and, if approved, to a daylong security training on prison culture. It took about four months to complete these steps and to have my name entered into the system computer as a "chaplaincy volunteer." During this time I submitted a proposal to the chaplain describing how I thought the meditation class would be conducted, and what equipment—a cushion, a bowl, and a painting of the Buddha—that I would bring in for the class. He scheduled me to come into the unit once a month, beginning the second week of July 2004.

For our first session, we sat on the concrete with no cushions or support. The men sat very still for nearly twenty or thirty minutes, occasionally rocking or shifting, but their eyes were closed. I chanted the *mani* mantra, rang the gong, made a dedication for our practice, and we exchanged bows.

The men stretched their legs, one lay down on his back for a few moments, and we regrouped for a short Dharma talk on the Four Thoughts to Change the Mind. On each of the thoughts, there was discussion, and the men were eager to show that they knew something about the Dharma they had read about, but they seemed to have very little sense of what it means to actually practice. During the discussion, the inmate that sent me the letter expressed his gratitude for my coming with tears in his eyes. He said even though he had been studying the Dharma for years, it was the first time in his life he had ever heard a Dharma talk, and the others all nodded their heads in agreement.

Following that first session we continued to meet once a month and the number of inmates attending slowly increased. I also heard from other inmates on the unit that were interested but could not attend the meetings, either because they were in closed custody (not able to move in population) or administrative segregation (one man, one cell, one hour a day for recreations, always shackled before leaving the cell). These men wanted me to come to their house (cell) for some teaching. The chaplain would not allow me to go anywhere on the unit to meet with inmates except in the classroom; however, he did offer that if I became a certified volunteer chaplain's assistant I would be able to go anywhere on the unit. The process to become certified involves forty hours of class work and a six-month internship under the direction of the chaplain. A year later, as a CVCA I began coming to the unit for one full day a week. The Buddhist group continues to meet in the afternoon and the roster has grown to over forty inmates.

Over the years the Buddhist service has taken on the look and feel of a traditional meditation hall. A Dharma bookstore donated some thangka paintings. A yoga studio donated some used meditation cushions, and the family of one of the inmates donated some carpet squares to protect their feet from the concrete floor. The laundry captain took our suggestion of recycling worn out blankets, stitching together layered fabric squares for added protection from the floor. Every week we set up a full altar with the thangka paintings, photos of our teachers, offering bowls, and three electric candles.

There is also a full library of books donated from various sources available for members to check out.

Several members of the group are serving quite long sentences, some for life, and this has allowed for a great deal of continuity at the core of the Stiles Unit Sacred Heart Sangha. Almost seven years later, most of the original eight are still very active. In the winter of 2008, one of the founding members handed me the book *Ethics for the New Millennium*, by the Dalai Lama, along with a *Study Guide* for the book distributed by the Dalai Lama Foundation. He suggested that this might be a good class to offer inmates, Buddhist and non-Buddhist. I took his suggestion to the Chaplaincy Administration in Huntsville and the class was approved. With the generous help of the Dalai Lama Foundation in making both the text and the study guides available, we set about organizing the class.

In an organizational meeting with eight interested inmates, mostly the original founders, we decided that inmate facilitators would take responsibility for running the ethics class. Each week we would cover one chapter using the key concepts offered in the study guide using a facilitator to lead each of the four or five breakout groups. During the first course the facilitators felt that the study guide should include examples of prison life instead of "free world" examples. Behaviors like reporting someone breaking the law that we may not think twice about outside of prison are a violation of the inmate code inside prison. Another big issue in prison is dispute resolution since no one wants a corrections officer to resolve an inmate-to-inmate conflict.

During the first offering of the ethics class, three facilitators created a *Study Guide for Inmates* adapting it from the one provided by the Dalai Lama Foundation. This team has also written a *Facilitators Guide* that contains an *Ethical Toolbox* of homework assignments for each chapter so that the class can be replicated at other prisons. Prisons in Texas, Maine, Rhode Island, and Massachusetts have volunteers that offer a form of the ethics class. Because it was difficult to get a Buddhist program established on the Stiles Unit, members of the Sacred Heart Sangha undertook creating outreach to other Buddhist inmates on units without a Buddhist chaplaincy volunteer. Their first effort was putting together a booklet on *An Inmates Guide to Buddhist Practice*. After several revisions, this booklet is available through Project Clear Light, a nonprofit outreach organization.

Working with a group of highly motivated, very intelligent individuals is both energizing and satisfying, but what does it mean that this group is all locked behind iron bars and coils of razor wire?

The hard truth is that prison is hell, and for some, this means for the rest of their lives. Coming to terms with this, and the reasons they are each there, is the cause for soul-searching and for seeking some degree of peace of mind. The promise of peace, serenity, and freedom is common to every spiritual tradition. Some traditions teach that this will happen in some other time or place. However, in the Buddhadharma, freedom, or spiritual awakening, is possible not just in this lifetime, but in this very moment. The challenge of prison chaplaincy is to guide and inspire inmates to practice in an environment that appears to contradict anything we might imagine as conducive to contemplation and meditation.

The sensory effects of a large number of people living confined in a relatively small space are sounds and smells that never stop. The noise is almost constant, with the sounds of talking, yelling, radios playing, doors slamming, traffic going in and out, and the day room where the TV is always on and inmates play very animated domino games, slamming down the pieces and yelling over every move. The only possibility for some degree of relative quiet is between 11:00 p.m. and 3:00 a.m. when the first call-out for breakfast is announced.

Proximity is possibly more pervasive than sound. Inmates are literally within arms reach of another person at all times. Eating, sleeping, sitting, walking, and going to the bathroom are all public events. The only time an inmate has any degree of personal privacy is taking a shower.

Along with proximity comes smells. There is a very distinct smell that comes from caged men. Even with regular hygiene, the smell is there; it's not really offensive, just distinct. A crucial aspect of proximity is getting a good celli (cellmate), the one person that is most immediate to inmates' most personal moments. There's always the possibility of getting paired with a "psych," someone that's mentally ill or even pathological.

Overcrowding causes friction, which creates confrontation. Even the slightest disrespect or offhand comment can instantly become a fight in prison. The threat and immediacy of violence is compounded by gangs that function as a single menacing entity using violence and intimidation to compete for power and control of the contraband markets. Fueling this are the few corrupt members of the prison staff that use the same tactics and profit from the same markets.

Anything and everything has a value and thus a market in prison, from necessities of soap and toothpaste to cell phones, drugs, and sex. Personal property is always at risk, either from a celli, another inmate trying to satisfy a debt, or from "shake-down" teams of security officers looking for contraband including drugs, tobacco, cell phones, or anything modified or not allowed by policy. In prison, anything that is not specifically stated in policy is not allowed; it's the opposite in the free world, if something is not written law, it's okay.

Prisons are filled with individuals that have repeatedly heard that they are bad, wrong, an offender, and the dregs of society. The prison culture reinforces this message. A great many inmates come from very troubled and dysfunctional backgrounds, saturated with judgment and negativity. One man shared that his father and uncles began taking him to the bar when he was five years old, making him drink beer so they could all get a good laugh at him staggering around and falling down. How does one convey to someone exposed to so much negativity that he is essentially good, whole, and complete, just as he is?

The truth of even the possibility of innate goodness is a slow take when surrounded by anger, violence, intimidation, and judgment. It has been my experience that for someone to practice in the context of such intense outer stimulus it begins with the willingness to recognize that everything we experience is an internal event, and that we have a choice in every moment how we will respond to whatever is arising in the mind.

My approach is that meditation is the method that allows us to be more present, aware of whatever we are experiencing without judging, comparing, or trying to change anything. Through meditation, we become more mindful, aware of what we are doing or about to do, saying or about to say, and with practice we are able to make real choices in real time.

The fact that someone shows up at a Buddhist meditation class, just that interest, is an expression of innate wisdom. The willingness to listen, to practice, read, and reflect is an expression of innate goodness. Becoming aware of a moment of joy, thinking about an absent loved one, talking with a friend, watching a bird in the recreation yard, or hearing music on the radio provides a glimmer of recognition that such moments are all expressions of goodness.

When nonvirtuous, troubling, disturbing thoughts continue to arise, the tendency is to fixate on these thoughts, identify with them, and feel that they define us. How do we work with them? It begins with the recognition that we are all conditioned, we have been conditioned, maybe even before we were born, and that the vast amount of our conditioning was not a conscious choice. We have learned to eat, walk, talk, and survive, but we have also been acculturated with attitudes, opinions, thoughts, and feelings. By being an observer of thoughts and the stories we tell ourselves we become aware of our conditioning, the conditioned nature of the mind. Each time we recognize and don't react to a conditioned thought, especially a nonvirtuous one, the power of that habitual thought is weakened. This is the healing, transformative power of awareness.

Every day in prison is an opportunity to witness all of the realms of samsara being played out. The contrast of present prison and future freedom is quite graphic. An inmate practitioner recognizes that projections into the future are a painful habit that causes greater suffering and dissatisfaction than the brief pleasure they afford. Thoughts of the past are often filled with regret, remorse, and guilt. With a little practice, the practitioner notices the stories that attempt to change the past. These projections and stories can arise anytime, while standing in line for chow or commissary, waiting for count to clear, lying in bed before falling asleep, or getting up. Mindfulness becomes an invaluable tool to recognize the tendency to judge and compare.

There is a good deal of racial and religious prejudice in prisons. Inmates, chaplains, and chaplaincy volunteers often find that Buddhists are not allowed to have a service in the prison chapel, a place they see only for Christian worship. My first experience of this came when I was asked, as a part of my certification internship, to offer a Christian service to the medium-custody inmates. Prior to the service, the inmate choir director, a very large, outspoken and charismatic black man, expressed to me his displeasure that a suitable Christian volunteer could not be found to lead their service, that they were stuck with a Buddhist instead.

The sermon I offered that morning was on "Turning the Other Cheek." I spoke about Jesus offering us such a simple but powerful means to move from nonvirtue to virtue, from seeing with an eye of material and emotional attachment, to seeing with an eye of spirit, love, and compassion for those that may wish us harm. By simply turning our head, we can be more mindful of the loving nature of all beings; we can recognize how easily we become conflicted by taking refuge in old, negative, and reactive habits of thought, and how easy it is to recognize goodness and wholeness. After the service, the choir director came over to me, took my hand, and invited me to come back again, anytime.

Regional chaplains, unit chaplains, volunteer chaplain assistants, and chaplaincy volunteers in Texas are under the direction of the Chaplaincy Department, a department of the Rehabilitation and Reentry Department of TDCJ. Programs are designated as Christian, Catholic, and Other. The "Other" includes Jewish, Muslim, Native American, Buddhist, Hindu, Jehovah's Witness, and Wiccan. My first impression of the chaplain on the Stiles Unit, a rather slight, wall-eyed evangelical Baptist with fifteen years on the unit, was that he was quite brusque, almost curt, with me. He worked with me to run the Buddhist program, but in a very perfunctory way, often emphasizing how busy and stressed he was having to always answer the phone and not getting anything done.

Despite his brevity, each time I came into the chapel I made it a point to say hello and to ask how he was doing. The answer was always the same, "Busy." I would come in for two hours to meet with the group and then leave. After a few meetings, as the men became more open in our discussions about prison life, some of the things they shared left me with a lot of questions about how things worked and the meanings of the terminology and slang they used. Since he is my immediate supervisor, I brought my questions to the chaplain, and our relationship began to change. As he realized that I was truly interested in this work he took more and more time to talk, and it evolved into a genuine friendship. I realized that he was more than willing to engage with someone interested in what for him was a calling and a passion. He has often expressed his appreciation for what I was bringing to the inmates through the Buddhist program.

My interest in chaplaincy work led me to traveling to other units around the state where there were ten or more inmates that called themselves Buddhist. My reception by most of the unit chaplains was professional and perfunctory, often holding to an interpretation of policy limiting attendees to inmates with "Buddhist" on their travel card, and not just anyone interested in Buddhism.

It came to my attention that the Chaplaincy Department in Huntsville had designated a number of "host units" for inmates that claimed Muslim, Native American, or Jewish as their religion. This means that inmates of these faiths that meet all the other qualifications can get reassigned to a unit that has a program to practice that faith. I took it upon myself to write a quite lengthy proposal to establish host units for Buddhist offenders and submitted it to the Chaplaincy Administration where it was summarily turned down. After three more revised attempts to get Buddhism designated, I was told that there just weren't enough Buddhist inmates to justify all the paperwork involved in doing the reclassification.

My efforts in working with the administration to get designation status for Buddhist programs led me to organize a not-for-profit organization, Project Clear Light, as the basis for what I envisioned as a statewide outreach to support Buddhist inmates. I hired an assistant to build a database of all the Buddhist inmates in Texas and we sent out periodic newsletters to all of them offering practice support.

In Texas there are over 160,000 incarcerated men and women in 110 prisons. There are 700 inmates in Texas that list their religion as Buddhist and less than a dozen Buddhist chaplaincy volunteers. This means there are still a large number of Buddhist inmates without access to either Dharma teachings or sangha practice.

The very positive response we received from our initial mailings led the Stiles group to produce the quarterly newsletter, *Angulimala*, that now includes contributions from inmates all over Texas. *Angulimala* is named after a mass murderer that—the early Buddhist canon tells us—became enlightened after attempting to kill the Buddha. Using typewriters purchased from the commissary, the editors offer insights into practice and updates on sangha activities. It also contains articles, letters, drawings, puzzles, and poems all written by inmates about what it means to be a practicing Buddhist in prison. Project Clear Light publishes and mails out the *Angulimala* to subscribers all over the country.

To answer the need for study materials and practice instructions for inmates without access to a program, a correspondence course on the Lojong teachings of Atisha has been developed by Project Clear Light and offered at no charge. These powerful teachings lay out the fundamental principles and practices for meditation in succinct and direct slogans. Participants are asked to write out and mail their insights and questions for each of the seven parts. Each letter is individually answered and over a hundred inmates are currently taking the course. Upon completion, the inmate receives a free mala and a Certificate of Completion along with a *Prayerbook* and *An Inmates Guide to Buddhist Practice*. Project Clear Light is listed by TDCJ as a source for information on Buddhism and publishes several booklets that are mailed to anyone requesting information about Buddhism and Buddhist practice.

Working as an engaged Buddhist in prison outreach is a powerful practice; it is a wonderful way to go deeper into the skillful means to both recognize and articulate what is helpful. There are not a lot of opportunities for the serious practitioner to teach, but serving as a prison chaplaincy volunteer is certainly one of them. I cannot imagine a more meaningful and appropriate situation in which to share our practice.

PART IV

Wielding Manjushri's Sword: The Arts
of College and Military Chaplaincy

May You Always Be a Student

Danny Fisher

I am a student.
I have been a student as long as I remember
And it is a pleasure to be a student.
It is a pleasure to learn that I don't know.
It is a pleasure to learn that I already know.
It is a pleasure to learn that I was mistaken.
It is a pleasure to learn from Great Masters.
It is a joy to learn by sharing what I learnt.
It is a joy to learn how to be what I am.
I seek to learn about the world around me.
I seek to learn about what I actually am.
I seek to learn how to be a proper human being.
Clouds show me the nature of my world.
Rivers show me the nature of myself.
Babies show me how to be more human.
I am a student.

Rev. Danny Fisher is a professor and coordinator of the Buddhist chaplaincy program at University of the West in Rosemead, California. Prior to his appointment at UWest, he served on the adjunct faculty for Antioch Education Abroad's Buddhist Studies in India program. Ordained as a lay Buddhist minister by the Buddhist Sangha Council of Southern California, Danny is also certified as a mindfulness meditation instructor by Naropa University (where he earned his master of divinity degree) in association with Shambhala International. In 2009, he became the first-ever Buddhist member of the National Association of College and University Chaplains. A blogger for *Shambhala Sun, Buddhadharma: The Practitioner's Quarterly,* and elephantjournal.com, he has also written for *Tricycle: The Buddhist Review, Inquiring Mind, Religion Dispatches, The Journal of Religion and Film,* and *The Journal of Buddhist Ethics.*

I will be a student as long as I live.

And it is a pleasure to be a student.

—"It Is a Pleasure to Be a Student" BY RINGU TULKU RINPOCHE

THE POEM ABOVE is one of many I have hung in strategic locations around my office at University of the West. From that office, I direct the master of divinity degree program in Buddhist chaplaincy, plan my courses, and write. I often find myself counseling students, staff, and faculty there as a campus chaplain of sorts. Members of the "UWest" community come to see me for counsel on a wide range of issues—from spiritual practice to personal relationships, stress, and mental health concerns. My pastoral responsibilities also include creating and offering frequent interfaith services on our campus, facilitating group processes for our students, helping to mediate conflicts, and organizing care services and pastoral visits for those who are ill and under medical care. Though active chaplaincy is not part of my official job description, I do it with enough regularity that I became the first Buddhist member of the National Association of College and University Chaplains in 2009.

The poems in my office inspire me as I do this work. While I find myself moved and motivated by each of the verses I have strewn about the office from the likes of Diane Di Prima, Chogyam Trungpa Rinpoche, Gary Snyder, Machig Labdron, Shantideva, and others, these lines from Ringu Tulku Rinpoche have unique relevance for me as a university chaplain:

> I am a student.
> I have been a student as long as I remember
> And it is a pleasure to be a student.

These lines resonate with my philosophy of life and inform my work, much of which is with students—mostly graduate students in the Religious Studies department, but some undergraduates from various corners of UWest as well. I get to touch base again and again with the pleasure of being a student myself. The practicalities of my job require that I understand "student" in the broadest possible context. In the same way that a hospital chaplain serves not only patients but also patients' families and hospital staff, the university chaplain serves not only students but also faculty, staff, and other members of the extended university community. Our younger students, like college-age students everywhere, tend to hear two things from their parents' generation. The first is that nagging question, "What are you going to do after you graduate?" The second is usually some reminder that their years in college are "the best years of their lives." Usually, this refers to that combination of relative freedom, youthful vitality, bountiful opportunity, and wonder that college students generally enjoy during their time in school.

Like hospital or other chaplains, I attend to the unique needs of those I serve. One way I serve students is to help them navigate questions, such as those asked by concerned parents. While I affirm their wishes that students appreciate this precious time—and my work is cut out for me at a Buddhist university where most are already operating with an acute awareness of impermanence—a lot of my efforts are directed at promoting another way of understanding their time in college as "the best years." Specifically, I try to encourage students (and by extension, others in the UWest community) to see the benefits of remaining students for the rest of their lives, in the way that Ringu Tulku Rinpoche talks about it.

Rinpoche points out the value of maintaining the learner's spirit even when specific roles and responsibilities change naturally over time. Of course, the students I work with are deeply in touch with that spirit by virtue of the fact that they *are* students. When one of them fills out a form that asks what she does, she identifies as "student." With the help of this temporary formal identity, these young people begin laying the foundation for a long-term informal identity as students of life. Of course—especially for those contending with comprehensive exams, theses, and the like—it is not always a pleasure to be a student in the literal sense. Rinpoche, though, goes on to remind us there are qualities unique to the role of student that are profoundly important to nurture in our spiritual lives:

It is a pleasure to learn that I don't know.
It is a pleasure to learn that I already know.
It is a pleasure to learn that I was mistaken.

First, Rinpoche speaks of the joy of learning that we don't know. This is the primary goal of education: providing students with knowledge they previously did not have. For students (or their professors) to discover they don't know is not always joyous. But I do not think Rinpoche is just talking about facts and theories students are expected to regurgitate and mull over on exams and papers. He also seems to allude to the significance of what the great Zen master Shunryu Suzuki Roshi termed "don't-know-mind." He's talking about keeping an open mind—a mind that is spacious, not rigid. In perhaps his most famous teaching, Suzuki Roshi said, "In the beginner's mind, there are many possibilities; in the expert's mind, there are few." When our minds are made up—tight, closed, sure of everything—we get further and further from seeing things as they truly are. Conversely, when our minds are open—supple, receptive, reflective—wakefulness dawns. In those moments when students are struggling with the more challenging aspects of academic life, when their work is critiqued, for example, I sometimes have found it helpful to reframe their current challenge in the space of don't-know mind. The mind that is open to anything is not defensive in the face of critique. It is comfortable with learning what it does not yet know. Not only is it okay to not know, not-knowing is a door to wisdom.

UWest is a small university (currently, just over 250 students) with a remarkable, vibrantly diverse international student body, representing many religious affiliations. In particular, we have large clusters of Eastern European Muslims, African Catholics, South Asian Hindus, quite a variety of Buddhists from around the globe, and more. Because of this plurality, UWest offers members of its community rich, rewarding, and often challenging opportunities for cross-cultural learning and communication. But it is not uncommon for me to counsel individuals and small groups around issues of conflict. I've learned over time to heed the wisdom of some long-standing members of the UWest community, who believe that conflict does not always have to be bad and can even enrich our cooperative spirit. One thing that I have noticed in these moments of stress is that tensions rise most often when we think we know everything about the other, even their culture and their motives. In counseling divided parties, I offer the suggestion that we can meet others in the spirit of "don't-know-mind." The mind of not-knowing provides a space, at the very least, to temper our reactions to some degree. At best, such an approach offers an invitation to deepen communication with others.

In the next line of this verse, Rinpoche speaks of the pleasure of "learning that we already know." On the surface, this can refer to the joys of discovering just how much scholastic learning we have done and are doing—we can often surprise ourselves with how much we have learned and are learning—but it can also be understood more deeply. It seems to acknowledge that part of the Buddhist tradition that teaches we are all fundamentally, intrinsically awake—that we have the ability to achieve enlightenment because, in a sense, we already are enlightened. With this comes the implicit and important spiritual lesson of self-acceptance: that we can accept ourselves as we are because at some level, we "already know." When I was a graduate student at Naropa University, one of my professors, Dharma teacher Reginald A. Ray, once said, "The spiritual path is not based on who we want to be, but who we already are. Actually, who we are is far richer, more joyful and satisfying than anything we could possibly want to be."

Self-acceptance is something quite a few young people I counsel struggle with. I have found it useful to suggest they look around at the friends they have made at UWest. In all likelihood, they will remain close with those friends for a long, long time—perhaps even for the rest of their lives. Depending on the age of the student, these may be some of their first adult friendships. And what typifies adult friendships? I think it is loving and appreciating others for exactly who they are, warts and all. I often ask students to consider the gift of acceptance that they give to their school friends and that their school friends give them. In recognizing this, students have a chance to consider the virtues of self-acceptance: if the friends that they cherish can accept them, then perhaps they can accept themselves.

Lastly, Rinpoche writes, "It is a pleasure to learn that I was mistaken." Here, I think he is speaking of the distinctive learning opportunities that arise out of making mistakes. In the context of higher education, their mistakes show students where their growing edges are, not just as budding scholars but also as well-integrated persons. Of course, mistakes also cost them "points" in terms of grades and standing within a cohort of students. This being the case, students tend to avoid mistakes as often as possible. In the context of spirituality, however, one's relationship to mistakes is somewhat different.

Within an academic culture that often equates excellence with a kind of perfection, I find it useful to remind students that mistakes in life can teach us in profound ways. Mistakes are not excuses to wallow in self-pity, to look at one's mistakes and pronounce oneself a "failure." This is a spiritual cop-out—a way of getting off the hook and avoiding the hard work of being a human being. I encourage students to look at their errors as a door to awareness of the places where they are stuck. Mistakes, like everything else, are opportunities, invitations to grow spiritually.

Because many of the students who come to see me are themselves Buddhists, I sometimes share a story from my graduate student days at Naropa University. In my first year there, I saw any mistake I made as a sign I was failing, not just in my studies but in my Dharma practice. I tried to avoid making mistakes at all costs, not wanting to sit with the suffering that came with the recognition I was not perfect. One of my teachers, Frank Berliner, seemed to pick up on this and said to me in class one day: "You know, Danny, it's called the *noble* truth of suffering, not the *shitty* truth of suffering." To me, his words were a revelation. I understood him to mean that as long as I insisted on shrinking from suffering instead of recognizing it as something that might teach me if I were brave enough to sit with it, progress on the path would not be possible. In this way, I began to relate to mistakes, however uncomfortable, in a different way—as precious teachers.

> It is a pleasure to learn from Great Masters.
> It is a joy to learn by sharing what I learnt.
> It is a joy to learn how to be what I am.

Rinpoche here alludes to the extraordinary learning that takes place between a spiritual teacher and a student, the strengthening of that learning through passing what you have learned on to others, and the ways in which greater authenticity emerges out of these processes. Learning from a teacher, teaching others, and becoming more genuine requires looking closely and listening deeply, trying to understand oneself and others exactly as they are, and responding from there. For me, this is what makes teachers great masters: they seek to truly understand students as they understand themselves, and be of benefit by helping them most fully be themselves.

I find this a useful principle in my work as both a chaplain and an educator of future chaplains. As Trungpa Rinpoche says: "If there are lots of clouds in front of the sun, your duty is to create wind so that the clouds can be removed and the clear sun can shine." Serving students collectively and individually in such a way that "the sun can shine" is my duty. As both a Buddhist minister and professor of chaplaincy/Buddhist theology, it is essential for me to maintain a daily practice and general "spiritual fitness" in order to do this as best I can. If I have any hope of being of benefit to others, I must do the work of being a student myself. This is not only true with regard to spirituality but is also consistent with the best practices in professional chaplaincy: Robert G. Anderson, in his essay "The Search for Spiritual/Cultural Competency in Chaplaincy Practice: Five Steps that Mark the Path," has written about the need for increased "spiritual/cultural competency," or the ability to "respond to the concerns and distresses expressed in uniquely spiritual and cultural ways by the person, family and kin in life transitions and crises," in the field, and that the way to begin developing this is through the chaplain's own "self-assessment and definition." To set an example for our MDiv students—whether it is in the classroom or practice space—I cannot fake it; I have to embody that which I preach if I want it to affect them.

The charges I received upon my ordination as a Buddhist minister by the Buddhist Sangha Council of Southern California were to (1) serve and support the Buddhist community widely, and (2) practice diligently in my own tradition of Buddhism. The second charge here implies that I show devotion to my teachers and rootedness with the lineage—it demands that I never forget the importance of those who taught me and my connection to them, and that I continue to show them the utmost respect. But I see the first aspect, with its explicit exhortation to Buddhist ecumenicism (and implicit suggestion of even wider, interfaith cooperation), as equally clear: it asks me to recognize teachers all around. As one of my precious teachers, Chökyi Nyima Rinpoche, has written in his book *Present Fresh Wakefulness*: "Appreciate other beings with this attitude: 'With the help of these beings, I can develop the precious enlightened attitude, bodhichitta. With the help of these beings, I can progress toward buddhahood. The fact that it is possible for me to train in the six *paramitas*, in the four means of magnetizing and so forth, and in the vast activities of a bodhisattva, is only possible because of other beings—so, thank you very much!'"

In addition, as a pastoral educator, I see having devotion for teachers and rootedness with lineage as meaning not only devotion to traditional Buddhist teachers and lineages, but also devotion to the teachers and curriculum of study at UWest and other institutions. The UWest curriculum is articulated as "knowledge of and the ability to apply Buddhist values; knowledge of the religions of the world; an understanding of how society, culture, language, and customs influence religious belief; knowledge of best practices in clinical settings; the ability to engage in critical, scholarly analysis of religious beliefs and practices; the ability to facilitate and construct opportunities for interreligious collaboration; and knowledge and practical skills for the application of spiritual care and counseling." Our MDiv students are part of the noble lineage of chaplains, theologians, engaged Buddhists, scholars, religious others, and all those who have helped shape our corner of the field—and I believe they show their devotion to them and rootedness in that lineage by their knowledge and application of that learning. As such, I see it as my responsibility as a professor to make sure the students are engaged with the materials that will provide them with knowledge and the skills to apply it.

In pastoral studies, I believe that a fairly wide variety of things can constitute materials to learn with: "the living human document," group process, scripture, scholarly sources, theology, spiritual practice, clinical experience, art, etc. On the one hand, I believe that much of the learning of spiritual caregivers and counselors will happen outside the university walls and will increase and develop through the years. From this perspective, much of what I do is about equipping students for their very personal journeys. On the other hand, I believe that students should emerge from their graduate education proficient in the nine areas of learning articulated by the Association of Professional Chaplains: ritual/liturgy, comparative religions, religious education, pastoral care and counseling, spiritual formation, religious history, institutional organization and administration, sacred literature, and theology/philosophy.

I seek to learn about the world around me.
I seek to learn about what I actually am.
I seek to learn how to be a proper human being.

Here, Rinpoche speaks of continuing to deepen our education. To me, these verses imply a certain humility: coming to understand that we have so much to learn, and that our education will necessarily be ongoing for the rest of our lives.

Perhaps one of the most powerful moments for me in my time at UWest came during the fall semester of 2010, a time when anti-Muslim sentiment in the US came to a flashpoint—quite literally in some cases. Terry Jones, the pastor behind the overexposed, stillborn "International Burn a Koran Day," may have been just a fringe figure. But he was symptomatic of America's mood at the time. There was the intense national debate about Park51 (the "Ground Zero mosque" that is neither at Ground Zero nor a mosque, but a community center that will occupy a building on nearby Park Place that used to be a Burlington Coat Factory). There were occurrences of violence at mosques in the southern United States. There was the finding that nearly one fifth of the country believed then that President Barack Obama was a "secret Muslim" (in actuality, he and his family are members of the United Church of Christ). All this offered a very disquieting glimpse into America's collective soul. As our UWest students in the master of divinity program and I prepared our September 11th interfaith memorial on campus, all this news weighed heavily on our minds. With the overshadowing of remembrances that year of September 11, 2001—a horrific national tragedy not even ten years past—as well as our significant Muslim population among the students, staff, and faculty, it seemed impossible for us to avoid talking about it.

I asked one of our students, Monica Sanford (of the much-beloved blogs "Buddhist in Nebraska" and "Dharma Cowgirl"), to reshape one of her blog posts into a central sermon of sorts. This decision dictated the shape of the rest of the service, so that other talks joined Monica's in directly alluding to current tensions in the US. In our planning, we had hoped to craft a service that sought to both acknowledge this somber event and offer healing for the rifts challenging our country and community. Monica spoke about first becoming aware of Park51, saying, "I thought, 'What a wonderful idea . . . [How better] to demonstrate the true spirit of America than by embracing the religion that was perverted in order to commit atrocities?" Another of our students, Holly Hisamoto, in a brief dedication, spoke eloquently about the importance of making the distinction between those who commit violent acts for their own ends in the name of religion and those who do not. (In a similar vein, would it be fair to hold all Buddhists responsible for the acts of Than Shwe and the other generals in Burma's atrocity-committing junta, who are all nominally Buddhist and invoke that whenever it serves their purposes?)

Perhaps the most powerful moment in the service came from Vanessa Karam—UWest's Coordinator of General Education and International Services Officer, and a practicing Muslim. Vanessa shared an old story retold in Farid Esack's book *On Being a Muslim: Finding a Religious Path in the World Today.*

> The story is told of a rabbi whose disciples were debating the question of when precisely "daylight" commenced. One proposed: "It is when one can see the difference between a sheep and a goat at a distance." Another suggested: "It is when you can see the difference between a fig tree and an olive tree at a distance." And so it went on. When they eventually asked the rabbi for his view, he said: "When one human being looks into the face of another and says: 'This is my sister' or 'this is my brother' then the night is over and the day has begun."

This seemed to me the most important "teaching moment" in our service in many respects. Being a proper human being, as the story Vanessa shared suggests, means recognizing our shared humanity, our deep connection to one another. As the head of the chaplaincy program at UWest, I felt so proud of my students and our staff and faculty for modeling this so well. They reminded our community that the night is only over when all of us—all of us, Buddhist and otherwise—recognize our connection and stand beside Muslim Americans and say, "This is my sister" or "this is my brother." That is when the day has begun. They reminded us what it is to be a proper human being.

Clouds show me the nature of my world.
Rivers show me the nature of myself.
Babies show me how to be more human.

In what is perhaps the most inscrutable part of Rinpoche's poem, he speaks of our nature as human beings by invoking images of the natural world. The ephemeral qualities of clouds remind us of ultimate reality, *shunyata*, emptiness. The movements of a river could suggest something about the busy quality of our minds as well as the possibilities for quietude in that movement of our minds. Finally, the image of a newborn suggests something about the importance of care and empathetic response to others. In addition, there seems to be another implicit reminder here about the importance of humility: being open and available to the lessons right in front of us.

In my efforts to remain a student despite my job description as a teacher, one moment in particular has affected me very deeply. When a member of our UWest community fell very ill and was hospitalized, I went with a group of monastic students to visit this person in the hospital. Ever the host, our friend rose from the hospital bed and sat in a chair to visit with us. But this friend wasn't quite ready for so much activity and suddenly became incontinent as we were sitting there. I was a little stunned at first, sort of frozen in place. My monastic colleagues, however, reacted immediately, naturally: one began to clean the mess with some nearby paper towels, while the other took our friend's hand and called out for the nurse. I was amazed; they were so attuned to our friend's needs in that situation, unfazed by any aspect of it.

I felt like I was watching the Buddhist canon come to life: in the *Vinaya Mahavagga*, the story is told of the Buddha attending to a monk with dysentery, cleaning him and caring for him. After caring for this sick man, the Buddha turns to the disciples who refused to help clean the sick man, "Let him who would look after me look after one who is sick." One could interpret this a number of ways, but here were monastics in front of me interpreting it literally—and not in a contrived way, but rather in a way that seemed as natural as breathing. They seemed to be caring for their friend as they might care for a Buddha. Whatever neurosis that kept me from responding vanished in that moment, and I walked hand in hand with our friend to the bathroom to clean up.

I often joke that I have more to learn from my students and our community at UWest than they have to learn from me. There's an element of self-flagellation to this, I'm sure, but it's my hope that I always remain receptive to the lessons of these remarkable people I am privileged to serve in my station as a university chaplain.

I am a student.
I will be a student as long as I live.
And it is a pleasure to be a student.

May you all be students for as long as you live.

Changing Our Mind, Transforming Our World

Ji Hyang Padma

The mind of the great sage of India
is intimately transmitted from west to east.
While human faculties are sharp or dull,
the Way has no northern or southern ancestors.
The spiritual source shines clear in the light;
the branching streams flow on in the dark . . .
—FROM "Sandokai"

THE POEM ABOVE is chanted each morning at San Francisco Zen Center. Sandokai can be translated as "merging of difference and unity," though this translation does not fully capture all the many nuances of that word. I am drawn to the last two lines, what David Bohm, a modern physicist, refers to as the explicate and implicate order of reality or what we refer to in Zen as form and emptiness. When describing form and emptiness in Zen, as in all Zen teaching, we convey the essence directly through images, darkness and light. Zen is like jazz—it works the spaces between the notes—and we develop an ear for that silence through sitting meditation. Within that deep listening, we touch the knowing that is within our entire body and

Ji Hyang Padma serves as director of Spirituality and Education Programs and Buddhist chaplain at Wellesley College. She also teaches at Babson College, Omega Institute, and Esalen Institute. Ji Hyang Padma has done intensive Zen training and teaching in Asia and North America for twenty years. Ji Hyang has also served as abbot of Cambridge Zen Center, as well as serving as a meditation teacher at Harvard University and Boston University. She is currently completing a PhD in transpersonal psychology.

mind. Practice develops our innate, subterranean tacit knowledge. Koan study and the study of teaching verses like Sandokai helps us access these levels of knowing consciously. They are designed to derail our linear thought so that we can connect with a deeper process, which is the core of Zen.

The last lines of the poem describe an inner process: for every word written, there is a depth against which our oars strike—an inarticulate, tacit body of knowledge that is coming to light. Whether we are considering science, technology, or liberal arts, through the practice of looking closely, we can see that these forms of explicit knowledge depend upon tacit knowing. The process of evaluating a work of art or composing music, the breakthroughs that characterize great science (such as Kekule's discovery of the shape of the benzene molecule), the art of relationship that characterizes transformative therapy—all these depend upon tacit knowing. Through contemplation we gain greater access to these subtle, subterranean ways of knowing. For this reason, the presence of mindfulness within higher education is essential. In the words of the Tao Te Ching:

> Thirty spokes share the wheel's hub;
> It is the center hole that makes it useful.

As a Zen teacher, my experience is that by creating space within, students are able to digest the information they have received so that it can become wisdom. Through mindfulness meditation, the mind is integrated with the heart and with the somatic ways of knowing.

DHARMA PRACTICE

At Wellesley College, together with my community, I hold meditation sittings several times a week and host lectures and ceremonies to provide spiritual care to our Buddhist community. Our speakers reflect the great diversity within our Buddhist group. Across my eleven years at Wellesley, I have enjoyed seeing so many students come into their own wisdom and beauty through Dharma practice. While my own practice is rooted in Zen tradition, I bring in teachings and practice that represent the depth and range of many Buddhist traditions, so that everyone finds moments of connection, and students are introduced to the Buddhadharma through a broad lens. Our altar has a statue of Kuan Yin, and I occasionally offer a course for our sangha on the divine feminine within Buddhism.

I find that for women especially, the power and energy of connecting with the divine feminine has the capacity to sharpen our perceptions of the awakened nature within our own body/mind and deepen our confidence in our potential for awakening. There are creative tensions in discussing Buddhism in relationship to the divine feminine. From a Buddhist perspective, all constructs, including gender, are seen as empty. At the same time, Mahayana Buddhist practice and teaching shows us the nonduality of the absolute and relative: all phenomena, just like this, are truth. As Rita Gross and Grace Schiresen, prominent Buddhist teachers, point out:

> The men who say let's not talk about gender because gender isn't real . . . don't go to the ladies' room, they go to the men's room.

In meditation practice, as we make contact with "just like this" truth, and as we notice that all the faces in the altar paintings are men, we may feel hungry to see realization in a woman's body. This is not merely a search for resemblance but a need to have our inner experience of the divine feminine mirrored, especially true on our college campus. When working with young women in a society that objectifies the feminine body, the presence of divine feminine images within Buddhism helps these women to see and know their own beauty. In discussing the archetype of the divine feminine with senior teachers across Buddhist lineages, we have seen that it takes innumerable forms. Some Tibetan teachings describe archetypal feminine energy as sharp, sensitive, quick to respond. These teachings also align feminine energy with emptiness. In Buddhism, emptiness refers to the way we are not separate from anything else in the universe. The archetype of the divine feminine in Buddhism thus can serve as a gateway to the ultimate unity, *prajna*, a way of knowing that is not separate from the known.

I have worked with hundreds of students over the years. Wellesley

College is one of the most diverse colleges on the East Coast, with students from a wide range of cultures and practice traditions. I will briefly describe the connections I have made with two of our students.

Tuyen, a Vietnamese American woman, was the first in her family to attend college. She struggled with self-confidence. Sometimes, she told me, it took her hours to write an email because she typed it again and again until it was perfect. She experienced high levels of anxiety, which was perhaps passed on in her family (her parents had experienced trauma in Vietnam) and which was compounded by the very rigorous premed track she had chosen. She experienced tension with her roommate and did not have enough confidence to address the situation directly or set clear boundaries. During finals period, one email she sent me was titled "Help" followed by twelve exclamation points. Over time, through practices of mindfulness, she was able to see her pattern of perfectionism and connect with the anxiety that underlay her procrastination, which allowed her to meet the deadlines for her coursework.

One day, at the end of a meditation session, Tuyen was able to engage her roommate and reach a resolution. In a conversation we had in the spring of her senior year, she told me, "I'm getting better at stepping into the unknown. It makes me feel like I can take charge of my own life." I asked her what that was like. Tuyen replied, "I have more confidence. When I am making a decision I trust it more . . . I am beginning to understand myself." Meditation practice helped Tuyen discover a centeredness and inner wholeness that was not dependent on conditions.

Another student, Anne, had a campus life experience very common to Wellesley students. Through her parents, she had some exposure to vipassana practice, which began when she was in middle school. She became curious about Buddhism, and practiced a bit with her family before arriving at Wellesley.

In Anne's words:

> In my senior year, I tackled a lot. You know, taking five classes, writing a thesis, acting in plays . . . and then I was sitting in on three other classes just for pure interest. And I felt really calm because of the practice I was doing every day with the other students. Just kind of taking everything one moment at a time, and being able to focus and engage with all of the stimulus.

For our goal-oriented student body, there is deep value in learning meditation, so they can relax and focus the mind and ground their emotions through the integrative practice of working with the breath. Within a rigorous college environment, meditation practice offers students a way of coming home to the body and extending to themselves unconditional presence and kindness. Students develop greater resilience and insight, which continue to benefit them as they enter the world.

INTERRELIGIOUS DIALOGUE

In addition to the core work of teaching Dharma and caring for our sangha, I am also part of a spiritual life team, which has been recognized nationally for its groundbreaking work in interreligious dialogue and diversity training. I have been part of the work of our Religious and Spiritual Life Team at Wellesley College since 1994. I was drawn to this work out of a sense of gratitude for having encountered the Dharma as a student here. My instinct to give something back through sharing meditation practice coincided auspiciously with Wellesley's adoption of a new chaplaincy model—a team that would together care for the spiritual life of the campus community.

In my worldview, this is a practice of upaya (skillful means), which develops greater multicultural awareness and conflict resolution skills within our campus communities and within our society as a whole. Upaya describes the infinite mediums through which original nature finds expression in this world. In Buddhism it gives us a way to appreciate the differences in practice and insight across lineages and to keep the channels of intra-Buddhist dialogue open. Skillful means shows us that the Dharma has a fluid expression, taking infinite and variegated form, just as water appears as an ocean or drops of rain.

Since Buddhism in America is already challenged to deepen connections within our diverse lineages, where do we begin to identify the common ground through which we, as Buddhists, can enter into dialogue with other wisdom traditions? It is comparatively easy to be open and present with practitioners of one's own tradition. In that relationship, we bring out the buddha nature within each other. There is a connection in giving and receiving the teaching that runs very deep, to the original root of what we are. However, coming together as chaplains of various faiths is more challenging. When our Buddhist communities converge out of the "ten directions," we have an unspoken understanding that together we take refuge in the Three Treasures and in silence. But finding a common language across traditions requires ongoing mindfulness and skillful means, so that not too much is lost in translation.

For instance, during my first year as Buddhist advisor, I knew that upon completing a month of *Kyol Che* (the winter intensive retreat in Korean Zen), my first day back at Wellesley would be a retreat with our religious and spiritual life team. I wondered what new forms of contemplation my colleagues would share with our circle. I was more than a little surprised when I discovered this retreat involved talking throughout the day. While other wisdom traditions have set holy days that are recorded on the campus calendars, we Buddhists are challenged to do the same since we do not have sacred days we universally share. On Wellesley campus we celebrate Buddha's Enlightenment Day on December 8.

However, East Asian celebrations follow the lunar calendar, which places Enlightenment Day on January 1. Of course, Theravadan communities celebrate this as Vesak in the spring. So it has been a challenge to create, out of many paths, one Buddhist community—and then again to share the teaching in a way that feels integral within a multifaith context.

And yet, there are some ways through. When our treasured connections to meditation, to sacred texts, to these ways of knowing, are foreign to each other, can we use this apparent separation as another opportunity to cut through illusion and attain nonduality? The appropriate response is clear in front of us: what we are most deeply called to do is to return to the deepest, pure elements of our practice and of our ministry—listening, openness, trust.

In 2005, I was fortunate to attend a symposium held at the Garrison Institute for university chaplains on contemplation and action. Father Thomas Keating, who developed Centering Prayer, was present and led one of the break-out sessions on contemplation. Centering Prayer, in its focus upon the inner experience of God, is possibly the closest Christian practice to sitting meditation. Father Keating had been clear that he believes that the experience of the Centering Prayer and the experience of sitting meditation are different. We reflected together on the nature of silence: Is it Christian silence or Buddhist silence? Over the weekend, we recognized a deep connection arising out of our monastic disciplines of silence. On the last day of the symposium, Father Keating said:

> In Christianity there is a personal God, whereas in Buddhism, God is impersonal . . . but perhaps God is beyond personal and impersonal . . .

Not personal, not impersonal—the sacred as a koan, a great mystery, which I revere and study and discover anew through Father Keating's eyes.

The day-to-day teamwork of our ministry is also a practice, which inexorably calls us to know ourselves better. How can we be present without any agenda, no matter how subtle or well intended? How can we stay connected to what is authentic and at the core of our own practice, while also holding space toward our shared direction of finding common ground? How can there be a mutuality that reflects the essential truth, that each person who steps into our life is our sister, our brother, our teacher? These are koans which I continue to live with and explore on a moment-to-moment basis.

Buddhist Pastoral Ministry in the Military

Thomas Dyer

The UNITED STATES MILITARY draws its service members from every facet of the general US population, so the military has always reflected current cultural trends. Likewise, Buddhism has become a rising phenomena in the US and, therefore, in the military as well. This shift has turned the attention of the Military Chaplain Corp (whose mission is to design ministries for the spiritual needs of all soldiers) to Buddhist pastoral ministry.

The Army authorized Buddhist chaplains in 1996, but it was not until 2008 that I became the first Buddhist Army chaplain, followed by Somya Malasri in 2010. Buddhism is still in its infancy in the US, and until recent years there were no education programs to qualify chaplains. At present, two Buddhist schools include military ministry training in their master's program: The University of the West in Rosemead, California, and Naropa University in Boulder, Colorado. The Buddhist Churches of America (BCA) functions as an endorsing agency for the Army, which is currently the only military agency endorsing Buddhist chaplains.

In order to become a Buddhist Army chaplain, I had to satisfy the Army's academic requirements with a bachelor's degree and a master's

Thomas Dyer began studying meditation in 2001, taking refuge in 2005, while a member of the Tennessee National Guard. On May 14, 2008, he became the first Buddhist chaplain in US Army history with the Army National Guard. In December of 2009, he deployed to Iraq to implement Buddhist ministry to soldiers, marines, sailors, airman, and Department of Defense employees in a combat setting. He returned from Iraq in July of 2010. Then on August 11, 2011, he was selected for active duty and is currently serving on full-time active duty in the US Army Chaplain Corps. He is currently a student of the monastic teachers Thich Hai Vien and Kempo Gawang Rinpoche, who both reside in Memphis, Tennessee.

degree in religious studies. The Army also requires that height and weight standards along with physical fitness standards be met. On top of that, Buddhist Churches of America requires verifiable Buddhist training before they will endorse a chaplain. My credentials include a master of divinity from a Christian seminary. In 2003, I began training directly under a monastic teacher. I am a student of Thich Hai Vien at the Pho-Da Temple in Memphis, Tennessee. BCA has recognized my training and current status as a student directly under a monastic teacher.

Once endorsed, a chaplain attends a three-month training course at Ft. Jackson, South Carolina. The course, called Chaplain's Officer Basic Course (CHBOLC), trains a chaplain in basic soldiering skills for a non-combat soldier. These skills include how to take cover if fired upon by small arms or rockets and how to deploy a gas mask in a chemical attack, which requires a trip to the gas chamber. There is further training in how to live in a deployed setting, such as Iraq or Afghanistan.

Being a Buddhist chaplain in the military means playing multiple roles: noncombat soldier, staff officer, battalion chaplain, and low-density chaplain. The Buddhist chaplain's education and training is designed to *provide* and *perform* religious coverage for all service members and all faith groups. In the military, Buddhism is considered "low-density"—meaning they do not have large numbers in one location or many fewer soldiers overall with these religious affiliations (as compared to the "high-density" faith group of Protestant Christianity). For this reason, when I embarked on a low-density ministry to Buddhist service members in a deployed setting, I needed to find ways to balance low-density ministry with battalion ministry and staff officer duties.

THE CHAPLAIN AS PROFESSIONAL STAFF OFFICER

One of my roles as an Army chaplain is professional staff officer, acting as special advisor to the commander of a battalion on the mental, emotional, and spiritual well-being of the soldiers. (A commander is in charge of three hundred to six hundred men and women.) When our unit first arrived in Iraq, for instance, I found one of our soldiers walking around the base confused. I realized she was experiencing some shock, so I advised the commander not to let her go outside the base on missions until she adjusted to being deployed in a combat setting. Another soldier was experiencing stress from the deployment and passed out in formation.

After a short period of adjustment, however, both individuals recovered and became stellar soldiers. On another occasion in Iraq, a platoon sergeant's leadership was too aggressive—yelling at the soldiers like they were in boot-camp, working them too hard and keeping them up too late under the guise of being at war. My advice to the commander was to counsel the platoon leader, essentially to calm him down so as not to diminish the effectiveness and morale of his platoon. In the weekly commander's meeting, which all the top officers of the battalion attended and at which I had an opportunity to speak, I always try to inspire virtue and emphasize how clear and calm leadership impact the effectiveness of the unit and the quality of life for the soldier.

I am in charge of managing the commander's religious program for soldiers. My responsibility is to make sure all the soldiers in the battalion have the opportunity to worship according to their faith group, e.g., Buddhist, Muslim, Jewish, Christian, Wiccan, and so on—while in Iraq, one soldier told me he was a practicing Jedi. As a chaplain, it is not my place to judge anyone's religious practice or preference, like telling the soldier it was strange to develop a religion from a Hollywood motion picture. My job was to help him. So I looked up a Jedi Temple Order website on the Internet and found the Jedi precepts. Strangely enough, these precepts were teaching virtues, such as love, wisdom, righteousness, and courage. In light of this, I told the soldier to print copies of the precepts, which he put in his soft hat and in his helmet and carried everywhere he went.

As professional staff officer, I am also responsible for managing the commander's suicide prevention and sexual assault prevention programs. While I was deployed, I monitored my soldiers for signs of suicide and sexual assault, which would require my immediate intervention. I also taught classes and training programs in Iraq in an effort to prevent suicide and sexual assault. I am happy to say our unit was successful in steering clear of these behaviors.

THE CHAPLAIN AS BATTALION CHAPLAIN

A Buddhist chaplain serves two missions. First is to serve as chaplain to all the soldiers in the battalion, which has two primary religious groups—Protestant Christian and "nonreligious preference," i.e., no religion declared or not practicing a specific religion. The second mission is to be a Buddhist chaplain to Buddhist soldiers. We consider Catholic, Jewish, Muslim, and Buddhist faiths "low-density" faith groups. There were no Jewish, Muslim, or Buddhist soldiers in my battalion of six hundred soldiers, which consisted of five Catholic soldiers, one Wiccan, and the remainder either Protestant Christian or nonreligious preference. My regiment of six thousand soldiers included six declared Buddhists, one Muslim, and two Jewish soldiers.

The Army Chaplain Corps has a motto: "Provide or Perform." This means my role as a religious leader is to *provide* religious coverage for soldiers outside of my faith group and to *perform* religious services and pastoral ministry for my own faith group. Since the majority of soldiers in my battalion are Protestant Christians, as a Buddhist chaplain, I cannot *perform* religious services for Christian soldiers. Instead, I *provide* religious coverage for Christian soldiers by ensuring they have the opportunity to attend Protestant worship services and providing access to a Christian chaplain for religious and pastoral counseling, if they request it.

I am responsible for the battalion's counseling needs—crisis, grief, marriage and family, spiritual, and life skills, for all faith groups, including atheist, agnostic, and nonreligious preference. This counseling is not specifically pastoral counseling or psychological therapy. It is *helping-counseling*, which is neither religious nor therapeutic but has to do with daily life problems. Young soldiers often struggle with relationships, finances, career decisions, and conflict with other soldiers. At times, as a battalion chaplain, I refer a Christian, Muslim, or Jewish soldier to a Christian, Muslim, or Jewish chaplain for pastoral counseling, again, if the soldier requests it. An authentic pastoral counseling experience between a soldier and a chaplain of his or her own faith group is irreplaceable.

I was invited to bases all over Iraq to visit Buddhist soldiers who had never had the opportunity to speak with a Buddhist chaplain. But there are also times I refer a soldier to Combat Stress or Behavior Health for professional psychological counseling. As a Buddhist chaplain, I am obliged to address the ministerial needs of every soldier in the battalion, whether part of a low-density or high-density religious group, and to balance these needs.

LOW-DENSITY MINISTRY PLAN

How does a Buddhist chaplain *perform* religious coverage for Buddhist soldiers? How does he *perform* religious services? How does a Buddhist chaplain *perform* pastoral counseling with a Buddhist soldier? When I was deployed, I was the only Buddhist chaplain in the entire armed forces in Iraq for all Buddhist service members: marines, airmen, sailors, and Army soldiers. Buddhist service members were deployed all over Iraq. How can a Buddhist chaplain *perform* religious services and pastoral ministry to Buddhist service members who are deployed all over a huge geographical area?

My chaplain "chain of command" operated on the principle of "Request and Accommodation" to protect the First Amendment rights of American military service members. If a Buddhist soldier *requested* to see me for pastoral counseling or *requested* a Buddhist religious service, it was my responsibility to travel to see the soldier or service member and *accommodate* with religious coverage.

In a deployed setting, such as Iraq or Afghanistan, low-density chaplains must have a *low-density ministry plan*. American soldiers are stationed all over Iraq and Afghanistan on Forwarding Operational Bases (FOBs). These bases may be anywhere from ten miles to hundreds of miles apart, and Buddhist soldiers (as well as other low-density soldiers) are scattered throughout these areas of operations. The Buddhist chaplain's "chain of command" must design a travel plan to provide widespread religious coverage. While I was in Iraq, since Christian chaplains cannot perform religious coverage for the Buddhist soldier, Christian chaplains or commanders provided religious coverage by inviting and hosting me to their base to provide religious coverage for Buddhist soldiers, which would also give me the opportunity to perform a Buddhist service and administer pastoral counseling to Buddhist soldiers.

In Iraq, I flew to different bases aboard a Black Hawk helicopter, where

I was usually hosted by the Christian chaplain, who would provide me with housing and arrange a location and time for the Buddhist religious service. The Christian chaplain escorted me around to visit the Buddhist soldiers. If the need for pastoral counseling arose, the Christian chaplain would provide a private place for me to meet with the soldier.

THE IMPORTANCE OF A BUDDHIST SERVICE

Soldiers in a deployed setting endure tremendous hardships. In the Middle East, for instance, the weather is extremely hot, at times up to 125 degrees, and the desert can produce extreme cold in the winter. Long periods of separation from family weigh heavily on soldiers. Military operations produce extended work hours, filled with noise and vibrations. Aircraft, helicopters, tanks, and other heavy equipment operate twenty-four hours a day. The terrain is brown, the uniforms are all the same, and the days are filled with repetition. At times, soldiers see, hear, and smell events in combat that most people never experience. This is the reality of a military deployment. Under these conditions, many soldiers turn to their faith for support.

In Iraq and Afghanistan, Protestant Christian soldiers can go to the chapel, gather and sing "Amazing Grace," and hear inspirational sermons. Catholic soldiers can go to Mass and receive spiritual sustenance from the Eucharist. Jewish and Muslim soldiers can enjoy a worship service in their tradition as well. Now, the same is true for Buddhist soldiers.

Buddhist soldiers returning from missions long to get out of the elements and come to a chapel. They should have the opportunity to practice their faith in the same manner as other faith groups. They relish the opportunity to sit in front of the altar with a Shakyamuni statue, smell the burning incense, and see the water or candle offering. Buddhist soldiers love to hear the calming sound of the bell calling them to meditation. They want the nutriment of the Buddhist faith and the healing power of meditation to protect their minds.

Many soldiers who attend a Buddhist service have "nonreligious preference" on their dog tags. Some are what we might call "bookstore Buddhists." They have come to Buddhism through reading the Dalai Lama or Thich Nhat Hanh, but they are not affiliated with a specific lineage.

Some soldiers who declare nonreligious preference come from Buddhist lineages but do not feel comfortable declaring their Buddhist faith while serving in the military. Offering a Buddhist service or meditation brings many of these undeclared Buddhists on the radar, which increases the potential for pastoral ministry.

It is important for a Buddhist chaplain to be extremely sensitive to different lineages, so a chaplain should provide a Buddhist service that can minister to all lineages. In Iraq, I found that soldiers enjoyed an altar with a statue of Shakyamuni, an incense burner, and a candle. I offered basic recitations such as the five precepts, Four Noble Truths, and the Eightfold Path. I provided fifteen-minute meditation along with "inviting the bell to sound." Also after the meditation and recitation, I offered a Dharma discussion—which the soldiers always seem to enjoy.

PASTORAL MINISTRY

Many Buddhist soldiers request pastoral counseling services from their Buddhist chaplain, so a low-density ministry plan and Buddhist services are indispensable. It is so important for soldiers to be able to speak with a chaplain who shares their faith perspective and can offer many different types of helping counseling. Much of spiritual counseling, also referred to in the Army as "pastoral ministry," looks the same among all the faith groups. All chaplains (Christian, Catholic, Muslim, Jewish, and Buddhist) will inspire religious soldiers to turn to their faith practice for encouragement and help while enduring the hardships of a deployment.

From the US constitutional perspective, a service member has the right to practice his or her faith while in the service. From the Army's strategic perspective, religion is a "combat multiplier," which means that religion is one of the most powerful forces to encourage, help, and sustain a soldier in combat. Mental, emotional, and spiritual health is sustained by religious practice, which helps the Army fulfill its missions. Religious practice is also a quality of life issue. A soldier's life experiences are better with some form of entertainment and religious practice, such as playing ping-pong at a recreation center and going to church or meditation. From the perspective of religious practitioners, devotion to faith is the most comforting force while serving in combat.

Deployment and, specifically, combat tend to make soldiers reflect on their spiritual condition. Pastoral ministry is very important on all these levels—constitutionally, strategically, qualitatively, and spiritually.

Although pastoral ministry may look similar among faith groups, Buddhist soldiers may struggle with unique issues. The Buddha taught *right livelihood*—and it was a common thread of most Buddhist lineages that military service was considered *wrong livelihood* and a vocation that would produce negative karma.

This is something I have reflected on often. It came to a head for me when I had the opportunity to meet the Dalai Lama, being introduced to him as the first Buddhist chaplain in US Army history. His Holiness stood back for a few seconds and looked at me with his big eyes. Suddenly he grabbed my right hand and pulled my face directly into his face, his eyes looking directly into my eyes—I felt the rim of his eyeglasses touching my forehead. Then he pulled back, squeezed my hand firmly, and gave an affirming grunt. I did not fully understand what had transpired, but the experience was forever imprinted on my mind. Later, when I asked my teacher, Thich Hai Vien, what had happened, he said His Holiness was looking into my eyes and mind to see if I had good motives and was sincere. I was relieved for the affirming grunt. The next day, I met His Holiness again, and this time I was wearing my Army dress uniform. When he approached me, he placed my two hands together and caressed them for a moment. Then he squeezed my hands and gave me another affirming grunt. Perhaps this experience was not a complete teaching on right livelihood, but it confirmed to me that motives are central to the quality of karma being generated.

And I try to bring awareness of this to Buddhist soldiers to whom I minister. When I performed Buddhist services in Iraq, I would ask the soldiers to bring their M16 rifles with them while we were sitting. As the soldiers held their weapons across their legs, we would pray or make aspirations that these weapons would only be used for good, to protect what is wonderful, beautiful, and right in the world. We would pray that one day the metal pieces of the weapon would transform and be made into a beautiful bell to call monks, nuns, and laymen to meditation. We would pray that one day the plastic pieces of the M16 would transform and be made into a cup from which the sick could take medicine. And I would remind the soldiers of the Dharma Seal of impermanence that is a universal truth: our enemies will not always be our enemies.

On one such occasion, we prayed that if our weapons had to be used, the round discharged from the rifle would go only where it needed to go for the greatest good. Later, one of the Buddhist soldiers approached me and, with a nervous and cracking voice, told me about his experience on a convoy traveling from central Iraq. While moving through a village, the lead truck thought there was an improvised explosive device (IED) in the road. The convoy commander directed the convoy to stop and be ready for small arms fire. The soldier was in the center gun truck manning a fifty-caliber machine gun.

Suddenly he saw a man lying down on a second floor balcony with an AK-47 pointed directly at him. The man began firing at him, and the soldier responded to his training by firing the machine gun and killing the man. In keeping with protocol, a special team was sent to investigate the incident. The soldier was determined to have performed correctly according to the rules of engagement. However the investigators found that the man's pregnant wife and six-year-old son had been inside the apartment and were killed as well. After finishing his story, the soldier said, "The round discharged from the weapon did not go where it needed to go." Then he leaned over in his chair with his elbows on his knees and his hands covering his face, crying.

The soldier also recounted a sutra from the Samyutta Nikaya. In short, the sutra says that if a warrior kills someone while exerting himself in battle, he will be reborn in hell. As a Buddhist chaplain, how could I help this Buddhist soldier? What could I say?

I found myself flashing back to 2009, when the Dalai Lama was invited to the Civil Rights Museum to receive the Freedom Award. I was asked to give the invocation at the event, which afforded me the opportunity to meet His Holiness a second time. After I spoke, I remained backstage so I could be close to the Dalai Lama when he spoke. Secret service agents were scrambling around and bomb-squad dogs were sniffing up and down. The Dalai Lama was escorted onto the stage and began to speak, and there was so much energy in the air. But when he said that every conflict has a peaceful solution, I felt conflicted.

I looked down at my Army uniform, and thought: Am I doing the right thing, being in the military? While I was thinking these thoughts, a Memphis Tactical Police Officer, carrying an M16 and walking a bomb-sniffing dog, was patrolling the back stage just behind a black curtain, in front of which His Holiness was teaching about love and compassion. No one in the audience was aware of the activity behind the curtain. There is my answer, I thought. The Dalai Lama is a precious jewel on the earth. I have the opportunity to meet him and listen to his teaching because the US State Department and the Memphis Police Department are preserving and protecting him. After the Dalai Lama spoke and received the Freedom Award, secret service agents escorted him out of the building, while Memphis Tactical Police snipers watched over him. What is good, beautiful, and right needs protection.

I shared this story with the suffering soldier and reminded him that although bad things happen in combat, this world cannot sustain itself without protecting forces. We talked about the good military has done and how US forces have responded to numerous disasters throughout the world. Then I affirmed him as a soldier, reminding him that his service is valuable and needed and that he responded well to his training—he did the right action at the right time. As a Buddhist soldier, if his motives are good, his karma is good. I gave him an Avalokiteshvara practice for himself and the people he had killed, told him I would contact some Buddhist teachers for their perspectives concerning the sutra he had mentioned—and counseled him to volunteer for humanitarian missions. The Army frequently conducted humanitarian missions while I was in Iraq, and I went on two of these missions. Before we went into the village, I was asked to offer a prayer and say a few words to my soldiers. I told them to remember the villagers are human beings who want what we want, that is, to be happy. Although we must maintain a posture of readiness and awareness as combat soldiers, if our eyes show love and our faces show openness, they will respond. Then I offered a prayer, and we proceeded outside of our base into a local village.

We distributed items like food, shoes, soccer balls, and water purification filters. What happened next was wonderful, something I will remember for the rest of my life: the villagers responded to our openness. The men were talking to the male soldiers, the women were talking to the female soldiers, and the children were running everywhere, playing with all the soldiers. It was absolutely electric. I saw a male soldier cry when a little Iraqi girl hugged him. I witnessed an Iraqi woman asking American soldiers to watch her toddler so she could carry her food home. When she went into the village, I watched the soldiers form a line to take turns holding the Iraqi toddler. Another time, a unit went into villages to fit children with disabilities for wheelchairs. One of the soldiers on the mission told me the most amazing thing he had ever done was to pick up an Iraqi child and place him in his new wheelchair.

In keeping with my promise to the soldier, I contacted one of Thich Nhat Hanh's nuns about whether a soldier who kills someone in combat will be reborn in hell. The correspondence I received from one of the senior monks at Plum Village said that the Buddha's teachings are to reduce suffering in the world; they are not permanent, fundamental doctrines to grasp after or cling to. The monk reaffirmed that motives are central to wholesome karma and even quoted Thich Nhat Hanh as saying he "wished more Buddhists would become nuclear scientists to help make the world a safer place." I shared these words with the soldier, and they were truly helpful.

But no matter how helpful the teachings are, the soldier will still suffer, and probably suffer throughout his entire life. Combat is ugly and messy, and it might be said that if the Buddhist soldier had not joined the military, he would not have invited the suffering into his life and brought his karma into question. Yet we must keep in mind that Buddhism is not dualistic, and whether a Buddhist or someone else is manning that machine gun, it is still someone who is connected to us. From the Buddhist point of view, we are all part of the same stream of existence. We are all suffering in some form or other as we move from birth, old age, sickness, and death. Collectively, we all must work together to do the best we can to reduce suffering in the world as individually we seek salvation, heaven, or enlightenment.

The world is complicated. Rather than think about being in the military as right livelihood or wrong livelihood, I think it is better to think about motives and the effort to reduce suffering by our thoughts and actions for ourselves and others. This is my mission as a Buddhist chaplain in the US Army. I want to inspire all soldiers, especially Buddhist soldiers, to see themselves as warrior-protectors. I want soldiers to start their military service motivated to protect what is good, beautiful, and right in the world and to protect civilians, women, and children. I want to help soldiers see how important it is to respect the civilian population when they are on deployments and to protect places of worship, schools, hospitals, works of art, and the culture of the people with whom they come in contact. In short, I feel Buddhists have the potential to contribute to the life of military service in unique and meaningful ways.

PART V

Living with Dying:
The Arts of End-of-Life Care

Spiritual Care with the Dying

Tenzin Chodron

THE FOCUS on preparing for death in Buddhism and the many teachings available on the dying process in the Tibetan tradition reinforce the need to understand death on a deeper and more profound level. Being part of the Karuna Hospice Service team in Brisbane, Australia, has given me an opportunity to learn to put those teachings into practice. It is an ongoing learning curve, often challenging, and an area of work I feel a strong affinity with.

Karuna offers end-of-life care to the dying in their own homes, through nursing, counseling, volunteer support, and spiritual care. Started by a Buddhist monk, Pende Hawter, in 1992, Karuna's work is based on Buddhist principles and values and is affiliated with the FPMT (Foundation for the Preservation of the Mahayana Tradition) through the guidance of Lama Zopa Rinpoche. In recent years His Holiness the Dalai Lama has visited and been connected with Karuna as its spiritual patron. As a Buddhist nun in the Tibetan tradition, I have been working with Karuna in the area of spiritual care since 2000.

In this chapter, I'd like to share a number of lessons I've learned from people I've met through my hospice work.

Tenzin Chodron is a Buddhist nun in the Tibetan tradition who, since ordaining in India in 1999, has studied Buddhist philosophy at Chenrezig Institute in Australia, while living within the Chenrezig Nuns Community. During this time she has worked with Karuna Hospice Service, offering spiritual care to those preparing for death, also developing and presenting educational courses for the wider community on spiritual care with the dying and Buddhism. In earlier years, Chodron received degrees in sociology and social work, focusing as a social worker and group facilitator in the areas of grief and loss, particularly with indigenous communities in Australia. Previous to this she studied and practiced extensively within psychosynthesis and the theosophical tradition before traveling to Tibet and embracing Tibetan Buddhism.

David was in his thirties, a surfing instructor who deeply loved his life by the ocean. He had attempted to combat the cancer overtaking his body using alternative approaches and everything offered by medical science, and he was not at all ready to face the prospect of dying.

David had no formal religion and was not particularly looking for any spiritual connection. He just wanted to be well again so he could get back to the waves. We met once, briefly, and lightly touched on some themes about preparing for death—it was not an area he wanted to explore. Following the visit, his condition deteriorated unexpectedly and quickly, and the next time I saw him he was actively dying. His mother and father were at his bedside—they seemed exhausted and had been sitting with David for days waiting for his final breath. He had been agitated and unable to settle.

David was unconscious and still appeared to be very agitated when I arrived. I asked his parents if they would like me to do some prayers and Buddhist practices, which they were happy to have done. I first placed some Kalachakra sand, blessed by the Dalai Lama at a Kalachakra cer-emony for world peace, on the crown of David's head, and then taped a small piece of paper with the *10 Powerful Mantras at the Time of Death*, face down, on the center of his chest. I also gently placed a blessing string from the Dalai Lama at David's neck and proceeded to do the Tibetan prayers traditionally associated with the time of dying.

In situations such as this where I don't know the family well, depend-ing on the family's wishes and the dying person's spiritual faith, I may quietly do prayers in the room as I sit with them—with the wish to create a compassionate presence and to request the blessings of enlightened beings for the dying person. On this occasion I had a feeling it would be useful not only to do the prayers so that everyone could clearly hear them, but also to chant various mantras and prayers in Tibetan—such as Medicine Buddha, Chenrezig, and others. I checked with David's parents about this and then began, sitting as closely as I could to David.

I noticed that with the chanting, David's agitation was settling. He seemed to respond to the sound. As I continued, his breathing began changing, with longer periods between the out-breath and the in-breath. After some time, as I reached the final dedications, still chanting in Tibetan, David's breathing stopped completely and I could see just a faint pulse in his neck. Then with the final moment of chanting, David's pulse stopped, in perfect timing with the end of the chant. The following moments were deeply peaceful and quiet.

It seemed as if the blessings of the enlightened beings were with David, and I was reminded of a teaching by the Dalai Lama in which he said that even if we have doubts about our own abilities and effectiveness as spiritual practitioners, we can have strong faith and rely on the power of holy beings and their blessings.

It's a very reassuring thought, especially in being with someone in the final stages of the dying process.

Motivation always plays a key role in the practice of spiritual care with the dying. Before visiting with a dying person, I take time to set a compassionate motivation for the visit, with the wish that it will be of greatest spiritual benefit for the person. Whether I meet with someone a number of times over a period of weeks or months, or meet them only once in the final hours of dying, the motivation forms an essential part of the process of care.

Here, let me share the story of Genevieve.

Genevieve was a woman in her early sixties who initially became involved with Karuna by attending a six-week introduction to a Buddhism course I was teaching as part of Karuna's community education program. As Genevieve began the course, she immediately felt an affinity with the Buddhist way of life. And at the end of the course when a refuge ceremony and the lay vows were offered by a Tibetan lama she took the opportunity to formally become a Buddhist.

Genevieve continued with Karuna by attending various educational courses and a weekly Medicine Buddha meditation group. As her illness progressed, she attempted as much as possible to hold off the inevitable and insidious decline that motor neuron disease (MND) offers its sufferers. We spent many hours together discussing Buddhist ideas on illness, karma, spiritual practices, and preparation for death, and she continued with daily practices, study, and meditation as best she could right through the term of her illness.

Genevieve had spent her earlier life as an elite athlete, achieving international recognition and acclaim in her profession. As someone who had valued and focused on intensive physical training, she found it particularly distressing to experience the loss of control of the body she identified so strongly with. She felt great fear at times as the illness progressed, and it was only through meditation, spiritual practice, and discussions about the spiritual path that she found relief.

It was a great lesson for me to experience the difference in her when we were meditating together with a compassionate motivation to benefit all beings, compared with other moments when she was in the clutches of fear and distress. And it brought home again and again the importance of transforming and awakening the mind to its true nature, especially in the face of such illness.

The nurses and volunteers worked with great compassion and kindness even as she was in intense mental distress. Thankfully in her final hours, Genevieve reconnected with the sense of peace she had struggled to find in the days leading up to her death.

At Genevieve's request, following her death we held a Buddhist funeral, in addition to a traditional puja—an offering and chanting ceremony—on the seventh day after her death; another puja on the forty-ninth day, and prayers and dedications for her during those forty-nine days, in accordance with the Tibetan tradition, and as part of our practice of continuing spiritual care after death.

Most of the people who receive end-of-life care from Karuna are not Buddhist. So in offering spiritual care we use a universal approach, one that recognizes the underlying spiritual needs of each dying person, and goes beyond traditional religious boundaries. We attempt to adapt to each situation and spiritual need as it presents itself, drawing from our Buddhist values while respecting the dying person's own beliefs. Sometimes we offer spiritual care to someone who has no spiritual affiliation—like a man who told me he believed "your lights go out and that's it." And sometimes we offer care to someone who has very strongly defined religious beliefs. Our philosophy of care is that, regardless of where a person falls in the spectrum of beliefs and practices, she deserves full support to find her own unique personal connection and meaning while preparing to die.

Consider the case of Margaret.

Margaret was a strong, outspoken, and forthright woman in her sixties who was cared for by Karuna at home, and who introduced herself to me as a "pre–Vatican II Catholic." Having been raised Catholic myself, I immediately felt the impact of that statement. The Vatican II Council had brought in many reforms and changes to the Catholic Church in the 1960s, attempting to bring the Church into the modern era, moving away from the traditional Latin Mass and strict practices. So identifying as a "pre–Vatican II Catholic" suggested a very conservative approach to the Church and life. At that point, as a Buddhist nun, I wondered if I would be able to serve Margaret's spiritual needs in preparing for death. I thought she might prefer to speak to a Catholic nun, which I arranged; a visit from a priest with similar views, although tricky to find, was also arranged.

To my surprise, she did not ask for the nun and priest after that. Rather, she wanted to continue our connection, and our relationship continued to develop and deepen over the months before her death. We spoke openly together about her needs in preparing herself and her family for her death. I found it helpful to draw on my Catholic upbringing and still knew the words to a number of the prayers Margaret liked to recite daily. Our visits included lively discussions and recitations of traditional Catholic prayers, which she found comforting. It was far more important to use words and concepts that were meaningful to Margaret than attempt to use Buddhist prayers and concepts that may have upset her mind. My motivation was to have compassion and focus on what would be spiritually beneficial for her. Buddhism doesn't suit everyone, but, as the Dalai Lama points out so often, the qualities of compassion and loving-kindness can be brought to every situation.

Margaret asked me to be with her through the dying process, and as she was dying I gently recited into her ear the prayers she was familiar with, so that as her consciousness was withdrawing, she would be reminded of her own deep faith and have confidence on her journey.

Another person I worked with was an older woman named Olivia. When I first met Olivia it was in her home, which was jam-packed full of expensive furniture and antiques, overloaded with collectibles, and bursting at the seams with valuable things that had obviously been gathered over many years. Material things were very important to her. As she walked into the living room and we greeted each other, she looked extremely thin and unwell, one arm hanging loosely by her side as the other clutched onto a metal pole on wheels holding a portable "drip," which was her only source of sustenance. She had a tumor at her throat that prevented her from being able to drink and a tumor in her stomach that prevented her from eating. She appeared completely drained of life and vitality, and she was filled with anxiety.

As our conversation progressed I asked her if it would be alright to speak openly about death and dying. I often ask permission to do this, when it seems an appropriate time. Usually it is part of the natural flow of the discussion and most people seeking the care of hospice are ready to talk openly, but on this occasion Olivia vehemently said, "No, I'm too scared." At that point she was just over a week away from her death.

I was wondering how I was going to work with this when the thought occurred to me to give her the small Tibetan wrist mala I had with me. Sometimes when people are overwhelmed with fear, offering something physical, as a sort of grounding, can be of benefit. The mala was something she could hold or wear. I explained it was blessed by a holy being, Lama Zopa Rinpoche, and that my belief was that it would bring blessings to her. I also gave her a picture of the Dalai Lama, whom she immediately recognized and connected with. I then taught her the mantra of compassion, *Om Mani Padme Hum*, and suggested she use it when she felt fearful to help her find a sense of peace.

I don't necessarily speak about the Tibetan tradition or Buddhist ideas with people, but in this situation it felt appropriate. I visited Olivia again a few days later—she was in bed with the mala on her wrist and the picture of the Dalai Lama with her. She had not taken the mala off since she had received it and had kept the picture close to her. She appeared completely different from the last visit—calm, at peace, smiling—and said, "I think God is calling me home now." She then asked me to help her say goodbye to her husband, something she could not even begin to consider doing previously. So the three of us sat together, and she spoke beautifully, telling him how much she appreciated sharing her life with him.

The experience with Olivia showed me very clearly that it's not always necessary or appropriate to explore the fear of death. Although for some people an exploration of fear or grief or anger can be a turning point, each situation is different. I have found that having discussions about inspirational people, whether they are Christian saints, enlightened buddhas, or inspirational and compassionate people still living, can be helpful in lifting the mind from a difficult place.

If the dying person has a particular religious belief, then invoking the presence and blessings of that tradition through a brief meditation can also be very meaningful and healing. In other situations a simple breathing meditation or visualization can help settle the mind. Sometimes I use a physical representation such as a consecrated stupa, a structure that symbolically represents the enlightened mind and the blessings of the buddhas, while doing prayers at the bedside of a dying person.

DEVELOPING COURAGE

One of the saddest experiences I've encountered in working with Karuna is the death of a young mother, previously separated from her partner, leaving a young boy of six.

Jennifer was determined not to die. She did not want to speak about death, hear about it, or think about it in any way. She was going to heal herself of the cancer in her body and she was adamant that this illness was a temporary setback she would recover from. She also did not want to speak with her little six-year-old son about it—as far as he was concerned, she was sick and soon would be well again. It was simply unbearable for her to consider any other possibility.

As Jennifer's condition deteriorated, she was slowly beginning to recognize the possibility that she was actually facing the end of her life and beginning to think about what that would mean. Then, although the doctors had thought she would live for a number of months, she died suddenly one night.

I felt such deep sadness for Jennifer and her beautiful little son, for the suddenness of his grief and loss—and very sad that we had not been able to create a more gentle preparation for him in the loss of his mother, even with the limitations of understanding that a six-year-old has about death. A process of opening had started within Jennifer that was not able to reach its conclusion, and it strongly brought home to me the reality that death can happen at any time; it doesn't wait for us to be prepared and ready to go. It can be messy and untidy and leave many loose ends that both loved ones and professional and volunteer careers need to work through.

The experience with Jennifer taught me about developing the courage to discuss death directly. I often speak about Jennifer and the experience of her son to other young mothers who are facing the end of their life.

She touches them and teaches them through her story, which helps with the sometimes heartbreaking task they face in talking with their children about what is unfolding.

Another person I will never forget is William. William was in his seventies, had no spiritual beliefs, and was in the last days of his life when he asked for a visit from "someone ordained." He did not care what tradition the person was ordained in, just that they be ordained. It was an unexpected request given his lack of belief in any faith tradition. As he was being cared for by Karuna at home, I was contacted.

When we began our discussion, William talked about an incident that had happened over sixty-five years ago that had troubled him all his life. It occurred when he was six or seven years old, involving himself and another little boy. William had never spoken about the incident to anyone, and many years later, the other boy grew up and married William's sister, becoming his brother-in-law.

Throughout his life, William carried a deep sense of guilt and remorse about his actions in this incident. William felt he needed to confess this before he died, as it represented something important and unresolved in his life that went far beyond the experience of two little boys. After we had discussed this together and William had expressed the pain he had been carrying, it seemed he needed further closure and I suggested we call his brother-in-law, who was also now an elderly man, so that he could speak with him directly. We arranged another visit, this time involving his brother-in-law, myself, and William's sister, who was his main caregiver in this final stage of his illness. We sat together and William spoke with great honesty and tenderness, apologizing to his brother-in-law for what had happened. Without any hesitation, his brother-in-law gave William the forgiveness he was seeking and said the incident had been lost long ago in his memory. But the process that happened between them represented a deep resolution for William and gave him a sense of peace—he then died two days later.

Not all issues of forgiveness are resolved in such a way, and not all dying people are willing to seek or offer forgiveness for perceived wrongs, even as they face death. It can, however, be very healing to work through an issue of forgiveness with someone at the end of life, even if the person to be forgiven knows nothing about it or has passed away.

I've often spoken to people about one of the end-of-life practices that is recommended by the Buddhist tradition, the practice of generosity. Generosity helps to prepare the mind for letting go at the time of death and also creates positive potential for future happiness. When I think of the power of generosity to transform the mind, I think of Sandra. She was a single woman in her forties who was in the last months of her life when we met, while she was being cared for by Karuna at home. Over the course of several visits, she spoke openly about death and dying, her wishes for the time of death and after, and her concerns and fears as she faced the end of life. We discussed many issues connected with current and past relationships, and her grief over saying goodbye to loved ones and the life she knew.

Sandra wanted to prepare her mind for death and was interested in using the practice of generosity before her death as part of her spiritual path. As she didn't have children or a partner, she decided to leave all of her savings to various charities that she had carefully considered and chosen. She arranged how all of this was to take place and was so inspired by the thought of giving that the grief she felt at leaving was completely dispelled. She told me on our last visit together that she was so excited about being able to help so many different people she just wanted to die now so they would benefit.

I learned so much from how Sandra faced her grief and transformed it into compassion toward others. She brought a great deal of healing to her own mind, a deeper sense of meaning to her death, and happily benefited the lives of many other people she never knew.

I have found that, generally, those who have some sort of religious or spiritual faith are able to approach death with greater stability and confidence, and with less distress, than those with no faith. This is not always the case of course—some people have doubts arise as they approach death and need support to reconnect with their faith. It seems, though, that if people have integrated their faith into their daily life, then their experience of the dying process becomes an expression of that integration and provides a source of strength to deal with unfamiliar terrain.

One elderly woman who was near death told me she had been meditating for many years, had focused on developing her inner life, and had no fear of dying. She was ready and looking forward to the adventure! She showed how a strong inner life gives confidence in approaching death, and not only helps to overcome fear, but also gives a greater ability to utilize the spiritual opportunity that the dying process offers.

Dying people are often interested in reflecting with others on what will happen during the actual dying process. For most people, the dying process itself is an unknown, something that is not discussed in daily life and that remains hidden from view in our culture. A dying person often wants to know: What will happen? How will it feel? What will it look like? Many times, when it has seemed to be useful, I have spoken about the teachings from the Tibetan tradition on what is known as the dissolution of the elements—the process the body goes through as it gradually shuts down during the various stages of dying, and the corresponding process experienced by the mind as it withdraws to more and more subtle levels of consciousness before finally leaving the body. I have found that a discussion such as this can help to settle fear in the mind and be of benefit in preparing for the dying process, both for the dying person and also for his or her family and caregivers.

When talking about preparation for death, I often use a well-known analogy of the movement of a wave coming to shore. Once the wave has started to build, there is nothing you can do to stop the momentum. You can stand there with your arms up trying to hold it back, but you may end up being dumped on the sand or rocks. Or you dive into the wave, and learn how to surf it into shore. I have met people who have surfed the wave beautifully, preparing for death with acceptance and honesty, physically, emotionally, and spiritually—facing both the expected and unexpected challenges as they arise. These people inspire me. Then there are those who try to hold the wave back. They challenge me to remain present with the fear, grief, and intensity of emotion surrounding dying, and with the physical discomfort and suffering that can also occur. It reinforces the need for me to practice more deeply and to face the realities of death, including my own death, with greater honesty and awareness.

Working in the area of death and dying has been a great blessing in my life. There is something extraordinary and very moving in being with someone during his or her last days, when the possibility of a deeper and more subtle connection is present. Sometimes with moments of silence, sometimes with prayer or meditation, sometimes with laughter or deep sadness, our connectedness and shared humanity emerges.

Community and Compassion in Care of the Dying

Joan Halifax

WHEN WE SPEAK about community in being with dying, the question is always, "For whom does it matter?" The feminist and philosopher Simone Weil reminds us that a community who loves asks, "What are you going through?" Many individuals, including those who give direct care and those who simply care, can surround a dying person. Although we might think our work is just with the dying person, I believe we need to open ourselves to the possibility that the community is a great resource of support and healing as well as a potential source of challenges to dying well. For those of us who work with dying people, we recognize that an important dimension of our work is to identify the community, which can include patient, family, friends, pets, and volunteer and professional caregivers. Who are those that care?

Roshi Joan Halifax is a Buddhist teacher, Zen priest, anthropologist, and author. She is founder, abbot, and head teacher of Upaya Zen Center, a Buddhist monastery in Santa Fe, New Mexico. She has worked in the area of death and dying for over forty years and is director of the Project on Being with Dying. For the past twenty-five years, she has been active in environmental work. A founding teacher of the Zen Peacemaker Order, her work and practice for more than three decades has focused on engaged Buddhism. Of late, Roshi Joan Halifax is a distinguished invited scholar to the Library of Congress and the only woman and Buddhist to be on the Advisory Council for the Tony Blair Foundation. She is founder and director of the Upaya Prison Project that develops programs on meditation for prisoners. She is founder of the Ojai Foundation, was an honorary research fellow at Harvard University, and has taught in many universities, monasteries, and medical centers around the world. She studied for a decade with Zen teacher Seung Sahn and was a teacher in the Kwan Um Zen School. She received the lamp transmission from Thich Nhat Hanh, and was given inka by Roshi Bernie Glassman.

The Buddhist story of Kisagotami reminds us it is the community that can teach us about the truth of life, death, and impermanence. Kisagotami came from a poor family. When she married, she went to the household of her husband, where she was not treated well until the birth of her son. But her son died suddenly when he was a little boy. Out of her mind with sorrow, she could not accept the truth of his passing. She carried his body from house to house, begging for a cure for him. Some people laughed at her. Some turned their backs on her. Others asked contemptuously, "Why do you want to give medicine to the dead?"

Finally, a kind, elderly man suggested she go see the Buddha, who was giving a talk nearby. The wise man saw she had lost her mind from grieving. He told her the Buddha alone would know what to do for her and her son. Clutching the body of her dead son to her hip, she approached the Buddha for help. "Please give me medicine for my son," she begged. The Sage saw deeply into her tragic misunderstanding, and told her to return to her village and collect tiny grains of mustard seed from those families who had not been touched by death.

Relieved, Kisagotami returned to the village. The first household she visited was still mourning the loss of one of its members. The next household knew death as well. And the next and the next. Finally she saw this was the same for every household in the village. She realized not one person had escaped the touch of death.

Realizing the truth of impermanence and the inevitability of death through the experience of her community, she took her son's body to the burning ground and offered him to the fire. She then returned to the Buddha empty handed: no son, no tiny grains of mustard seed. She had discovered from her community that not one family, not one individual, had escaped death, and all were linked by bonds of loss.

I believe we cannot do this work of being with dying outside some form of community. We learn to care by being cared for by our parents. Later, our friends and families give us care and give us the chance to care. We receive support, give care, train in compassion, and find respite in and through our communities. Our greatest lessons come from our relationships with each other, and we will all part from each other sooner or later. Because of this, we know loss and grief. Like Kisagotami, some of us have learned that all of us know death in one way or another, and if we are lucky, we find that meeting the community in death may create a community in life.

The Pew Health Professions Commission created a useful model of caregiving based in a vision of community. In their development of the model of relationship-centered care, the commission identified at least three types of relationships in the extended community around a sick or dying person that make a difference. The first is the relationship between the dying person and the healthcare professional. The second is the relationship between the community and the healthcare professional. And the third is the relationship between all of the healthcare practitioners. There are other relationships that need to be worked with as well: between community members themselves, meaning family, friends, and volunteers; between community members and the dying person; and even between dying people themselves, like women who have end-stage breast cancer, in which case people who share a diagnosis can become allied and a support system for each other.

This might seem like an overwhelming job for a busy healthcare professional or a volunteer caregiver. Obviously, it is not entirely within range for either of these individuals. But I believe it really helps to have a map of where those are who care and are giving care. Often it is in the cracks between these complex relationships that the support system around the dying person breaks down. And it can be so helpful to know not only who cares but how they care and how they feel about caring.

In this regard, the Pew Commission outlined three distinct areas that get expressed through these relationships: values, knowledge, and skills. Values in the practitioner/patient relationship are those related to respect and appreciation for all aspects of the patient's and community's life. Knowledge includes self-knowledge, knowledge of health beliefs in the community, knowledge of conflicts and problem areas in the community, and knowledge of effective communication. And a practitioner's skills need to include the ability to listen to and assess what will serve the dying person and her community.

In the community/practitioner relationship, values include respect for the community's integrity and diversity, support for community and individual health, open-mindedness, honesty, responsibility, and a commitment to work for the well-being of the community. A healthcare practitioner needs to be aware of community dynamics, including myths and misperceptions about community; the history of the community, including relationships with other healthcare practitioners; and ways that care can be better brought to the community. Skills include willingness to participate in community development and skills of assessment, communication, learning, teaching, collaboration, and teamwork.

In the relationship among healthcare practitioners, values include self-awareness, appreciation of diversity, a sense of mission, openness, humility, trust, empathy, and support. Self-knowledge, knowledge of diverse healing approaches, and knowledge of team building, team dynamics, and power inequities across professions can be invaluable. Skills include self-exploration, learning, communication, listening, teamwork, and the skill to resolve conflicts.

Many of the same values, knowledge areas, and skills that involve health care professionals can be brought into focus when considering and fostering the relationships between community or family members and between the dying person and his or her community and peers.

The work of community development is often not insignificant. I have seen some pretty sorry mishaps around dying people because relationships were not recognized, understood, or tended. In a way, having been a student of anthropology has made me aware that the community is a great resource and is often neglected. What follows are some of the areas that might give us an enriched perspective as we work with dying. For example, we might want to discover the beliefs, customs, and culture that a community shares or an individual has around dying and death, illness, and loss. This includes the community of healthcare practitioners tending the dying person, because their worldviews affect how they will give care. And we may want to learn what kind of support strategies, psychological approaches, cultural sensitivities, and spiritual and religious practices are appropriate for a community, for the one who is dying, and for a family going through the loss of a loved one so that we can support the giving of care in a way that is culturally and psychologically sensitive.

Often there is more diversity of beliefs and behaviors in a family and community than we might suspect. Sometimes community members' belief systems are so divergent that they are a source of conflict. Here is where our communication skills are important, as well as skills that help engender greater tolerance among community members. And some of what we do is to help the community members find the most appropriate way to communicate about their shared hope that the dying person will live and die well.

Consider the case of Anna: When Anna was dying, she found herself in the middle-world between orthodox medicine and unconventional health beliefs and practices. Her large support community was also in an intense communication process of working with these two worlds. The community included healers, physicians, very educated family members, friends in the research and medical world, spiritual teachers, and artists.

This was quite a rich weave of individuals. When I saw what was going on, I wondered how Anna and her husband Matthew would find their way through the complexity of differences, as well as help the people around them from entering into conflict. This one and that one were convinced they had the cure for Anna. Others stated emphatically that there was no cure for her aggressive brain tumor. With a torrent of information and opinions, the two did what was typical for them. They opened themselves to all possibilities, and also relied on their intuition, sense of rightness, intelligence, and good hearts. They also kept all communication lines open, clear, and very active.

When I walked into their home two months before Anna died, I myself was a bit overwhelmed by the flood of advice, information, and people. Folks were arriving on her doorstep to heal her. People all over the world were praying for her. Diets of every kind were being explored. The best medical specialists were on line helping her.

Fortunately, she was a physician and had a skillful, kind, and firm way of approaching the territory of diametrically opposing opinions. And her husband Matthew had a remarkable amount of energy and graced Anna with complete devotion. He also had a good sense of humor that often took the sting out of difficult situations. Anna was the one who went to the healer but chose not to follow his advice to put aside certain medical interventions. It was her call to have radiation and her call to stop. She was in the middle of a mandala of care, but she was also taking the lead.

In this situation, the center of this large community of compassion was a brilliant young doctor who had years of experience with spiritual practice and who was now dying of a glioblastoma. The greater community of family, friends, healers, and doctors was woven into a firm net by Anna's and her husband's skills and patience, their diligent communication with a great many people who cared, and their willingness to accept all who came to them.

As a caregiver, I can offer many different types of support in a community. I can be at the very edge of the situation or near the middle. My work, however, is the work of discovery, of helping to uncover the rich spiritual basis of each person's life and the life of the community and supporting and strengthening the opening of faith for all. With Anna, Matthew, and their community, I tried to learn what would serve, what would ease, what would be genuinely helpful. It was a path of discovery, and I discovered that the most important thing I could do was to bear witness, listen to them and their friends in an unbiased way as they sorted through questions and options. They themselves were the best caregivers they could have, with their good motivation, intelligence, and courage to face whatever was arising.

Around the time of Anna's sickness, I was sitting with the koan called Kyogen's "Man in a Tree." Koans are teaching stories from China used in Zen to deepen practice. This koan is from the Gateless Barrier, Case 5, and goes like this:

> It is like a person up a tree who hangs from a branch by their mouth. Their hands cannot grasp a bough; their feet can't touch the tree. Someone else comes underneath the tree and asks the meaning of Bodhidharma's coming from the West. If the person does not answer, they do not meet the questioner's need. If they answer, they lose their life. At such a time how should they answer?

This is our life: caught between a rock and a hard place. What do we do? The trouble is, we are always looking for solutions. Sitting with Anna, I felt like this man in a tree. There was no solution to Anna's sickness and suffering. This was the first noble truth being lived in the course of dying. I could only hang from the branch with my mouth wrapped around it, knowing that even looking for a solution was an admission of defeat. As long as I had hope, I would be approaching Anna with old logic and ideas about something being better than the time we had together, as it was.

From Anna and Matthew, and many others over the years, I have learned to accept "things as they are," be it the truth of suffering or differing views and beliefs about suffering and sickness. It is usually not our faith guiding the dying person and the community. We are this man in the tree, being with the impossible, where there is no solution. And in this regard, we, as caregivers, whether professional caregivers or family members or friends, often find ourselves in a community of differences. In the best of all possible worlds, we manifest the openness of reconciliation between opposing opinions, hopes, and aspirations that allows for respect and kindness to flourish.

In the end, as caregivers, we need to be guided by the faith and beliefs of the dying person as we are present for that person. When it comes to what is right for the dying person, our challenge is to familiarize ourselves with the particulars of different faiths and to encourage and be with whatever spiritual approaches are appropriate to a community and to the dying individual. That is why I often ask: What guides and supports you in your life? What do you have faith in? What really matters to you?

A good part of our work is to help communities and individuals realize that dying and death are a normal part of life. This we can do through education and the calm and accepting way in which we serve the community and the dying person. Becoming aware of attitudes toward death and dying is very important in this process. There are six common responses to death: fear, denial, defiance, sorrow, acceptance, and realization. Often there is a great deal of variability in how people relate to dying and death, sometimes from moment to moment. Our job is to accept even the most unaccepting and unacceptable and to realize that this is normal, too.

Dying and death almost always evoke some aspect of spirituality in the lives of individuals and communities. Active dying, anticipatory grief, and near-death experiences can provoke profound existential questions. Meaningfulness, reconciliation, normalization, and transcendence are experiences that can open as an individual is dying. Our practice is to help there be openness to the spiritual dimensions that arise in the course of dying and to encourage, when possible, the development of a sense of meaningfulness, of love and courage, in the dying individual and in the community as well.

We must also understand that dying and death is a rite of passage, a developmental phase in human life, that offers the possibility for profound maturation for individuals as well as communities. As a rite of passage, dying can be understood as having three phases: separation, threshold experiences, and incorporation. These three phases are present from diagnosis to dying. With an anthropological model, death and grieving can be reimagined as a process of initiation.

Dying, whether recognized as a rite of passage or not, often involves intense psycho-spiritual experiences. Some of these experiences may be pleasant, even inspiring. Some are unpleasant and terrifying. When a wall is hit, as it often is, we must be prepared to work with the hard and gritty aspects of dying for the dying person as well as the community. These include pain, obsessive suffering, denial, negative (and positive) transference, depression, anger, blame, shame, judgmental mind, preferential mind, hallucinations and visions, confusion, fear, grief (including anticipatory grief), and loss. These low-tide experiences are really where a community can learn and bond.

There are a number of ways to remind and educate people about the spiritual dimension of their experience. One of my favorites is storytelling. I use anecdotes, folk stories, and myths as a way to bring people closer to the truth of dying. One of the stories I tell is of the centaur Chiron, whose wound sent him looking for a cure, then brought him to helping the least fortunate, and finally became the gateway to his death and transformation. It is a story that can give suffering and death meaning. Communities have long been healed through the medium of narrative, the medium of story.

I also work with what I call learning moments, those moments that unlock the possibility for deeper exploration of an emotional topic. For example, David, one man I worked with who was dying of a brain tumor, asked what would be done with his body immediately after he died. His question gave his family and friends the chance to sit with him and explore what David wanted and what might be possible. Here we used council as a way to explore this issue.

Because of my background as an anthropologist, I am also interested in how cross-cultural sensitivity can be cultivated as we work with those dying people and communities who are from a culture other than our own. There are many differing customs; culturally determined needs; cultural perceptions of illness, dying, and death; culturally appropriate interventions; gender and age issues; nuances of the caregiver/patient relationship; belief systems; and religious and spiritual practices that shape our relationship to the community and to the person with a life-limiting illness. We can offend others without realizing it by violating boundaries that are culturally determined. We can also have the mind of not-knowing and be open to learning how to best help, even when we do not quite understand what is the right thing to do.

Consider the case of Sita, a young East Indian woman who was dying of breast cancer, which she had suffered from since she was twenty-six years old. My coworker Kathryn was giving support to Sita and her family as Sita was going through active dying. Kathryn had a lot to learn because of the cultural differences between Sita's family and herself. Their gender issues, religious beliefs, and customs around dying were new to Kathryn. Fortunately, she was very careful to find out how best to be with this rather volatile family.

When repeatedly pressed for an opinion by the family, the hospice nurses communicated that Sita displayed many of the physical signs of impending death and would probably die within three to five days. Upon hearing this, Sita's family began their ritual funeral preparations, including letting the male relatives know that they should shave their heads and begin to fast. They painted traditional colors on Sita's forehead and along her hairline as she lay in a coma. They also arranged for a restaurant to serve traditional foods for the breaking-fast gathering that would take place after she died.

On the day it was assumed Sita would die, Kathryn came to the house to support her and her family. Instead of finding a deathbed scene, Kathryn found Sita sitting up in bed playing cards! Sita put down her cards when she saw Kathryn. Distraught, she asked Kathryn if she too thought that she was dying. And again, she insisted: "Did you really think I was dying, Kathryn?" Kathryn quickly realized that Sita was deeply troubled because the family had been so quick to mobilize for her death. She feared that everyone wanted her to hurry up and die. After all, they had been in this crisis for five years.

It was up to Kathryn to help the family through this awkward situation. Kathryn's sensitivity to cultural and gender issues played an important part in helping bridge the differences between the dying woman and her husband and family.

Just as Kathryn was prepared to enter the awkward, we must be prepared to explore with dying people and their community issues related to quality of life, including the use of interventions attempting to prolong life and issues concerning suicide and assisted suicide. I believe that our own beliefs and feelings about these issues are not what is important. We must help to create trust and make it safe for people to openly explore and discuss these controversial and difficult matters. This includes understanding advance directives and how to set them up with the hope they will be followed. We want to help people be prepared for the best and the worst, to see realistically the many possible outcomes in the event of resuscitation or the use of extreme interventions. We also want to be fully present at the moment of death and to have the family and community prepared as well by creating an atmosphere of safety and trust.

One of the most powerful and potentially bonding moments in the dying/death process is being with the body after death. I often give family members and friends printed guidelines on care of the body after death. This information can give a community the opportunity to offer respect to the body by bathing it and by sitting with it as is the custom in many cultures.

In some cultures, practices can be done after death for the benefit of the deceased. These include intercessory prayer and the Tibetan practice of consciousness transference at the time of death. Other practices are directly related to working with those who are grieving. Sometimes volunteer caregivers do funerals and memorial services and can help a community to design and facilitate them. We also sit with family members and friends and bear witness to grief. Finally, in this work of education and practice, we know how to work with our own feelings about loss and death, and we help others to do so.

One area that is often neglected is self-care or care of the caregiver. We know that the more peaceful, stable, open, and accepting caregivers are, the better it is for them, the dying person, and the communities they serve.

Here are some goals for the dying person and community that may help guide our work:

► Develop and maintain an open and healthy relationship between the dying person and all community members based on humanistic and spiritual values

► Foster partnerships among community members in support of the dying person

► Help create a safe space around the dying person

► Develop a spiritual basis for the work with the dying person and the community

► Use or develop effective psycho-spiritual strategies for working with issues and symptoms

► Foster good communication strategies

► Help the community prepare for an uncertain future

► Facilitate continuity within the community

Awakening Kindness:

END-OF-LIFE CARE IN A SOCIAL MODEL HOSPICE

Randy Sunday

AS THE NATION'S volatile economy falls and rises for some, for the most vulnerable, their distress is uninterrupted and they bear the brunt of society's inequities. They are the first to lose access to healthcare, and especially at the end of life, they are the ones most likely to die alone and forgotten. It is the mission of Sarah House, where I work, to care for the dying poor. Sarah House is one of the only "social model" hospices in the nation in contrast to "medical models" that receive support from Medicare. We receive no federal or state funds for end-of-life care. Even so, in 2010, we were recognized with the Outstanding Program Award from the California Hospice and Palliative Care Association, the organization of our medical model peers. Sarah House provides care for the increasingly more numerous homeless people, veterans, women, and, in general, more low-income individuals in need of a place to die with dignity and peace.

Although Sarah House is not affiliated with any particular religious tradition, we embrace the spiritual values of unlimited friendliness and

Randy Sunday grew up in Texas as the son of a Presbyterian minister and a nonprofit activist. He was a George F. Baker Scholar and received a BA with honors from Rhodes College. In 1973 he became a student of Chogyam Trungpa and also studied with his Vajra Regent, Osel Tendzin. For ten years, Randy served as director of Dharmadhatu Meditation Center and was founding president of the Buddhist Council of New York. For the past thirteen years, he has been the executive director of Sarah House, an end-of-life care home or hospice residence for the low-income and homeless.

compassion as our common foundation for care. In Buddhist terms, it is the discipline of generosity that affords the skillful means for acting with loving-kindness. Likewise, loving-kindness, in a cycle of positive reinforcement, deepens generosity. As the first *paramita* or transcendent virtue of the bodhisattva path, generosity is traditionally expressed in three ways: through material offering, through saving life and protection from fear, and through the gift of the Buddhadharma. The essence of generosity's transcendent nature is nonattachment. During a Buddhist-Christian conference, Chogyam Trungpa Rinpoche explained:

> The Sanskrit word *dana*, which at its Indo-European root is related to "donation," is translated as "generosity." Generosity, or giving in, is very important in Buddhism. Dana is connected with devotion and the appreciation of sacredness. Sacredness is not a religious concept alone, but it is an expression of general openness: how to be kind, how to kiss someone, how to express the emotion of giving. So real generosity comes from developing a general sense of kindness. We have to understand the real meaning of dana. You give yourself, not just a gift, and you are able to give without expecting anything in return.

Generosity is the basis that transcends selfish actions and runs through all great traditions. As is said in *The Sutra of the Recollection of the Noble Three Jewels*, "Generosity is the virtue that produces peace." This is the foundation of awakening kindness at Sarah House.

Our agency began in Santa Barbara in 1989, founded by a public health administrator named Alice Heath who despaired at the thought of young gay men dying of AIDS, alone in their apartments. Prior to that, she created Hospice of Santa Barbara in 1974, the second hospice established in the United States. Our first home was called Heath House and opened as a two-story Victorian in 1991. Those early days of crisis were marked by many who moved in and never moved out, usually dying within six weeks. Like all truly successful community campaigns, our nonprofit was born of consensus and love, with individuals determined to drive past a bottom line, who never wavered in response to the dire need for shelter, comfort, and love. Some noble individuals gave all they could to open

Heath House, and the agency's lineage includes, in particular, many women. They could not stand by as their sons and brothers suffered. I have no doubt they were like other women and men from whom "homes of the heart" arose, dedicated to alleviating the pain and sorrows of many who were ignored and even despised.

By 1994, the need for AIDS housing had grown and a second one-story called Sarah House was built. Then in 1997, the miraculous success of protease inhibitors combined into "cocktails" suddenly and rapidly began to diminish the mortality rate of those with HIV. The remaining residents of Heath House were moved into Sarah House with its eight bedrooms before the cost of two homes could capsize the agency. The medications not only weakened the virus but they also eradicated some of the ugly opportunistic infections that attacked the compromised immune systems.

By 2003, other licensed HIV/AIDS houses in California were closing with the drop in demand for residential care. Rather than lose the invaluable resources of our staff and home, we expanded our mission to care for the non-HIV dying poor. We wrote and sponsored state legislation that sailed through committees and both legislative houses. On January 1, 2005, Sarah House opened as the first "social model" hospice in California, if not the nation.

Dr. Balfour Mount, a true pioneer in palliative care and former head of that department at McGill University Medical School, explains the essential elements of a "social model":

> What is needed is excellence in control of pain and other symptoms, but once that foundational need has been taken care of, we need to have attention to all those other domains that are so specific to that patient and family. What's been found is that these needs may be most effectively addressed in a home-like atmosphere. The critical factor is the quality of the relationship of caregivers, a home-like atmosphere, and people who will be really present and accompany the person who is ill and their family through this potentially difficult period.

At Sarah House, we care strictly for the low-income and homeless. Our residents are our neighbors, sometimes living alone and sometimes with family who cannot manage the stress of caring for someone who is dying. They are families with children or grandchildren and jobs and their own physical limitations, or a wife or husband incapable of tending to their beloved. Grown children enter Sarah House for the first time pushing their father in a wheelchair, afraid and guilty. A typical family member feels she is negligent because she must turn her loved one's care over to strangers. But after a couple of hours, we are used to seeing the tension in her shoulders drop and her face relax. We feel as if our part has been done when we hear her say, "I think I'll go home and take a nap." This is the trust we wish to inspire in the families we serve, along with the understanding that we will love family and friends as we do the resident, with unlimited friendliness. Debbie, the house manager and most senior staff member, expressed the essence of unlimited friendliness when she said there is only one formula that has worked since we first opened in 1991—"Someone knocks on our front door. We welcome them in, and love them as long as they are with us."

As a Buddhist, I have found that this work is a powerful reminder that "death is real and comes without warning." At Sarah House, every resident must have a hospice diagnosis of less than six months to live, but there are times when a resident's departure is more precipitous than expected and the staff is left startled and sad. Even though the average stay at Sarah House is three weeks, some arrive and even die in a single day. There is a shocking scenario in which a resident begins his last days with a trip to the emergency room and is quickly referred to the sixth floor until he can be discharged to a place to die. Some of our residents have been so quickly squeezed through the process that they never return home to pick up books and treasured items.

We have an eight-bedroom home, with a flowering garden of Princess Diana roses, ginger plants, and dwarf citrus trees. We consciously decided to keep the beds to a minimum to sustain an environment that feels homelike, rather than institutional. A tiered fountain's watery melody is enough to cut the din of the nearby freeway. The backyard has statues of St. Francis, Buddha, Kuan Yin, and a giant sea turtle (which is both a Taoist and Native American image). The home-like atmosphere is one of welcome and warmth, with the scent of fresh pastries and *chile relleno*, rather than the sterile smell of Pine-Sol. The design is spacious and accommodating to circulation and sunlight, with lots of room for laughter and poignant shared moments.

Each bedroom is decorated by the resident, sometimes looking like your grandmother's, sometimes covered with photos or Elvis paintings on velvet. Each bedroom has access to the garden, a sink and a fridge, cabinets and a closet, and is bigger than a dorm room. We appreciate the personal decor as each individual's style is a window into a life. We also have common areas for residents and loved ones to be together, or smaller niche environments for a moment of quiet solitude.

There is a high-ceilinged living room with a TV at one end and a fireplace at the other; a dining room with a refectory style table you might find in a seminary; and a spacious country kitchen open to all for making a sandwich or heating leftovers. We have lots of local art and there's always at least one dog around. A cappella choirs rehearse in the great room weekly and musicians seem to appear as spontaneously as the fresh fruit, vegetables, casseroles, and cookies. As you enter, there is a ledge for memorials with photos, memorabilia, candles, incense, and flowers. It really feels like a big family home and invariably a departing visitor remarks, "This is not at all what I expected."

We embrace each resident as he or she enters our home and we offer comfort foods, comfortable surroundings, comfort TV and music, and the comfort of friendship, whatever distance is required so that each individual can enjoy this final passage according to the needs of her personal journey. It is not markedly Buddhist by any means, but it is whatever is needed. At one point a Protestant chaplain and ardent meditator told me he wished we could be fully Buddhist, but I explained that's hardly whom we serve. There are few requests for any specific spiritual direction here, simply a need for loving-kindness, and a call to provide for whatever journey is necessary.

At the end of life, rituals become particularly important. One of our residents, Cathie, reclaimed her Native American heritage in her last days with a naming ritual. We all joined in a ceremony in which she became Cathie Coral Two Feathers. We make an effort to celebrate birthdays and traditional holidays, celebrations often involving the whole house. We derive special satisfaction in discovering each person's unique preferences for these occasions. Music or cheerfully corny theater is often involved, with tastes ranging from Motown to musical comedy show tunes. There are also daily rituals that our staff takes care to support. For one resident, the daily ritual is scrutiny of the fish tank. For another it is the 3:30 snack of "fin & haddie" that reminds her of her British upbringing.

There are also those moments that defy preconception. The moment might be contained by the group as in a spontaneous gathering of a drumming circle, the annual reading of the names of those who have passed in the previous twelve months, or the creative construction of this year's altar for the Day of the Dead. Or it could be the last minutes alone with a resident spent in silence and simply tucking in the bedclothes and adjusting the blinds. Time's importance slips away and the space is imbued with tenderness and an equanimity of both sadness and peace.

After someone dies we will ask the loved ones if they would like to join us in bathing the body. Once the shock of the suggestion subsides, a brother or daughter, for instance, will join us and spend the quiet time bathing the body in water scented with *yerba santé*. After the body is dried, the water is poured on one of the plants in the garden with a contemplation of the cycle of life. And then, when the young men from the mortuary arrive to take the body, everyone walks beside the gurney, usually arm in arm and hand in hand. It is an exquisite moment, unforgettable in its simplicity. At these times too, there is often singing.

When one of our homeless friends died, the memorial was held in the living room. His companions from the street, "rough sleepers" with their own pure language, stood and spoke on Billy's behalf, recalling their own special brand of fellowship. When the time came for the more formal ritual, the Episcopal minister deferred to what he had already seen and heard, a genuine voice of the human spirit. He said, "I have nothing to add. Surely, this is what the kingdom of heaven must look like."

In the Tibetan tradition, we are cautioned to guard against expressing too much emotion when near someone who is dying so that we do not inadvertently stir up attachment in the departing consciousness. In my experience, this mindful presence helps create a ground for release of the immediate grasping and fixation for all who are gathered, presumably the dying resident as well, and can shift instead to an appreciation for all that was genuine and good in the deceased. Prior to the death, during the entire stay of each resident, there is a natural development of trust and truthfulness among the residents, their family and friends, and the staff. The Tibetan Buddhist teachers I have known emphasize the foremost need for cultivating trust. Just as my father's counsel from his days as an Army chaplain was "to not make promises that you can't keep," my teachers have taught it is important to be true. As insubstantiality approaches, there is great transparency and all that is artificial is more obvious. This can lead to more freedom in expression by the resident, but it also requires straightforwardness and sensitivity by the caregivers, as it did in the case of Mrs. Culroddy.

Mrs. Culroddy was expected to die momentarily after four days of being seemingly comatose. While Debbie drove ninety miles to LAX to pick up her son and daughter from New York, Paloma, one of our volunteers, was finishing her bed bath. As she was being gently turned, Mrs. Culroddy opened her eyes and thanked Paloma for all her care. Wide-eyed, Paloma gasped. Mrs. Culroddy said, "I know, I have heard it all, and thank you for the fresh flowers you brought me yesterday." Paloma had been told that hearing is the last sense to go and always spoke to a resident as if fully conscious.

The physical layout of a hospice is certainly a vital element of the atmosphere, but the heart of the matter is our staff and their relationships with the residents. The house manager and staff are fond of saying, "We are Sarah House." This phrase helps remind us that we are a family supporting one another through burnout, compassion fatigue, and tough times. The staff are consummate caregivers who embrace each new resident with open arms and warmth, and tend to him or her as they would a cherished family member. For new funders, we often have to speak in organizational language and identify the loving-kindness of the caregivers as the service or product of the agency. More simply and directly put, it is our caregivers' belief that "We are the medicine." Each of our resident assistants seems to me to embody this phrase: they are what they do. They have each followed a unique path to our doors to discover that they have a genuine calling for this work. As the hospice director, I enjoy visiting Sarah House almost every day and basking in its environment of consideration and joy. I am not sure that the resident assistants even realize how much the house is like a sacred space.

This reminds me of Shunryu Suzuki Roshi's description of his return to Eiheiji monastery in Japan after time away.

> I heard the various sounds of practice—the bells and the monks reciting the sutra—and I had a deep feeling. There were tears flowing out of my eyes, nose, and mouth! It is the people who are outside of the monastery who feel its atmosphere. Those who are practicing actually do not feel anything. I think this is true for everything. When we hear the sound of the pine trees on a windy day. Perhaps the wind is just blowing, and the pine tree is just standing in the wind. That is all they are doing. But the people who listen to the wind in the tree will write a poem, or feel something unusual. That is, I think, the way everything is.

The experience at Sarah House can be remarkable in that it is so basic or elemental and familiar as an experience that everyone shares. It is absorbing to the point that it is independent of contrast. As another Buddhist teacher instructed, it is like the feeling of rain on your face without any thoughts about that feeling. For the staff, Sarah House and the residents are dear, but what they do so customarily is commonplace, it's simply how they are. For visitors, it is in the transition of coming or going that they see the difference.

We believe that the relationship between resident and caregiver is paramount, but it does not mean that one needs a registered nurse to help someone die a good death. When we proposed the bill to allow care for non-HIV patients we were challenged by legislators who asked how we could care for the dying without a registered nurse present twenty-four hours a day. For fifteen years we cared for those dying of AIDS without an RN, and wondered what was the difference? They had no answer. In fact, it is possible to be overtrained and inadvertently overlook the humanity of the person being cared for.

Our resident assistants tend to hold someone's hand rather than feel for a pulse, stroke a forehead before checking for fever. Medical standards are observed and each resident is also attended by visits from a registered nurse from a Medicare certified hospice agency. The local hospital would not permit patients to be discharged to Sarah House unless their vice president in charge of quality control and risk management shared confidence in our work. The work we do is also more cost-effective as our daily bed expense is half that of the medical model, but not receiving Medicare means we are continually raising funds and rely on the kindness and generosity of our community.

On the office door at Sarah House, this quote from the Dalai Lama is posted:

> When caring for someone who is seriously ill, it is important to cultivate positive attitudes like compassion, love, and tolerance. Real care of the sick does not begin with costly procedures, but with the simple gift of affection and love. In the practice of healing, a kind heart is as valuable as medical training, because it is the source of happiness for both oneself and others. People respond to kindness even when medicine is ineffective, and in turn cultivating a kind heart is a cause of our own health.

Although a resident with severe anxiety in the wee hours of the morning might elsewhere encounter a medical response of a dose of Ativan or Roxinol, our more favored prescription is to bring a mug of hot herbal tea, hold a hand, and read a poem by Mary Oliver, perhaps.

I am reminded of the schizophrenic woman brought to us by her attendants at the mental health facility who did not want her to die in impersonal isolation. As she entered her room at Sarah House, she said, "I respond very well to kindness."

In the context of care, I understand the second aspect of dana or protection from fear as helping the resident open to the fear of dying. This courage is shared through the constancy of affection, which creates a longer hull for riding the waves of emotionality and unpredictable changes. The trust that develops between the staff and the residents is all-important, and with their steady presence the caregivers can support a family or patient as they try to understand dying as a process that everyone must pass through, without exception. This sense of protection from fear slides into the third, more spiritual aspect. In general, at Sarah House, our explicit efforts toward care are part of the first and second aspects of dana or generosity. First, we offer material offerings of food and shelter, and secondly, the saving or care of life and protection from fear. The third aspect, the gift of Dharma, is also made but it is unspoken and in fact often invisible—because most of the staff are not Buddhists.

While the staff spiritually aspires to offer from the heart an uncontrived and unconditional friendship and compassion through the discipline of generosity, it is not done as if they are Buddhists. Nevertheless, the staff has recently begun to cultivate stability of mind through meditation. There is weekly practice at the house. Several staff members also attended programs at Metta Institute, and *metta* or *maitri* "prayers" are often said at staff meetings and at the bedside of residents. This has been by the individual staff member's choice, not from anyone's direction.

From my experience as a Buddhist practitioner, I see residents reach out in times of confusion and be met by staff with a compassionate curiosity that, exactly like mindfulness, is willing to explore every corner. This gentle touch, physically, emotionally, lets us observe pleasure and pain and the gaps in between where we catch glimpses of the human heart.

During the final naked passage into death, it is not hard to see the innate decency that we all hold, whether one comes from a house with a street address or from under a bridge with no blood kin. Vulnerability is shared by all—but far from being weakness, vulnerability or "the soft spot," as Trungpa Rinpoche describes bodhichitta, the awakened heart, is our very strength and beauty. Our "soft spot" is the unconditioned potential that is ultimately, if not immediately, expressed as compassion and love for others. Once glimpsed, that kindness awakens further with every breath. Being with the dying, it is possible to see that tender humanity as it manifests both as fear and fearlessness. The role of the caregiver, Buddhist or not, is to help each person relax into his or her basic nature. I believe that the physical, psychological, and spiritual discipline of generosity is truly a meaningful and transcendent discipline for guiding those efforts.

Although a commitment to loving-kindness surely happens in many hospice settings, for Sarah House it is central to our care and our fundamental attitude of who we are as a "social model." The level of care we provide *is* who we are.

The Buddha said there are 84,000 dharmas that guide students to enlightenment; there are many skillful means to address the diverse needs of individuals. Similarly, for caregivers, there are many skillful means to serve the dying and many ways to share friendship and love with patients and their families. I feel fortunate for having found the Dharma and my teachers, who have shown me some of these skillful means. Each has given me a discipline of meditation and awareness with which I can seal my life with practice and my work with compassion. As I strive to do so, I aspire to bring simplicity to my life and the lives of others and awaken the kindness that is the natural expression of an open heart. If you are ever in Santa Barbara, please visit.

We would love to show you the house and garden, and share a cup of tea and a poem with you.

Being a Compassionate Presence:

THE CONTEMPLATIVE APPROACH TO END-OF-LIFE CARE

Kirsten Deleo

RE YOU DEAD YET?" her high-pitch voice hurled across the room. "Are you dead yet . . . *you* in the corner?" She glared at me, wide awake, ready to engage. I had been sitting quietly in her room assuming she was asleep. The physician had pointed to the chair in the corner across from her bed before he shut the door behind him with a resounding bang. I had a sinking feeling in my body. I was a fresh hospice volunteer and novice meditator. I followed the direction of his finger and sat down on the chair. I did what was expected: straightened my back and sat in silence.

Amanda, an old lady with tufts of white hair, had lived all her life on the streets before she was admitted to hospice. She was ill tempered and moody. They had put her in a single room and whoever entered was quickly dismissed with insults. I was prepared that it was just a matter of time, before I too would be "dismissed." For now the situation seemed safe. I was wrong. She wasn't asleep but had watched me with great curiosity from the corner of her eyes.

Kirsten Deleo has been active in the hospice movement since the early '90s. She is a trained counselor and offers seminars and retreats for healthcare professionals and the public in Europe and the US under the auspices of Rigpa's Spiritual Care Program, a nondenominational outreach program. She is on the faculty of the "Contemplative End-of-Life Care Certificate Program," a specialized professional training offered through Spiritual Care and Naropa University. Kirsten studies under Sogyal Rinpoche and under his guidance completed a three-year meditation retreat. Together with her husband, Jeff, she lives in upstate New York near Rigpa's retreat center, the Center for Wisdom and Compassion.

She said, "Annoying, huh? Having a corpse like me sitting here?" I responded to my surprise, "Yeah!" She growled with a big grin, "Dead people don't do it for me."

I had to chuckle. My naïve image of the somber and near-saintly hospice worker was blown away, and I felt the great relief of a burden dropping off my shoulders. Sparring with someone made her feel alive. She was dying, but I was the dead person in the room. "Me neither!" I laughed. Her grin exposed an even bigger smile, along with missing front teeth. She had found a friend.

Extending our compassionate presence to another fellow human being is a simple act. There is nothing special about it. It requires a willingness to be aware, open, and loving. This is not always easy. We are required to drop our habitual ways of doing things and any agendas we may have, and instead rely on a compassionate intuition that extends from our practice. We may think that we can do "compassionate presence" by assuming the right outer appearance, as I did when I sat down in Amanda's room. The truth is, we cannot *do* "compassionate presence"; we can only *be* a compassionate presence.

Contemplative practices are an effective and profound way to cultivate the ability to be nonjudgmentally open with all that arises; to be compassionately present. The contemplative approach to care is practical, down-to-earth, dynamic, and engaging, offering us greater understanding and insight. Anyone can learn and benefit from contemplative resources and skills such as mindfulness, meditation, and compassion. One does not have to become a Buddhist to benefit from these skills. We can all learn, step-by-step, how to be present with ourselves. When we show up in our own lives, we become fully present for others.

The premise of the contemplative approach is that, if you want to be useful to others, the place to start is with yourself, beginning with your own mind. Meditation practice gives us a window into observing and understanding the mind and its nature, and therefore it is an excellent basis for effective care. Meditative practice can help us preserve our sanity and connect to our basic goodness. This can be therapeutic and deeply healing for the caregiver as well as the receiver of care.

The contemplative approach is to inspire a quiet revolution within ourselves and the way we care. In the words of Sogyal Rinpoche, "a quiet revolution in the whole way we look at death and care for the dying and the whole way we look at life and care for the living" is urgently needed. A quiet revolution is one that asks us to look within and transform ourselves and thereby those we accompany. After the publication of *The Tibetan Book of Living and Dying*, our sangha received requests from healthcare professionals from around the world to provide training programs on how to apply the understanding and methods offered in this book to life and work. This was the birth of Rigpa's Spiritual Care Program, an international, nondenominational outreach program I work for.

As with many others serving in this field, I have been motivated by a vision for change. Hiding behind technological advances and "progressive thinking," our society remains ill at ease with the realities of illness, aging, dying, and death. It is not that modern medicine has failed us. We simply expect too much of it, believing we are invincible. We narrowly define *care* as "cure." Yet modern science cannot cure all things. Until we face the whole of life and death, we inhibit our ability to truly heal, physically, emotionally, and spiritually.

One way we can contribute to the quiet revolution is by embracing suffering, impermanence, and death as inescapable facts of life. At first glance, this may seem counterintuitive to the wish to preserve life and alleviate suffering. But the opposite is true. If we fail to acknowledge the truth of impermanence, we also fail to uphold the needs of people at the most vulnerable times in their life. We desperately need a more compassionate approach to care as well as an education that encompasses all aspects of care, addressing the greater questions of living and dying. Spiritual care is not a luxury but a necessity.

His Holiness the Dalai Lama defines spirituality as "to be concerned with those qualities of the human spirit—such as love and compassion, patience, tolerance, forgiveness, contentment, a sense of responsibility, a sense of harmony—which bring happiness to both self and others." Contemplative or spiritual care is applying these essential good qualities of the human spirit in practical ways to our everyday life while caring for others in need, whatever our role or capacity.

We don't usually think of caring for another person as a spiritual interaction. Yet, whether we care for the body, make a cup of tea, or simply listen, caring is spiritual work. The way we talk to people, touch and gaze at them, the whole *quality* of our presence, can make them feel whole and remind them of their sense of purpose and meaning. And they, in turn, reflect this purpose back to us.

Spiritual needs are universal and include:

- ▸ Connection and love
- ▸ Forgiveness and reconciliation
- ▸ Accepting and transcending suffering
- ▸ Finding refuge or a source of peace

These needs are not limited to end-of-life issues, nor are they necessarily religious. Throughout our development we continuously wrestle with them, in one way or another. Christine Longaker, a pioneer in the hospice movement and one of the founders of the Spiritual Care Program, calls these needs the four tasks of living and dying. As we work through these needs, they become a resource to us. The confidence we embody when we have faced them ourselves is the most valuable asset we can bring to those facing death, loss, or bereavement.

The spiritual care approach is not about us providing something to the other. On the most profound level, it is a way of being and an understanding of a deeper inner dimension of who we are. It springs from the recognition and appreciation that there is a fundamental openness, clarity, and love, a spiritual essence that lies within each of us. This essence is untouched by suffering and pain and is the source of intelligence, wisdom, and boundless compassion. The more we come in touch with it, the more natural confidence we have to be present in an unafraid and honest manner. Our presence then radiates from a much vaster source. This can free us as well as the person we are accompanying, allowing us to be more flexible, spacious, and discerning, thus affecting their well-being and spiritual future.

The key to unlocking this inner source of wisdom and compassion and to enhancing our basic good human qualities is through contemplative practice. This is well-known in the Buddhist tradition, and scientific research is now beginning to discover the positive effects of meditation training on a physiological level. The new field of "contemplative neuroscience" shows multilevel benefits of meditation. Studies of long-term meditators indicate that basic human qualities can be deliberately cultivated through mental training.

Training in meditation involves a radical shift from *doing* to *being*. Angela, a pediatrician in a major city hospital, is a graduate of our certificate program in contemplative end-of-life care. Recently, in a meeting with medical residents at her hospital, she shared how hard it has been for her when medicine left nothing more to offer.

"No words of comfort can reach the parents nor take away their pain when they lose their baby. 'What can I *do or say?* What can I *offer* when nothing else can be done?' I kept asking myself. I was trained to do, to fix . . . I felt helpless and inadequate."

The residents fell silent as she continued, "My meditation and extending loving-kindness helped me to gently befriend myself and accept these feelings. It is an ongoing process. I was astounded when I realized that being present is actually a skill that I can learn and practice. I am learning to show up in these extremely painful situations because I am more in touch with myself. Believe me, these situations have not become any easier, just more workable. I am a big talker, and it is still hard to listen and receive in silence. Still, my confidence in offering my presence and heart is growing. To be present in those heartbreaking moments, I know I am offering the best of me to my patients. This does not deplete me, but nourishes me."

It is said the entire teachings of the Buddha can be summed up in one line: "to train or tame our mind." It is not about taming someone else's mind, but our own. Most of the time, our monkey-like mind jumps from one thought to the next, continually looking for something to do, completely lost in the jungle of ceaseless thinking. Our mind is so well trained in multitasking and distraction that we have forgotten how to be present.

In the practice of meditation, we gradually learn to become more present. We get to know our own mind, how it functions, and begin to see its true nature beyond thoughts and emotions. This can heal our feelings of fragmentation and anxiety. The word "heal" derives from the same root as the word "whole." By training to allow our mind to simply be at ease and let thoughts go by like the clouds in the sky, we move closer to a sense of wholeness.

Meditation does not introduce us to anything new that we did not have. It reveals to us that which always has been present and available in us, our pure awareness. Getting in touch with this pure awareness and learning to rest in it, however much we can, gives us genuine confidence. It creates the stability and courage to face the mental, emotional, physical, and spiritual distress we witness without becoming bogged down by it. Cultivating natural openness, clarity, and presence of mind, we are less likely to fall prey to seeing patients as their diagnosis. It also supports clinical decision-making. We learn to be less reactive, less judgmental, and so become better observers, uniquely attuned to what is truly needed while taking full advantage of our professional expertise and life experience.

Mindfulness, awareness, and spaciousness—qualities we cultivate in meditation training—are essential to good care. Mindfulness helps us to stay focused without becoming fixated. Awareness enables us to keep the big picture without losing the details. Spaciousness gives us stability and a healthy sense of groundedness, which makes us less speedy, more open and kind. It also brings a sense of humor and light-heartedness when needed. Through contemplative practices such as meditation, we learn how to be. Just to be. By doing less you can actually accomplish more.

Being with the dying is a powerful way of deepening our own spiritual practice and understanding. We discover a surprising capacity for love and compassion we may never have suspected, propelling us forward on the path. Compassion is not a sentimental feeling. True compassion is linked to our innate wisdom or intelligence. In fact, it can promote clinical competence and is a protection against burnout. By cultivating an altruistic attitude, we find ourselves getting far less emotionally involved and carried away by our feelings and narrow self-concerns. But in all of this, it is crucial that extending loving compassion begin with extending love to yourself. How else can we expect ourselves to love another person if we do not first experience some degree of self-acceptance? The practice of loving-kindness can unblock the love that is hidden within.

At the beginning of our longer professional training programs, we ask participants not to reveal their professions. This usually raises some eyebrows and you can see inquisitive looks on people's faces. If I do not know what they do, how can I relate to the person sitting next to me? Job titles, resumes, roles, and responsibilities do not define who we are. This becomes clear when it comes to dying. Our roles can keep us at a safe distance, especially from those we are trying to serve. If we see ourselves only as the caregiver, care becomes a process of *giving* while failing to realize how much there is to *receive*.

I worked for many years at one of the last nursing facilities with open wards. In the hospice ward, I experienced viscerally for the first time how we all face aging, illness, and dying. The hospice ward was one large room with twenty-eight beds. Men at one end, women at the other, each separated from the others by only a flimsy curtain. The patients came from very diverse cultural and spiritual backgrounds. The suffering of the entire world seemed to be enclosed by the four walls of this ward. It made my heart ache. Despite the sadness, there was an underlying feeling that we are all connected, that no one was alone in his or her suffering. Here I learned what it meant to "bear witness" and about our human brokenness.

There is always a temptation to ignore our relationship to death and jump into the role of the helper with a dualistic attitude of "*I* am helping *you*." This kind of strategy can give us the illusion that we are "bullet-proof," and so death, pain, and suffering cannot "hit" us. Yet this strategy is a sure way of ending up feeling burnt out and resentful.

It is normal to try to shield ourselves from suffering. Suffering scares us and nobody wants to feel pain. However, the awareness of our own suffering is the link that connects us to others and, moreover, to our own heart. It is essential that we examine our attitudes and reactions to suffering and cultivate a greater sense of self-awareness, because our attitudes will be reflected in the way we care. This is where the contemplative approach can be of great benefit. We learn to make friends with our human condition and get to know our own mind. Through listening, contemplation, reflection, and meditation we are moving closer to the genuine heart of compassion.

When giving care, we need to become mindful of our motivation and if necessary adjust it. Through this kind of examination, we might, for example, realize that we are sitting at someone's bedside out of a false sense of duty or obligation. Knowing our motivation is important when we consider that, when nearing the moment of death, a dying person is highly sensitive and his or her mind can become atmospheric. I vividly remember Peter. Entering his room, I felt as if I had entered his mind. It was clear that whatever was on my mind deeply affected him. I decided to use the walk down the hallway to his room as a chance to clear my mind, and before I pressed the handle of his door I paused and set my intention for my visit. This kind of on-the-spot meditation, when there is no time to sit down between seeing people, can be an effective tool to integrate the mindfulness and awareness of meditation into the caregiving context.

John, a dear sangha member suffering from AIDS, had decided to leave the hospital to die at home supported by his sangha and a few close friends. When I came over to visit him the first afternoon he was home, he pulled me close. I gently held him and I asked him how I could help. "*Just be my friend*," he said with some sadness. The simplicity of his statement touched me. His words brought home what caring is all about. If we can just stop for a minute and view the person in front of us as "just another you," as just another human being with the same hopes and same fears, it will immediately soften our hearts. This will help us to put ourselves in that person's shoes; to get a sense of what the world looks like from that person's perspective and what he or she needs.

There are so many tender and magical moments when we can connect with the essence of another person, if we are receptive. We can connect through our shared humanity and love. There is also the opportunity to recognize the potential for enlightenment. We may glimpse people's buddha nature at the core of their being, however clouded it appears by their mental or emotional states, or however disfigured they are by physical illness.

Cecile Saunders, a pioneer of modern hospice, tells the moving story that illustrates the need to care genuinely. "I once asked a man who knew he was dying what he needed above all in those who were caring for him. He said, 'For someone to look as if they are trying to understand me.' Indeed, it is impossible to understand fully another person, but I never forget that he did not ask for success but only that someone should care enough to try."

You do not have to be perfect; you only need to care enough to try.

When we try to extend our care and love, we might quickly realize that we are not always skillful. We may end up imposing "a right way" to die, which can be quite subtle. We may take things personally, especially when the person exhibits strong emotions, or our help is refused. Or the sick person becomes a "charity project" that needs *our* help. We can avoid these pitfalls by blending the trust in our absolute nature with a levelheaded humility and an appreciation of where we are at on the path. It is important that we work compassionately with our limitations, with what we still need to learn and understand.

Do not expect too much of yourself or fear making mistakes. We can probably recall situations when "well-meaning" help felt more like a nuisance than a support. Looking into the mirror of death and our states of mind, we begin to see how much the mechanism of hope and fear has a firm grip on us. This certainly doesn't feel comfortable, but is, in fact, good news. Good news, because it gives us the chance to see what is truly going on instead of feeling mired by our concepts and fantasies of ourselves.

Caring for a terminally ill person is in itself a profound contemplation of our own mortality. I find it helpful to remember that we are all in this together. With every passing moment we are moving closer to death. To make friends with this truth is not easy. Yet when we do, we begin to become fearless about our own death. When the dying person gazes at us he or she does not wish to see fear reflected in our eyes, but confidence and love.

Those who courageously face their fears and transform difficulties into a source of strength are true "spiritual warriors." "To be a spiritual warrior," says Sogyal Rinpoche, "means to develop a special kind of courage, one that is innately intelligent, gentle and fearless. Spiritual warriors can still be frightened, but even so they are courageous enough to taste the suffering, to relate clearly to their fundamental fear, and to draw out without evasion the lessons from difficulties."

It takes courage to care without prepackaged formulas and to feel vulnerable, and remain present with *what is*. Dying is not a medical event but a sacred process. Creating a safe and inspiring environment has less to do with the outer space than with the space we have made within us. Care that comes from a deeper insight of who we truly are has the power to dispel fear and anxiety, and to inspire true confidence in those we care for. This kind of care has the power to transform our society and change the way we live and die.

Finding Acceptance at the Heart of Things

Carlyle Coash

W HAT IS THE MEANING of all this?"

It is the first time I have seen Tom without his bandages and I am finding it hard to focus on the question he has just written on the yellow legal pad he keeps by his bed.

The cancer that began in Tom's throat has now eaten away much of the right side of his face. It is only a matter of time before it eats away an artery in his neck or causes a hemorrhage in his brain. The bandage that keeps his jaw in place, and usually serves as a barrier to keep the hospital care staff from the full effect of how the cancer manifests, has been removed so that the wound can be cleaned. The experience leaves nothing to the imagination.

It becomes clear he has little room for denial or avoidance of his condition.

Every day he is literally watching himself decay. His teeth fall out as his jaw disintegrates. His ability to speak is long gone, and he relies on piles of notebooks to get his concerns across. When I visit, more often than

Carlyle Coash, MA, BCC, has been a part of spiritual care practice since 2000, beginning in Boulder, Colorado. He has worked in hospice, hospitals, and as part of a palliative care team at Kaiser San Jose Medical Center, where he was also the manager of spiritual care. He is board certified with the Association of Professional Chaplains and was one of the first Buddhist practitioners to be designated as such. Until 2011, Carlyle had been the section leader for the Spiritual Caregiving Section of the National Council of Hospice and Palliative Professionals (NCHPP). NCHPP represents the professional disciplines within end-of-life care and is part of the National Hospice and Palliative Care Organization. He also served on NHPCO's ethics committee and was chair of their educational subcommittee. Most recently he served as hospice director for Zen Hospice Project in San Francisco.

not I see panic in his eyes. Suddenly, seeing him so exposed, I understand truly what that panic is about.

I take a long deep breath in. I look at him directly and do not turn away. As I breathe in, I acknowledge the suffering he seems to be experiencing. I think about the discomfort and pain of the wound, not to mention the emotional stress, and how that might feel. I imagine what it must be like for him to look in a mirror, or to see the expressions of others who visit throughout the day.

In that moment, I realize I am also suffering. Every so often a patient I visit cuts right to the core of something inside. We are the same age and this could be my situation as much as his. I feel helpless with his panic, with his whole situation. He wants me to teach him about Buddhism, about meditation. With his jaw hanging in pieces it all feels impossible. What can I possibly offer him that will be of any help?

I breathe in. I let the feelings of sadness and fear come inside. They are dark and sticky. I let them touch my heart and they help me stay open. My heart welcomes them, and they take hold. I imagine a strong light growing in my chest that balances the darkness coming in. The fear begins to feel more workable. I want to make these dark aspects welcome, with nothing turned away.

Then, I breathe out.

I offer both of us as much loving-kindness as I can. The light in my chest is what I offer to him. My breath is glowing with it, filling the room with any and all hopefulness I can find within me. I try to transform the energy from the fear and apprehension in the room, and in me, into this loving-kindness. I use that light within me to make medicine of the poison I breathe in, to remove it of its harmful properties.

I might not be able to do much for Tom, but I can do this.

I draw upon any and all experiences of joy and peacefulness in my life and offer it to him. Any moment of ease I have had, may it be his. Any experiences of true kindness, may he experience them. All of the love and support I have been given in my life, I ask that he receive as much. May he always know that he is loved. May I be able to take on his burden, so as to soothe his suffering for even a moment.

Scary thought. Take on his suffering? It seems a little radical, but somehow I trust I could. When I read the stories of the great teachers, this is usually the kind of approach they embody. They are selfless, with a tireless energy to end the suffering of others. How far would I be willing to go to ease the suffering of another? How tightly do I hold on to my own comfort, my own sense of self? What do I lose by giving him all my happiness? What do I gain?

Breathe in suffering. Breathe out kindness.

I come back to this over and over.

All I can do is stay focused on him. I try to witness him, without pity, offering as much kindness as possible. I figure I owe him that much—one being to another. He at least deserves that I do not turn away, and so I stay right there. I look at his wound and try to stay grounded.

Tom's question—"What is the meaning of all this?"—is a more difficult matter.

As a chaplain, I am often asked, "Why is this happening? What is the purpose of my suffering? What is the meaning?" I have found the answers to these questions elusive. To answer would suggest I know the reason, and if I have learned anything in the last ten years as a chaplain, it is that I do not know. These are primal questions, full of complexity. They reside at the core of what it means to be alive and exist. And fairness has little to do with it. My role is to explore the questions, not to provide easy answers.

"What is the meaning of all this?"

"I wish I knew, Tom. I wish I knew."

So begins our visit together.

THE TEXTURE OF BUDDHISM IN SPIRITUAL CARE

My purpose in this section is to explore what it means to provide Buddhist spiritual care, or rather spiritual care from a Buddhist perspective. I say this because spiritual care is inherently interfaith, certainly in the medical setting. Although I am informed by my Buddhist practice, my role is as an interfaith chaplain. I do not represent just one particular faith or perspective. I must hold a broader view.

This approach of broader view was embodied in my Clinical Pastoral Education training, which encouraged dynamic interchange with other faiths. The training taught me how to reside in my own practice while reaching out to others, versing myself in other perspectives. This means at times that I pray to God, or help a family baptize a child who has died. It means I explore aspects of faith very different from my own. Being of service to others requires stepping out of the familiar.

At the same time I need to understand where the boundaries are to this stepping out. Does this mean I am everything to every person, a jack of all trades to everyone's spiritual needs? No. Sometimes what the person needs is a rabbi or the Catholic priest, and then my job is to make sure the person receives that support. It is important to be able to get out of your own way and pay attention to what the other person truly needs.

Often what is needed from me is not my Buddhist practice. Those I serve, whether in the hospital or hospice, need someone who represents faith and meaning. They need counsel, someone willing to explore difficult questions. They need a way to confess misdeeds and poor choices without judgment and shame. They need someone who can hold them in prayer or silence, weaving the story of meaning into what happens next. They need someone to be a sounding board, an intermediary to the greater universe that surrounds us. They need a companion.

So that is what I try to do. I arrive and bring my whole self. I bring how I am feeling and what I am thinking. Before I step into a visit I take account of these things, so that I can be aware of where I might be limited. I look for ways to be of service, to be a voice for stories and meanings that patients are struggling to express or convey. This requires a minimum of agenda and letting go of hope for any kind of outcome. This can be challenging because the standard in the medical setting is to be able to demonstrate what a problem is, provide an intervention, and monitor outcome for each aspect of a patient's care. Yet, as a chaplain, there are times when a visit's only visible outcome is that I held a person's hand.

For me, spiritual care is not an academic exercise.

It is not something that can be studied from a distance. Rather, it requires clinical skill, including an ongoing study of culture, meaning, and the role of faith. To be a caregiver you need to engage in interaction, either at the bedside, the prison cell, the homeless shelter, the war zone, or after a natural disaster. Spiritual care takes place in countless settings and it is in the moment of direct contact that it truly comes alive.

What I find so amazing is that the majority of these moments are ordinary. My work, in hospice and the hospital, is rarely dramatic. Often there is silence, for example when watching the breath leave the body for the last time. It is these silences that elicit intimacy: the sharing of a memory, moments of laughter and of connection. It is here that the heart of spiritual care beats, these simple gaps in the movement of things. This is because the small moment is where the truth often resides. It is here that the person shares his fears or what is weighing on him, while watching his favorite TV program or playing cards. The pressure is off. We are simply residing together and there is a trust that I might understand because I am human too. It occurs also because I am willing to just sit down with the person and be ordinary. I let him take the lead and, as I have said, I try not to get in the way.

In the end, spiritual care is practical. In the midst of the large existential questions are mostly ones that focus on simple needs. What will happen to my body? Will it be peaceful? Will it hurt? Will I see my loved ones when I get there? Will you make sure my wife is okay?

The ordinary moment is perfect for questions like that. My role is to explore these questions, often reflecting the question back to the person. The answer is usually within. Sometimes what is being asked for is forgiveness. Serious illness places the edges of our lives much closer so that we look hard at the choices we made. It makes us wonder if the illness has occurred as a result of a misdeed or a harsh word spoken. I have watched many patients struggle with these edges, and it can be a lonely place.

Offering companionship can soften the sharpness, allowing for grace to be present as well.

THE CASITA (LITTLE HOUSE) MODEL OF CARE

Over time I have worked with a variety of different models for practicing spiritual care. Models can be helpful, in that they place a frame around the work, providing a reference while working in the field. A model should ground you, acting as a touchstone if you get off track.

A few years ago I came across a model for resilience that was developed in South America called the Casita Model—*casita* means "little house." I found it in a book titled *Resilience in Palliative Care*, edited by Barbara

Monroe and David Oliviere. For purposes here, Tony Newman offers a definition of resilience that might be helpful: "a universal capacity for a person, group, or community to prevent, minimize, or overcome damaging effects of adversity." Although the book by Monroe and Oliviere looks at the role resilience plays in the management of serious illness, I found it to be an essential resource for the work of spiritual care. I say this because resilience is needed not only for people with illness but also for their family and for the professionals providing the care to those people. The stronger their resilience, the more people can manage complex symptoms, and emotions and spiritual issues they will likely face during a crisis or illness. Therefore this notion of resilience infuses all aspects of spiritual care, and the model provides a perfect template from which to work.

CASITA RESIDENCE BUILDING

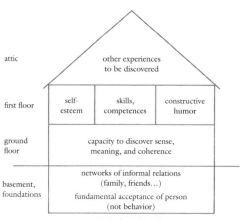

The Casita Model, developed by Stefan Vanistendael, utilizes the image of a house to explore what is key for our ability to be resilient through change. The model requires us to look beyond problems to the positive elements that help us rebuild life. As Vanistendael himself says, "the search for positives is not a denial of what goes wrong, but a more inclusive and realistic view of the situation, not exclusively determined by problems."

What struck me immediately when I saw the model for the first time was the foundation of the "little house": "fundamental acceptance of the person (not behavior)."

It seemed to me a very Buddhist notion, and I was curious how it would apply to my work in spiritual care. In Buddhism, there is an elemental idea that each and every being—at its core—embodies wisdom and compassion. In order to become awakened, one must perceive this innate nature with clarity and equanimity. Similarly it is felt that in order to truly cultivate resilience, a person must feel that in some way she is truly accepted for her being-ness. A person has value, has meaning, simply because she is a living being. That is the only requirement. If this knowledge is instilled at some foundational moment of a person's development, she will be able to manage change and transition in a very direct way. The behavior, in many ways, is incidental to this being-ness. It is neurosis and habit, rather than an essential quality.

For me, there was something easily transferable to the direct care experience from the structure of this model. The model is holistic, with an open-ended aspect to allow for continued discovery and learning. Yet, at the core is the message of acceptance, meeting people right where they are. This foundation of the house, acceptance, is especially useful when I am working with people who challenge me emotionally. At times I must work with people whose values or beliefs are radically different than my own. I have been asked to visit many people that normally I might never spend time with. I have been yelled at, punched, dismissed for being too young, being male, being white, being Buddhist. Still I continue to show up. Even if I never see that person again, I try to keep him/her in mind and offer kindness.

That is not to say I am successful all the time. There are times when the connection you make with someone opens a vulnerable side in yourself that is important to acknowledge. After months of getting to know Tom, he started to decline. His family was concerned about his going to heaven, so they wanted to discourage his interest in anything outside of their beliefs. As a result I was banned from visiting because of my Buddhist practice. I had experienced this many times before, yet this time it hit me deeply. It was hard to not focus on the behavior of his family. I felt hurt and discarded, especially after spending significant time with them as well. In that case, it was hard to see past the behavior and to see past my own ego.

After a while, I was able to see that they were grieving. They wanted to protect their son. The illness and the effects of the cancer were outside their control. But who visited Tom in his last moments was not. Despite my sadness at being asked to leave Tom's side, I made sure I took the time to reflect on the effect this situation was having on me. This kind of reflection is crucial to the work of spiritual care, as well as any caregiving profession. I am part of the same continuum of change as Tom and his family. To not acknowledge this creates the illusion I am somehow separate from them. I am not. And when I put myself in their shoes, I had to admit I might have done the same thing. Allowing myself to see their perspective kept me connected to them.

For me this is at the core of my work in spiritual care—the fundamental acceptance of people. Acceptance that they suffer, that they have emotions, and that they are impermanent. Finding that acceptance initiates a thread of connection and allows me to stay open. If I am simply cranking out numbers of visits to serve outcome reporting, the practice becomes lifeless. The model of problem, intervention, and outcome runs counter to spiritual meaning making, a process which is often very grey. The challenge is how to manage both the medical model approach and this grey, ineffable process. Both are important, and the role of the clinically trained chaplain is to assist in these two realities relating to each other.

THE ROLE OF SPIRITUAL CARE

Acceptance leads to connection. Connection is also present at the basement level of the Casita, as community or a "network of informal relations." It is through community that we are seen. Community becomes especially important to people who are facing serious illness or death due to the particular challenges they face. It is not uncommon for friends and family to pull away from a person who is dying, uncomfortable about how to speak to or support their loved one. At the time that connection is most needed, a dying person is often at risk of isolation. With this risk factor in play, my role is to foster and nourish whatever network the dying person has in place. This network can be powerful. I have often witnessed a person transform at the end of his/her life when community starts to gather, even if the community is just a couple of people.

Dying can be an isolating experience. If you think the person who is sick does not notice the withdrawal of his friends and family, he does. I have heard many people say to me, "Why did they stop visiting? Aren't I still the same person?" I think this isolation occurs in some part because death is scary and unknown, unequivocal in its directness. No matter how much we try to control the outcome, the outcome is still the same. We will all die. For most of us, this experience is overwhelming. In a sense the person dying is a direct mirror of what we are fearful of, and so people pull way. Community and connection is essential for someone in those moments of crisis.

I remember speaking with a chaplain in Kenya, who told me the story of a woman he visited who had been diagnosed with cancer. Since knowledge of the disease is often limited in rural areas, members of her village stayed away from her for fear she was contagious. As a result she had not been touched or communicated with in weeks. Neighbors would leave her food, but would stay away. When he and the nurse came to visit, the first thing they did was cook her a meal and help her take a bath. She asked for the chaplain to offer a prayer and as was his custom, he placed his hands on the top of her head. She reached up and placed her hands over his. When he was done, he went to take away his hands and she held on. She shared how hard it had been to not have touch, to be held, to be facing this alone. As her tears flowed, she expressed her gratitude for this care they had provided, stronger than any medicine she needed.

For me this links into the ground floor of the model, which looks at the importance of having the "capacity to discover sense, meaning, and coherence." Each level builds on the next, so the foundation of acceptance and community creates the ground for meaning making. From there the first floor can flourish, as self-esteem and basic skills take shape. It also follows that humor plays a role, especially in the ability to find levity in the midst of struggle. This helps us move through, rather than becoming stuck. Finally in the top part of the Casita Model is the ability for "other experiences to be discovered." It is a dynamic process, allowing for movement and new experiences to feed the ground and foundation.

As I look at the role of spiritual care, it is this dynamic process I am asked to support and participate in. It is why I have found this model so helpful. It provides a framework to which I can look to see where the person I am working with, or myself, is strong and where things might be stuck. What does this person have to draw on? So often people in crisis forget how much they already have. Part of the practice of spiritual care is reconnecting them to that awareness so that they can find healing.

PRACTICE IN ACTION

I have worked in hospitals, hospices, as part of palliative care teams, and with many patients. In all of this I would say that my most recent time at Zen Hospice Project came closest to how I feel spiritual care, and caregiving for that matter, should be practiced. Given my connection to the Casita Model, it seems fitting that my main focus of work was supporting the operation of their six-bed Guest House in San Francisco. There is a way in which spiritual care is infused in all aspects of practice there, so that a holistic care model can be created. It is also where I have seen the elements of the Casita Model manifest.

When the house reopened, our first resident was a forty-nine-year-old woman diagnosed with lung cancer. With her came a strong community of support: her family and church friends, who filled her room with prayer and attentiveness to the care she needed. A key part of this community was her nine-year-old daughter, June.

At first we saw June infrequently. There was concern for her and how the decline of her mother might affect her. So she had visits from the hospice social workers, our staff, and other concerned parties. She said she was all right, feeling a little uncomfortable with the attention. We soon realized that what she needed was for all of us to relax.

After a few days, she started visiting the house more. She would sit in the dining room doing her homework. She colored and drew pictures, and on occasion someone would sit and do some coloring with her. We slowly got to know each other. One day, the four-year-old granddaughter of another resident came by for a visit and they became fast friends. They sat at the kitchen table, the four-year-old sitting in June's lap helping with her with a book report. It felt magical.

Soon it was common for June to play a kind of hide and seek with whoever was in the house. I was nominated several times to participate. To be honest it was less like "hide and seek" and more like "hide and creep." Instead of hiding she would creep up quietly behind you to see how close she could get before you noticed. Very fun.

Just before we opened, a local farmer who grows dahlias offered to provide the Guest House every week with a fresh batch from his farm. About three weeks into June's mother's stay, he sent four large buckets to the house that were brimming with stems. Vibrant colors filled the house. Reds, oranges, pinks, purples, violets. It was quite marvelous.

As I was leaving for the day, I noticed that June was busily working with the buckets of flowers. At the time I had forgotten that the flowers were donations to the house and as I saw her working I assumed they had arrived for her mother. My last image of June for the day was of her carrying vases full of colorful dahlias up the stairs to the second floor. Each vase seemed almost half her size, but she wanted no help in carrying them. I thought to myself that her mother would be in for a great treat that night.

It took me until the next day to realize, as I visited the resident's rooms, that June had a different purpose in mind. She had created special arrangements for each resident in the house and brought the bouquets upstairs to them, one by one. My heart broke open.

She was providing care to us.

As her mother's health declined, she continued to connect with the staff and volunteers. We let her be just as she needed to be. We accepted her. We did not try and push an agenda of support on her. She drew pictures for us and spent time talking with the nurses at the nurses' station. You could tell she was very sensitive to the changes her mother was going through. Even after her mother's death, she was participating— expressing emotion and grieving.

To step into suffering with another is perhaps our greatest act of kindness. When this happens at the end of life, you will meet the profound teacher. There is none that will teach you more or keep your heart more steady. Everything you have ever learned, studied, practiced, and understood is for the moment of death. Serving those in that state is sacred. Embrace it as much as you can. I have, and it is certainly where I have learned the most and deepened the most. The best part is that there is still more to learn. You will not be disappointed.

A Little Nowness

Ginger Brooks

WHEN I WAS TWENTY, my father died in an Intensive Care Unit, where he had been from the time of his admission to the hospital. During those two weeks he was there, I wasn't allowed to see him because, I was told, he "looked so bad." But my experience of his death had elements of the mystical, and through it, I woke to a larger world of change and suffering. I felt that I *belonged* to this world in a way I had not before.

Some forty years later I am a chaplain. I am not a "Buddhist chaplain"— I am a hospice chaplain. If I identify myself as a Buddhist chaplain, an interfaith chaplain, or a Protestant chaplain, I risk inviting preconceptions on the part of my patients. In fact, we "chaplains" at the hospice in Boulder where I work prefer to introduce ourselves simply as "members of the spiritual care (or spiritual support) team."

For centuries "chaplain" described a Christian minister, so my colleagues and I agree (as do many chaplains nationwide) that "spiritual care" is a broader and therefore more useful name for the support that we offer. Because of its connotations, i.e., its Christian origin and association with the church, the designation "chaplain" actually closes a door

Ginger Brooks began meditation practice in Cambridge, Massachusetts, in 1975, under the direction of Chogyam Trungpa Rinpoche. In Nova Scotia, she worked part time for Shambhala International and participated in raising a son. She is ordained as an upadhyaya in the Shambhala Buddhist tradition, where she is an active meditation instructor. She studies Iyengar Yoga, and works full time as a member of an interdisciplinary team, providing spiritual support to patients and their families, at Family Hospice in Boulder, Colorado.

for many people. This is not hard to understand, given our increasingly multicultural and secular America. Most patients and families, however, do accept a *bringer of spiritual support* with gratitude and a measure of trust.

I believe the essence of spiritual care is connecting with the spirit or *spiritedness* of a person. Most elderly hospice patients have little social support. Their families are grown and dispersed, they have lost one or more spouses, and they have long ago slipped away from their church communities. Even so, some patients are comforted by the words and music of the church, and for these I am happy reading the Bible, praying, and singing.

Rarely do the very old and very sick care to talk theology.

Many no longer talk much, if at all. At the end, beliefs once held about life and death and God and salvation tend to be important only insofar as these beliefs have served them well as their lives have unfolded. Beliefs have either nurtured the strengths of acceptance and love and trust, or they have not. And if they have not, from my own observation, it is never too late.

In hospice, everyone has a job, a role. The nurse's job is to control pain and anxiety with drugs and with empathy and affection. A CNA (certified nurse assistant) helps maintain the dignity of the body with the same empathy and affection (and CNAs seem to have a corner on humor). The social worker looks for practical solutions to problems in the system and acts as a skilled counselor when patient/families need to heal relationships. As chaplain, my role on the team is to be the person *with nothing to do*, who stays present to the patient or family member.

All team members support the *spiritedness* of the patient and family and participate in a deeper level of care than a job description might suggest. As a chaplain, I feel my job is to hold and communicate the view that there is no problem with what is happening, that nothing needs repair. We are here to surrender to the reality of dying, not to resist it. Surrender also knows that there is no "good" death, no best way to die. There is only *this* death, as it is in fact unfolding. It means that we may mitigate pain and distress, but, finally, we have no alternative to what is happening. For me, being with the choicelessness that is the situation, being temporarily suspended from the mind that hopes for something better and fears something worse, is clicking in to *nowness*. Nowness doesn't know struggle, is devoid of hope and fear. In nowness, past and future dissolve into the present-tense realm in which magic happens—the simple and profound ordinary magic of opening to the beauty, the *is-ness* of life.

From that perspective, I feel a responsibility, often frustrated, to actively resist the tendency of the hospice team to medicalize the end of life. Some days the members of such a team seem like crusaders for the perfect, pain-free, peaceful end of life.

Personally though, I think that the body's final struggles also have the power to illuminate. I think of the altered, often difficult breathing at the end of life as labor analogous to childbirth, another of life's transitions. Even so, I am also not sure that morphine and Ativan, those drugs that "control symptoms" so well, inherently present an obstacle to the dying person's experience of the illumination possible at the time of death.

On the other hand, some of the more drug-free deaths that I have witnessed seemed to result in a sense that the patient died with more awareness of the love cradling her, of what she is leaving, or perhaps taking with her. But terminal agitation can be so hard to witness, and verbal communication with the patient is usually not possible by the time it sets in. Even some patients and families who have wanted to be very conservative with the use of these powerful drugs give in when their loved one begins to show signs of agitation.

I believe that for all of us to accept the inner struggle of dying is to open to a deeper dimension of being. We can learn to appreciate the goodness of the process, if not as a potential for awakening, at least as an expression of inconceivable profound truth. We can have faith in the rightness of what is. We can be awake to the heart of life in death. In one sense, the profound lessons of death are ordinary lessons. Almost everyone involved in a serious loss experiences, if only briefly, how the inconceivable truth of it releases us from petty concerns, scrubs us raw, makes us feel life's preciousness.

As a chaplain, I hold the view that we are all capable of finding confidence in dying and that the exquisite fruit of the struggle for the dying person and the family and friends is always there in the choiceless reality of what is happening. The chaplain can be the guardian of the space around the dying, modeling peace and acceptance, confirming the rightness of what is with her presence and perhaps her words. I have seen how this curtails anxiety and the busyness that attends it and prepares the ground for acceptance.

This heart-full allegiance to *now* can help the family to settle down or to let go.

The family may feel ready for their loved one's death but are uncertain how to relate to the patient if he or she is unconscious or only partly conscious. Or perhaps death is close, but no one wants to name it. There is free floating fear. My Buddhist teacher once said that the dying are often confused about what is happening, so there is that uncertainty, too. I have learned to trust myself to feel things out and then, with gentleness, do what is necessary to bring anxieties and uncertainties down from the ether into the earthy simplicity of what is happening.

One of our patients, a man admitted only the day before, lay dying with two sisters present. The sisters were very tender but afraid and restless, not knowing how to be with their brother, not knowing for sure if he was actually dying, and not knowing whether he understood what was happening to him.

I asked them to tell me a little about him. He was a single man, a bank president who had done very well. His family was from rural Kansas. They were proud of his accomplishments but felt a little estranged because his lifestyle was so different from theirs. He was not intimate with anyone in the family, but other siblings were on their way from out of town and the family was rallying around. He had not been a churchgoer but the sisters thought that he "probably believed in God." I kept asking questions until I sensed they had come closer to their brother through remembering him.

The patient himself was barely conscious.

I leaned over him and asked him if he knew that he was at the end of his life. He indicated that he heard me. I reminded him that everyone dies, that it is a natural thing, and that this was his time. With assurances that everything was going as it should, and that everyone could just go along with it, I invited the sisters to tell him whatever they wanted. Then I told him that we were going to bless him for the journey he was about to take. I used traditional anointing oil and invited the family to participate. The sisters put oil on his face, hands, feet. We all saw him change, relax. The sisters were crying with relief. They just hadn't known how to step in.

I think this story demonstrates the simplicity of the chaplain's role: to show that you can be with death; you can go past fear and be with dying; you can be intimate with the *ugliness* of death. This love and acceptance communicates itself, so that the dying person knows you are *with* them. As this story suggests, a chaplain may take family members by the hand both literally and figuratively and bring them into this space of choicelessness, of acceptance, where nowness dawns. When this happens, it can be a kind of initiation for all of us, and we share the warm space of oneness together. You could say that the experience is there for the taking if you can be with what is.

Sometimes, of course, especially when relationships are complicated, people are unable to do this. I am careful to follow the signs. Sometimes, if I can get one family member to come close to the patient, those hanging back out of fear will follow.

Saint John of the Cross said that all human beings have to cross the river of suffering, but the boat they cross with is love. This is often what being the chaplain at the deathbed feels like—we are all being contained in a vessel of love. And we are, all of us, crossing. I do my best to communicate trust and acceptance, knowing that love is what is there at the end of the argument with death.

The dying process, and what a chaplain might bring to the deathbed situation, is such a potent time. But much of my activity as a chaplain consists of just being a friend, a hand to hold, a "bringer of kindness," as one of my chaplain colleagues puts it. Sometimes the friend is a counselor, a person to complain to, or a minister bringing the sacraments, scripture, prayer, or blessing. Sometimes I am just another pair of eyes and ears for the hospice team or the family. In general, I am willing to accept whatever role or projection a patient or family member assigns me.

Every patient is unique, but I have usually found it effective to begin by inquiring into what is happening to them now. I do not try to cheer people up. Rather, I acknowledge and normalize their experience.

Acknowledging their suffering often leads to a connection to their humor or their innate positivity.

Some chaplains try to guide their patient through a process of reflection on the imminence of their own death, as if there were a point when a person chooses to accept dying or not. Perhaps a little guidance of this kind can be beneficial, but it is not something that I do any longer. I have faith, based on my years of experience working with the dying, that simply acknowledging change as it happens is enough. Realizing impermanence often comes in spurts, and with these windows on truth, many are able to surrender their pride and accept the love and help of others with less complaint.

Chaplains I have worked with are comfortable with silence. Silence provides a space to observe and listen and enter a patient's world, if the invitation is there. That world may contain memories of happiness or of pain and regret. There may be sadness present or complaint. Sometimes there is acceptance, appreciation, and love. It is always a lonely space, but it is that aloneness which makes true connection possible if it is going to happen.

I would say that the common characteristic shared by the aged and the ill is loneliness and isolation. The natural loneliness of the end of life is compounded when our elders have to give up living independently for assisted living and nursing facilities. In the nursing facility especially, they have been lifted completely out of their *context*. The family visit may be reduced to just one hour per week. When the loved one whose brain is aging is no longer the person she used to be, the family often views her as no longer a person. Many elderly people, with loss upon loss and with a sense of continually losing, no longer know who they are.

Patients may or may not engage with me in reflecting on their life or past regrets. Many who are aware they are near the end have no interest in sharing memories, even happy ones. I often ask people if life seems like a dream. I usually get a response or a look says, "Oh, you know how it is."

WWII veterans, especially, struggle with painful memories and the terrible mood swings that go with them. At the end of their lives they may be sharing these memories for the first time and need special patience and kindness. I have become very close to a ninety-five-year-old veteran named Ted, a loving, gentle, courtly, and self-reflective man of faith. During the war he always refused to carry a personal weapon, but he faithfully performed his service as a combat captain responsible for keeping the big guns in position at the lines of battle. Now he cycles through agonies of remorse about the killing that he was responsible for. Now, after two years of listening to his repetitive traumatic memories, his hospice team just tries to redirect him.

Perhaps the deeper issue for him is his disappointment that, despite what he calls his "lucky" life and despite his moral integrity, long history of traditional church-centered faith and devotion to family, and ideals of community and country, it has all ended in this—loneliness (despite a very involved daughter) and helplessness. He says, "I don't know who I am anymore." For a time, I tried to explore the meaning of faith with him, but soon realized that talking and thinking about beliefs doesn't really help. Through people like Ted, I have discovered the power of liturgy or ritual in my practice as a chaplain.

Ted's belief in a God who aided and protected him gave him strength to walk through life. As his mind began to slip and his beliefs began to dissolve in the face of his present situation, he made efforts to shore things up. He read and reread Norman Vincent Peale and other books on positive thinking but finally gave that up, complaining that he can no longer "control his mind." One day, on a hunch that he might be receptive, I brought Communion to him, something rarely shared in his tradition. I have found this sacrament to be a very powerful way to feed the spirit, when we experience together the blessing of connecting to the numinous. I liken it to identifying with the enlightened qualities of the *yidam* in my Vajrayana tradition.

Of my deceased patients, the one I miss most is the devout and brilliant Episcopalian, a former private school headmaster, with whom I shared weekly Communion for eight months. His dementia was fairly advanced, and he lived in a typical nursing home, not a pleasant place. He often thought he was on a cruise ship, his privileged background following him wherever he went. He didn't complain to me or to anyone else (according to family and facility staff), and he had nothing but praise for everyone and everything. He thought the canned tomato soup in the nursing home dining room was the "most superb" he ever had.

Typical of families of patients who were once very accomplished, this man's children found it difficult to witness his decline. He was simply not the man he once was, and they were looking forward to the end of "his suffering."

Although Communion is served weekly in the Episcopal Church, this patient had never experienced it one-on-one. Together we marveled at its depth. Each time, sometimes in the middle of the liturgy, he would exclaim that he was hearing and feeling parts of it for the first time, and he would tell me in what ways it was new for him. Each week when I read to him, it was as though I, too, was feeling and hearing it for the first time, and I would tell him how it was new for me. The nondualism of Christ's words from the service, "Abide in me as I in you," doesn't get much clearer. With those lines the sacred began to be present for him, and I followed him there.

For this wonderful man, the increasing signs of the impermanence of his body and limitations of his mind were becoming a gateway to a more profound consciousness. He referred to feelings of "completeness" or "oneness." He said he was looking forward to the "love that is beyond the stars," but I think he had found it. He was so grateful for our meetings.

I thanked him as well, always thinking, "You have no idea, Lane, how grateful *I* am."

With Lane, sacred presence was like a net falling over us or like a field of ordinary magic at the boundary of thinking mind. This experience of the sacred is the treasure of nowness. I have found that the very ill, at the end of their lives, stripped of pretense and hope, are most likely to step into this territory.

It may take the shape of a mere moment of fully meeting another, but I like to think that, too, is blessing.

Ten Slogans to Guide Contemplative Care

Victoria Howard

I HAVE WORKED as a hospice caregiver, in the Shambhala tradition, for over thirty years. And as part of Dana Home Care, I've also been involved in the training of hospice volunteers. In our tradition, we use ten *lojong* slogans that summarize and guide a contemplative caregiver's role.

Here are the slogans:

> Without armor, full of delight.
> All situations are passing memory.
> No escape, no problem.
> Notice everything, respect everything.
> Let the situation speak for itself.
> Take the blame yourself.
> Don't expect things to go your way.
> Be grateful to everyone.
> Be steady, don't go up and down.
> Rely on a cheerful frame of mind.

Victoria Howard, PhD, is a minister in the Shambhala Buddhist tradition and was core faculty in the master of divinity program at Naropa University until her retirement in 2010. She has worked extensively in the fields of elder and hospice care, serving as clinical director for Windhorse Family and Elder Care and as a volunteer trainer for Hospice of Boulder and Broomfield Counties. She has also helped to develop small group residences for frail elders and has specialized in applying contemplative principles and approaches in all of her professional work.

These slogans have, for me, acted as guides in my work with the dying. While I can't take credit for the slogans, the commentary that follows is my own.

Without Armor, Full of Delight.

When we enter a new situation or meet someone for the first time, it is important that we present ourselves naturally. We do not need to hide behind some idea of professionalism. We do not need to worry about what people are thinking of us. We can just relax and our relaxation will invite theirs. When people are new to each other, there is always an atmosphere of uncertainty. If we drop our shyness and defensiveness, that energy can be stimulating. This fresh encounter could be anything. We are challenged by the opportunity and delighted to explore further.

All Situations Are Passing Memory.

Spending time with someone, engaging in relationship, we do our best to understand and to be helpful. It is like sailing a boat—the wind blows this way and we tack accordingly. The wind shifts direction and we adjust. People that we are working with give us feedback. Sometimes they smile. Sometimes they complain.

It is a balancing act that is never quite perfect. We cannot be too attached to our victories or too disheartened by our failures. There will be many situations where we can do nothing and some in which we actually do harm. All of these experiences become memories, intangible and haunting. They are neither true nor not true, but remembering can serve to open our hearts.

No Escape, No Problem.

In any relationship there will be moments of claustrophobia. We may feel bored or restless, trapped by this person, hopeless in the face of his or her situation. We may have trouble staying awake when we are with such people or have difficulty listening to their words. None of this is a problem. We simply note what we are experiencing and return to the sensation of our feet on the floor, our butt on the chair. It might help to glance out a window or follow our breath as it goes out into the room. As we refocus our attention, questions will arise. "Why do I feel this way and what is the other person feeling?" We can lean into our curiosity now that we have come back.

Notice Everything, Respect Everything.

When we engage with a person, we are together in an environment. It could be the person's home, a hospital room, or an office. Perhaps we are in a coffee shop or driving in a car. The point is that our communication is always influenced by our context. In a person's home and even in a hospital room, the objects and arrangement of the space tell a story. People react differently in different environments. Someone who has difficulty talking face to face may open up while riding beside you in a car. By observing how people relate to their surroundings we learn about their preferences and their habits. We can attune ourselves to a person by respectful attention to these details.

Let the Situation Speak for Itself.

In any encounter and in any environment, we are tempted to try to manage by labeling things as this or that. "This person is depressed," or "This household is dysfunctional." Interpretations and opinions come up for us. They may be accurate or inaccurate, but they are just thoughts. We can note them without becoming involved with them. We do not need to interpret reality for the people that we are working with. They have their own intelligence. We can trust them to see and to learn. We can accompany them in that process. We do not have to control the situation. It will speak for itself, further and further, if we let it.

Take the Blame Yourself.

People are rarely comfortable about needing help. They may feel vulnerable, anxious about what is happening, worried about what will come next. The atmosphere can be fraught. As caregivers, we are like lightning rods, taking in this charge and grounding it with our presence. The people that we work with are in pain of one kind or another. They are in the grip of something beyond their control. They may push us away or they might blame us. They may be unable to relate at all. Whatever their behavior, we do not need to become defensive or apologetic. It is not about us, but we can let it penetrate us. We can breathe in the intensity of people's dilemma. We can feel what they cannot bear and in so doing bring them ease.

Don't Expect Things to Go Your Way.

Expectations are a tricky business. If we fear the worst, it can become a self-fulfilling prophecy. If we think that we know what will happen, we may not notice what is actually taking place. Expectations are assumptions that can obscure our direct perception. They narrow our view. At the same time, we all have hopes and ambitions. Aspiring to help is based on the assumption that such a thing is possible. When expectations come up, we can see them for what they are and not take them too seriously. We can remind ourselves that we really do not know. Remembering this, we can wait and see, thus sparing ourselves frustration and disappointment. It could be that the outcome, while not what we expected, is better than we could have imagined.

Be Grateful to Everyone.

We aspire to be more skilled as helpers and every interaction is a lesson. We learn from the feedback that the world gives us. Our mistakes are often the greatest teachings. Some encounters may be difficult. There will be people who do not appreciate our good intentions, people who do not like us at all. We may be rejected because of our religion or the color of our skin. Even shocking and hurtful moments are full of information. They can awaken us to the diversity of human perspectives, to the fact that not everyone sees the world as we do. We will also have experiences of unexpected kindness and stunning bravery. Other people will surprise us and we will surprise ourselves. All of these moments are gifts, further instruction about the nature of reality.

Be Steady, Don't Go Up and Down.

The people that we work with are in transition. Something has happened. Some change has taken place. They are knocked off balance. What we have to offer them is our steadiness. We have seen other people in similar situations. We understand that difficult passages occur in every life. Even dying is a normal process, something to be expected. In these heightened moments, we can fall back on ordinary comforts—a cup of tea, simple conversation. If we are in the person's home, we can tend to the environment, open curtains, tidy. We can use our words and our actions to bring calm. Once things settle somewhat, we can inquire further. There is no rush.

Rely on a Cheerful Frame of Mind.

We do this work because we love it. It pleases us to try to help. We are interested in the people we encounter and we can be certain that we will learn from each situation.

Some days are harder than others. We will attend suffering and we will feel it. We are honored by that intimacy. We can come back to our original inspiration, remembering the great kindness of those who have helped us. We can taste the joy of human goodness, feel it in our own heart. We can trust that problems will come up. They will bring challenge and freshness. We are so fortunate in our life and we bring our contentment with us. We rely on it and we extend it to others.

Reflecting on these slogans and those early years at Dana Home Care, my friend Ann Cason recently reminded me of Trungpa Rinpoche's opening statement at one of our supervision sessions: "This is warrior's work. Any questions?"

PART VI

The Pastoral Role of the Dharma Teacher:
The Arts of Ministry

Thus I Have Listened:

A REFLECTION ON LISTENING AS SPIRITUAL CARE

Willa Miller

CHARLENE LOOKS at me with a long gaze, longer than would be comfortable if I were sitting across from her at a coffee shop. But we are not at a coffee shop. We are in the interview room, a room designated during silent retreats as a place where teacher and student can meet intimately for short periods to discuss a student's practice. Gazes are not uncommon. Silence is not uncommon.

Charlene is about sixty, with strong blue eyes. She wears a tie-died T-shirt that says "I'm on Island Time." She has just told me about her cancer, in her liver, in her brain. She has told me that she is getting her affairs in order and that she wishes to start living a more spiritual life, in her last few months or years, however long she has. How can she do that, she wonders. I have only known Charlene for several days, but I am already inspired by her. She signed up for this death and dying retreat, where we are now, keeping silence, eating vegetarian food, meditating. The retreat enrollment was restricted to experienced meditators, those who had already finished a program of study. But hearing of her

Willa Miller, MA, is a *lama* (Buddhist minister) in the Tibetan tradition. She is the founder and director of Natural Dharma Fellowship, a nonprofit organization in the Boston area dedicated to transmitting the practices of Tibetan meditation for use in everyday life. Her books before this one include *Essence of Ambrosia*, a translation of a work by Taranatha, and *Everyday Dharma*, a practical guide for getting started on the spiritual path. She lives in Cambridge, Massachusetts, where she is working toward a doctorate in religion at Harvard University.

prognosis, I could not say no. We, the young and healthy, are interested in reflecting on the inevitability of death. She, on the other hand, was living the inevitability of death. She was on Island Time now, and she deserved to be spending it here, perhaps more than anyone.

She muses, "I have been trying to figure out if I should forgive my brother, while I still have time left." I have learned from her the extent of harm her brother brought to her and her sister, and it is hard for me to feel forgiveness myself. I ask her, "What do you think you should do? What are you feeling?" She shares that she is still very angry at him, as he continues to make the family's life difficult. I nod in acknowledgment of her pain, her anger. I notice my own anger rising at this brother of hers I have never met. I breathe into that feeling and remember my commitment to being here now, to witnessing her. I refocus and listen.

Encounters like this were not what I anticipated when I began to step into the ministerial duties of being a lama, a Tibetan Buddhist minister, several years ago. I had generally been led to believe, if not by words by implication, that this role wholly entailed teaching the Dharma. It was, I imagined, a role about transmission of Buddhist truths from one generation to another, guiding others in practices of meditation, and explaining the fine points of Buddhist philosophy. It was about being adept at ritual.

In reality, it turned out to be about many other things, unspoken and unexpected. In reality, being a Dharma teacher has turned out to be about cultivating relationship with sangha, about interfaith dialogue, about sitting at bedsides, and about praying for and with people. In many cases, it is about performing christenings, weddings, and funerals, about being self-employed, and about public speaking. It is also about listening attentively to the stories of others, and bearing witness to their joys and sorrows. In short, being a lama in America is not primarily about being a Dharma teacher and ritual adept—at least not for many of us. It is—to a greater or lesser extent, depending on the inclination of the individual—about being a friend, a community organizer, and a spiritual caregiver, in many contexts.

Many of us who start down the path to become a Buddhist teacher are on this path long before we know it. We consider ourselves students of the Dharma, here primary to learn, to develop skills, to deepen in meditation. In my case, it was far from my mind that I would end up in the role of teacher, much less a role involving pastoral duties, what the fields of ministry and chaplaincy sometimes refer to as "spiritual care." This role snuck up on me, and I expect that is how it is for many others. Suddenly, the duties are there, and we are thrust into the role without training. Suddenly someone like Charlene is sitting right there, needing a listener and friend, requesting spiritual care. And because these needs are not likely to disappear, it is time for Buddhist communities in the West to more actively acknowledge and prepare students-in-training for the particular skills needed *in reality* for Buddhist teachers.

The term "spiritual care" is fairly new to me since working as a teaching fellow at Harvard Divinity School, but as soon as I heard it, I recognized it as what we are often doing in the role of Buddhist teacher. The term "spiritual care" captures the reality that, in order to thrive, humans need more than medical and psychological care. There is some part of us that is nourished and cared for by spiritual practice, spiritual community, and spiritual presence in our lives.

In the area of spiritual care, ministers, pastors, lamas, and roshis have much to offer, and that is quickly recognized by a sangha. Whether in Asia or here in the West, Buddhist teachers fulfill that role for many congregations. We do not inhabit a one-way context. We live in a relational context. Dharma teachers are friends and witnesses. We are often called to hear stories, comfort those in pain, and witness growth. People who come to our teachings do not just look to us for wisdom. They seek someone to reflect with them on the vicissitude of life. They look to us to be heard and seen. They look to us to be acknowledged and loved. They seek to be witnessed. To witness is very different from simply teaching. To be a witness involves being really present to others, listening to others, developing the capacity to be in skillful relationship. Even teachers who try to limit their duties to the formal Dharma hall, or to the podium, find themselves—either willingly or not—in relational contexts in which witnessing plays an important role (or should).

To witness is to be permeable, to be willing to look and listen. Over time, as I find myself in the role of witness, listening has floated to the top of my priority list of things to "learn how to do better." It was not always high on my list. In fact, it was not even on my radar. I have not always been a good listener, and I do not claim to be one now. Rather, I see listening, like Dharma learning and teaching, as a lifelong practice needing consistent cultivation.

We are sometimes led to believe that Buddhism has an answer for everything—but a willingness to listen often leads us to discover otherwise. Providing answers may not be as effective as asking questions and listening to experiences. Remarkable things happen when we leave space for an answer, or nonanswer, to emerge on its own. Formal training as a lama, or at least the training I went through to become a Tibetan Buddhist minister, has many gaps in it. One of those gaps is exploring this possibility, that our Buddhism might be made better by many acts of deep and careful listening.

Now, as I began to explore the possibility that listening can be a deep spiritual cultivation in itself for Buddhist teachers, I also began to wonder: Are there indigenous Buddhist models of listening that we can turn to for inspiration? If we turn to conventional roles within the sangha, the Buddha or the guru is cast in the role of teacher, and the congregation is generally cast in the role of the community of listeners. In seeking to recast the Dharma teacher in the role of Dharma *listener*, are there scriptures that we can rely on?

I think there may be many such scriptures. But in this chapter, I will just explore one, a source that has been useful for me as I take up listening as a practice: it is the section on "The Three Defects of Listening" in Patrul Rinpoche's *Words of My Perfect Teacher*. In this book we find an ancient way of talking about listening that can inform our modern practice of Buddhist ministry.

The three so-called "defects" of listening are (1) listening like an upside-down pot, (2) listening like a pot with holes in it, and (3) listening like a pot containing poison. In Patrul's discussion of the "three defects," the student is the listener, and three analogies are used to illustrate how this hypothetical student *should not* listen to a Buddhist teaching. One should not listen like an upside-down pot, a broken pot, or a poison-filled pot. Implicit in this presentation, however, is its positive counterpoint: how one *should* listen, what we might call today good listening practices. These good listening practices have value for a minister listening to his or her student, or chaplain listening to a patient.

ATTENTIVE LISTENING

The first of the "three defects" of listening is "listening like an upside-down pot." This concerns receptivity in the practice of listening.

Patrul starts with advice on the effective practice of listening—the intact and upturned pot—a mind directed without distraction: "listen to what is being said and do not let yourself be distracted by anything else." This is a definition of attentive listening, a practice of listening that has also been a major point of exploration in modern contexts by Buddhist caregivers, in connection with meditation practice. Attentive listening is focused enough so that outer and inner distractions fail to break the mind's tether to the verbal content heard.

To choose attention over distraction is a mental discipline, a force of intention that compels our mind to stay with what is spoken and not anticipate a future response. We might see this first quality of listening as a commitment, on the part of the spiritual caregiver, to value our student or patient's speech, coming at us in the moment, similar to the way disciples value the speech of their guru. We can respect, in a deep and sustained way, the inner wisdom of the person we are hearing, and—in the deepest sense—trust his or her Buddha nature to find its way. If we see the other in this light, it becomes easier to choose the act of listening over the outer and inner distractions that vie for our attention: thoughts, judgments, feelings, obsessions, sounds, physical sensations, and so forth.

This kind of discipline is greatly aided by curiosity. If we are genuinely curious about the internal world of another person, we will stay with the story, because we care to know the outcome. We care to know what the person cares about. If we are curious, we no longer are required to be there but rather *want* to be there, in the presence of our student's suffering or joy. This kind of curiosity can be cultivated, I believe, but it does require a certain kind of humility. We cannot maintain curiosity if we are constantly concerned about sharing who we are and what we know. Good listening begins with letting go of the need to be heard ourselves, in favor of entering the world of another for a time.

Drawing a parallel between our meditation practice and listening *while we are listening* can help with the quality of our attention. Listening can be a kind of meditation in this way. It is the quality of attention that turns the "pot" of our mind into a sound vessel, capable of retaining what is heard. And like meditation, simply paying attention makes the act of listening rewarding both for the listener and for the one listened to. To be in the vicinity of this quality of attention is to be truly heard.

Attentive listening has a potential to go beyond mental attention to paying bodily and emotional attention. Patrul Rinpoche says it like this:

> When listening to the teachings, you should be like a deer so entranced by the sound of the *vina* that it does not notice the hidden hunter shooting his poisoned arrow. Put your hands together, palm to palm, and listen, every pore on your body tingling and your eyes wet with tears, never letting any other thought get in the way.

Good listening is a somatic experience; it is an attention of the entire body and emotions. It involves our posture, emotion, and feeling. If we were to take this into the context of our work with pastoral counseling, this would mean being attentive to, even disciplined with, our posture when we listen. How are we sitting? How are we standing? Are we fidgeting? Although our palms may not be joined literally, we can assume a posture of attentive respect, as the basis for our listening practice. We can meet the story of the other with the readiness of a disciple, not with preconceived notions of what the other should or should not do, might or might not say.

Furthermore, when we listen, we can learn to be attentive to how a story we are hearing manifests *in* our body. We can turn our attention to how our body feels in the presence of a particular story. Sometimes this is more powerful than listening to our thoughts about a story. I believe that, in some cases, the body is more truthful and intuitive than the mind. For example, once in an interview, I was listening to a student talk about her relationship with her mother and noticed a visceral sense of discomfort in my body that I could not put into words. Over time, I became conscious that the discomfort came from the fact that some kind of transference was occurring. This student felt that I was her mother, and the story was a story that she anticipated would play out between us. This is the first time that I "felt" transference and was aware of it. Lorne

Ladner, a Buddhist psychotherapist who emphasizes empathy in deep listening, says, "In a sense, our bodies are like antennae or satellite dishes pointed at each other, picking up on subtle emotions that the conscious mind is not likely to see." The body is a kind of radar that is constantly listening to its environment. As caregivers, we can learn to fine-tune our radar to listen more completely to what is being communicated by our students, clients, or patients.

LISTENING WITH RETENTION

The second defect of listening is to listen like a pot with holes in it. Patrul Rinpoche describes this type of listening:

> If you listen without remembering anything that you hear or understand, you will be like a pot with a leak: however much liquid is poured into it, nothing can stay. No matter how many teachings you hear, you can never assimilate them or put them into practice.

The second defect of listening is to listen without retention and without processing what you hear. When we listen, we need to retain what we hear and knit it together with our past experiences, so that we can respond appropriately. Listening is the initial act of hearing the story. Assimilation of that story relies on memory—the retention and processing of our past experiences with relationships, with this person and with others. Based on our own past experiences, we can imagine what life must be like for them, and then we can empathize authentically. In some sources, this kind of listening process is identified as "active listening," because instead of listening passively we make an effort to process what we hear in relation to our knowledge and memories. When we listen actively, we allow ourselves to get involved. In this space, the very interaction becomes a moment of training that offers us information and understanding to be enacted in this and our future acts of caregiving. For me the process of active listening involves an attitude that I call "compassionate responsiveness." Compassionate responsiveness is not so much a set of actions or beliefs as it is an *energy* of receptivity paired with a willingness to feel with our student, to come alongside him or her in a moment of difficulty. To be compassionately responsive means to put ourselves in another's shoes for a moment, long enough to understand what an appropriate response might look like.

LISTENING WITH RIGHT MOTIVATION

The third defect is to listen like a pot containing poison. The third defect of listening pertains to what is already in our mind before we even begin to listen: our attitude, our motivation, and our emotions. When we begin to listen, we can inquire into our present state of mind and our motivation. Are we a clear vessel, or are we bringing a charge into the room? Why are we listening? What do we hope to accomplish? Regarding the attitude, Patrul specifies the wrong attitude as one that wishes to glorify oneself and vilify others, who are the source of knowledge. We can instead aim to be respectful and selfless listeners, to practice what the Quakers call "devout listening." What would it mean for a Buddhist minister or chaplain to listen devoutly? I recently volunteered at Boston Medical Center as a hospital chaplain, and often found myself sitting with drug addicts who were in the hospital to be treated for conditions brought on by their addictions to crack, meth, and alcohol: infected veins, overdoses, kidney failure. The first few times I sat with addicts, it was very difficult for me not to define them by their addictions or dismiss them as somehow less important or virtuous than the last patient I had visited. It was difficult for me to listen to the stories of craving and relapse without feeling numb. Just as Patrul Rinpoche calls for his students to notice their subtle attitudes of disrespect and vilification, we also can be attentive to how we approach and identify a person we are listening to: Are we respectful, or are we subject to unconscious prejudices? Is the person in front of me my first priority, or am I caught up with self-concern? To what degree is my practice of listening colored by my own hopes and fears?

I have found it helpful to think of listening as can an act of generosity, of *dana*, in which attention is offered to another. Just as with the practice of dana, the fewer expectations we have when giving our attention, the greater the merits. I find it helpful to recall the concept of being free of the so-called three spheres: free of a listener, of someone listened to, and of the act of listening. In this way, we can begin to imagine a listening that is nondual. We cultivate a generous, open, and free state of being, of which the practice of attentive listening is not the cause, but rather is a natural outcome.

To notice motivation means that we must train to simultaneously listen to ourselves and to the other. Listening to oneself means to notice what is in the mind even before we begin to listen. Are we starting out "mixed with poison"? If so, it is possible the quality of our presence may be diminished by our inner desires, turmoil, aggressions, and confusion. So it is important that we look into our mind, if we are able, before we listen, because in the act of pastoral care we are responsible for self-regulation of our emotional state. No one is going to regulate that for us.

I remember a moment when I was sitting with a relative who was facing the early onset of dementia. He had been a professor, erudite and intelligent, and a gem of a person. I had not seen him in years, so my shock was considerable when I reunited with him to see a man diminished, slow and confused, having difficulty recollecting where we had last met, my name, and even memories shared recently. I found myself flooded with both love and sorrow, my heart sinking. In such moments, it is possible to continue to consider the needs of the person near us, and learn to set aside the feelings we are having in order to sustain a compassionate presence. My mentor and coeditor of this volume calls this "flagging," an ability to notice strong emotions coming up and "flag" them to address and process later. It seems important that we not ignore what comes up, without necessarily allowing what comes up to interrupt the flow of our presence.

Back in the interview room, Charlene asks me, "Will you hold my hands? Last time, before I left, you held my hands and it made me feel human." I take her hands in mine and we look at each other. She is smiling a big, sunny smile. It is not the smile of a dying person—it is the smile of life, the smile of someone savoring every moment as if it were her last. Because it might be. The room has a little Zen rock fountain in it. The fountain trickles. The air conditioner whirrs. I have spent a good deal more time in silence than in speech during the fifteen minutes of our interview. I have listened, with the occasional comment. Then Charlene squeezes my hands, lets go, still smiling wide. "I know what to do now," she says. "My brother has done terrible things. I cannot change that. But I can notice how I feel and work with that. I want to work myself to forgiveness before I die, but not for him. For me. That's my spiritual practice." She rises. The interview is over.

I leave interviews like this one in awe. I feel moved by the power of the human spirit to find its own way. I feel moved by the humanity and courage of the human heart. I am energized by Charlene's liveliness even as she is facing the sunset of her life. In this brief exchange, she has taught me what it means to listen to oneself and find the root of forgiveness.

It seems to me most of us first came to Buddhism with the fresh mind of people like Charlene, and with very basic needs. We did not initially come to Buddhism to learn rituals. We did not come seeking to chant long liturgies. More likely, like Charlene, we came to Buddhism seeking solace and freedom from our particular sufferings. And as we sought out freedom, we found ourselves in spiritual relationship, wishing to be heard, seen, and understood by our teachers and peers in a spiritual community. We longed to be heard and seen because we intuitively know that is the first step in a healing relationship. Thus we began the process of understanding the nature of our suffering, learning to relax deeply, and finding a ground on which to accept ourselves. Being heard is a critical step in the process of finding freedom. Being heard allows us to find our own avenue out of suffering and into the light. It helps us find self-acceptance. It helps us find solutions to our particular problems through our own experience. And down the line, if we are lucky enough to become listeners, we are blessed by the practice of witnessing, and sometimes we find the information we need to act skillfully.

My personal aspiration is that the younger generation of Buddhist teachers will deeply consider the role of listening in their ministry. If that happens, we may spawn a generation of Dharma listeners, who will do some teaching as well. On the contrary, if we do not cultivate good listening skills, we risk being isolated in our own world of "rightness" and undoing all the good our sharing of the Dharma has spread in the world. Listening, I believe, is one of the unsung gems of the Buddhist path that needs to be cultivated by every Buddhist leader as a conscious practice and uplifted as an expression of effective bodhisattva activity in the world.

Wrong Speech:

KNOWING WHEN IT'S BEST TO LIE

Lin Jensen

THE CALL CAME from Enloe Hospital at 3:30 on a fall afternoon. A Japanese Buddhist woman, Chinatsu, was dying. I would find her, I was told, in Room 302 of Enloe's oncology ward. Her family had gathered and had asked for me to come. I'd been the hospital's designated Buddhist spiritual caregiver for several years at the time, but this was a first, being told to hurry if I wanted to see the patient alive.

At the hospital, I took the elevator to the third floor only to discover that the patient had died a few moments earlier. The family, a ward nurse informed me, was waiting for me. Down the hall, twenty or more family members and friends of apparent Japanese descent were packed into a small waiting area. Among them was a young man in a suit and tie who greeted me with a bow and held open the door to a room where another dozen or more family members were gathered. When everyone from the waiting area had squeezed in behind me, we were all pressed tightly round the dead woman's bed.

Lin Jensen is Buddhist spiritual caregiver to Enloe Hospital and founder and teacher of the Chico Zen Sangha in Chico, California, where he writes and works on behalf of nonviolence and in defense of the earth. Four of Lin's books—*Bad Dog!*, *Pavement*, *Together Under One Roof*, and *Deep Down Things*—were each selected for the *Best Buddhist Writing* series.

A child of the Great Depression and WWII, Lin has seen the best and the worst that life offers. He writes with the wonder of how love and beauty take root in even the most barren places. His consolation is that no matter how difficult life can be, its sweetness is always with us.

The young man who'd first greeted me in the waiting area and who seemed to have taken me under his guidance was now at my side and whispered to me that most of the family were Shin Buddhists. I took it that he was suggesting how I ought to proceed. But I'm a Zen Buddhist and have scant familiarity with the Pure Land schools. I suppose that my first instance of wrong speech that afternoon was a lie of omission in that I didn't admit this rather significant shortcoming. Instead I was considering what would be best for me to do under the circumstances. But before I say anything more about what I did next, I need to tell you that, when it comes to lying, I'm not at all sure that I know when it's best to lie or even whether or not it's ever best to lie. Nonetheless, I put on my *rakasu*, clasped the palms of my hands together, and set out to make the best I could of what little I knew of Shin Buddhist ceremonial practices.

Seeing this, everyone grew still. An air of expectation and a hushed silence settled over the room. Less than an arm's length from me lay Chinatsu. Her eyes had been drawn closed and, though ravaged by the cancer that had killed her, I saw that she was quite beautiful, a woman in her late forties or early fifties judging by appearance. Having served for several years as senior Buddhist chaplain at High Desert State Prison in California where most of my students were Pure Land Buddhists, I did in fact know a little of Shin Buddhist practices. And so with my young advisor still at my side, I prayed that Amida Butsu, from his Western Paradise of Ultimate Bliss, would take Chinatsu into his care, that she too might reside in the Pure Land.

You should understand that I don't have any belief in a "pure land." I don't have a belief of that sort in anything. Zen is not a repository of belief, and the only pure land I know of is the dirt under my feet. And so my prayer for Chinatsu's deliverance was I suppose a great falsehood, but my intention in offering it was not necessarily so. If I was doing this simply to save face and not appear unqualified, then the patched together prayer was nothing other than falsehood of a self-serving sort. But if I was doing it because thirty or forty grieving family and friends were depending on me to enact an essential cultural tradition and because, like it or not, I was all they had at this hospital for a spiritual caregiver, then I'm not certain what sort of falsehood I was engaged in. But even as I went on, the question of motivation weighed on me, I looked at the faces gathered round the bed where Chinatsu lay dead, and I wasn't sure whether I was lying for their sake or for my own. I wasn't sure I wasn't lying to myself. But for all my uncertainty, I said some other prayers more or less of my own invention, and everyone seemed satisfied with how things were going.

I'd learned at one time or another that Japanese Shin Buddhism teaches that through the power of Amida's Vow, the recitation of Amida's name is sufficient for deliverance to the Pure Land, a grace bestowed on one who sincerely chants the name of Amida Butsu. At the prison, I'd run into some stiff resistance among the Shin Buddhists when I tried to teach them meditation, which they thought useless because for them salvific power lay solely in the recitation of Amida's name. Since Chinatsu could no longer chant on her own behalf, I thought maybe we'd all feel better if we chanted for her to help her on her way to the Pure Land. And so I began chanting "Namu Amida Butsu." My advisor seemed especially pleased with this and took over leading the chant with the whole room joining in with him. I chanted along too until as if by a signal they all quit at once. In the absence of sharing any belief in what I was chanting, I genuinely wished that everyone's hopes for Chinatsu's deliverance to the Pure Land would somehow be realized for them. For the moment I felt less false in what I was doing.

Following the chant, the room was silent once more. I asked then if anyone had anything they'd like to say to Chinatsu, and a few did, sometimes speaking in Japanese and then as a courtesy to me in English as well. Then a woman wearing a soft blue cap worked her way toward me from the rear of the group until she stood across from me on the opposite side of the bed. She said, "I think Chinatsu would like you to say something about God." A few others in the room murmured assent. It was only then that I saw—strung from Chinatsu's neck and partially hidden in the gown at her throat—a tiny cross. The woman that lay dead before me was not a Pure Land Buddhist. She was a Christian!

It was an absurd moment. I could only surmise that the Shin Buddhist practitioners in the room preferred that she be sent to the Pure Land rather than to a Christian heaven. As things stood, I might just as well have conducted a Zen ceremony. But now, if they wanted me to say something about God, that was something I could manage: fourteen years of childhood attendance at Trinity Episcopal Church in Orange, California, had given me enough Christian liturgy to get by on. After all, I'd just done a Pure Land ceremony about which I knew nearly nothing. At this point the whole event seemed to have taken on a trajectory of its own, of which I was no longer the pilot but just another passenger in a journey of unknown destination.

Inwardly, I asked that I not be false to myself; outwardly I went on with some prayers and other liturgy of the sort Reverend Hailwood might have recited in the sanctuary of the church so many years ago. I spoke the words of the Lord's Prayer, lines from the Twenty-Third Psalm, and the Apostle's Creed with its belief in a god as the maker of heaven and earth, the virgin birth of a god's son, the resurrection of the body, and the life everlasting, not a word of which I could any longer make myself believe. This was the last and perhaps most blatant lie of that afternoon in Room 302. But despite my nonbelief, the familiar words rolled out of me over Chinatsu and gathered about us in the room like a rising mist from ancient seas of past beliefs. I couldn't keep my eyes dry.

In the end, both the Pure Land Buddhists and the Christians seemed content with what had been done. They wouldn't let me go until they'd taken up a collection as an offering for my services. I left the hospital with a pocket stuffed with cash and an unresolved ambiguity regarding what I'd done. Or not done.

At one point in the Buddha's teaching on abstaining from false speech, he describes a person who speaks truth, saying, "He never knowingly speaks a lie, either for the sake of his own advantage, or for the sake of another person's advantage, or for the sake of any advantage whatsoever." The situation in Room 302 was one wherein a temptation to resort to falsehood for the sake of my advantage or for the advantage of those gathered in the room was virtually unavoidable. But is advantage what's really at stake when a lie is told out of concern to spare another's feelings or to soften a difficult time for someone? If someone benefits from a lie, it seems to me that the intention behind the lie and the nature of the benefit accrued needs to be weighed.

The Buddha's teaching of right speech is offered in the light of his teaching on the nature of right intention, a step in the Eightfold Path that I draw upon for guidance as much as upon anything traditional Dharma has given me. The Buddha taught that our choices of speech and action should be consonant with an intention of selflessness, kindness, and harmlessness. If I'm torn between truth and falsehood, I have to ask myself if the choice taken is self-serving or selfless, harsh or kind, harmful or harmless. Only then can I know what's best to do. Surely the ancient Buddhist precept of "Do not lie" is to be honored in the *spirit* of truth with an eye toward probable consequence. Right speech isn't a matter of legalized ethics. The mere fact of a lie is a quality unknown without consulting the heart's intent.

Zen concurs in seeking the heart's consent, and it does so because it's the circumstance of the given moment rather than any generalized rule—regardless of how applicable the rule might seem to be—that ultimately determines what needs to be done. George Orwell, in his classic essay "Politics and the English Language," lays down six rules of good writing having to do with the use of metaphor, brevity of expression, passive and active constructions, and so forth, but his sixth rule is "Break any of these rules sooner than say anything outright barbarous." Orwell speaks pure Zen when he frees the writer's pen from compliance with any preconceived rule. You can neither write nor live by rules.

When it comes to right speech with its injunction forbidding lying, what's needed is an Orwellian rule of exclusion, a rule that frees the heart to determine when it might be best to lie, perhaps something like "tell any lie rather than speak some pointlessly harsh truth." Nothing in a Buddhist rulebook will tell you when and how to do this, which is perhaps why Zen insists that you shoulder the responsibility on your own. That being so, I'm asked to feel my way into the moment and determine on the basis of that very moment what's best said or not said.

But it's essential that I be skeptical of my own advice to "feel my way." There are times when I choose not to tell the truth, judging that out of consideration for a fellow being it's best not to do so. But am I reading the circumstance rightly and am I truly acting out of selfless consideration? Am I assuming too much in supposing that I know what's best for another to be told? Am I being merely manipulative, imagining myself capable of skillful means that I may in fact lack? I ask these questions of myself precisely because of my very real conviction that, in the end, I have no alternative but to find my own way in this matter, consulting heart and intuition to determine when it's best to lie or not lie.

Yet however intuitive and sensitive to circumstance I imagine my feelings to be, they must be tempered by doubt and reasoned self-editing. Otherwise I can end up deceiving myself, acting upon self-interest while convincing myself otherwise. It's not enough to simply "feel" that it's best to withhold truth: the strongest and most convincing of feelings often spring from the vanity and fear that fuels attachment. The ego-self acts in its own defense, and when any of us abridges the precept regarding falsehood, we need to be searchingly honest about why we're doing so.

One of the Buddhist inmates I'm teaching at High Desert State Prison wrote me recently about "white lies." He'd been studying and practicing the Buddha's teachings of right speech, and he wondered if he was breaking the precept when an inmate read him a poem recently and asked him how he liked it. My student didn't like it much at all, thinking it too moralistic and obvious. But his fellow prisoner had been working on it for weeks, and so he told him what he wanted to hear, praising the poem's wholesome message and ignoring its obvious lack of performance as poetry. He wrote me because he was troubled by the lie he'd told.

"Have I done something wrong?" he asked.

What was I to tell him? None of us ever knows for certain whether what we've done is right or wrong and what the consequences of our actions will be. Very few choices you and I make are entirely wrong or right; most are some of both. Yet every choice we make, large or small, will have its corresponding consequence. The Buddha's teaching of dependent coarising states the certainty of consequence in the simplest terms: "This arising, that arises. This arising not, that arises not. This becoming, that becomes. This becoming not, that becomes not." Everything any one of us thinks, says, or does constitutes an arising, and it is assured that something will come of it.

And this is true of the inmate's little white lie as well. The best he and I can count on is a greater or lesser degree of probability that one consequence rather than another is likely to result. It's a sobering responsibility and one I weighed as carefully as I could before assuring my inmate student that he'd not done anything wrong. "You've acted within the spirit of not lying," I told him. "You were right to act on the truth of your heart."

This sort of lie gets told all the time.

Someone on the morning walk in the park greets you saying, "Great morning for a walk, isn't it?" and you reply, "Yes, great morning," though you're feeling cranky and out of sorts and the morning seems anything to you but great. I suppose you could tell this greeter how you really feel, but I've always felt it best not to dump my personal complaints on others without good reason.

Once my mother came home with a new hat. My mother was a beautiful woman and the hat looked horrid on her. She'd bought the hat for a luncheon she was having with some lady friends on the very day of her purchase. The first I saw of the hat was when she was at the door on her way to the luncheon and, obviously pleased with her purchase, she asked, "How do you like my new hat?" It looked awful on her, but I said, "You look great, Mom." I lied. I'd lie again under the same circumstances. What *was* the truth at that juncture? What about the truth of simple affection for my mother and concern that she have a good time at her luncheon? My guess is that her lady friends didn't think the hat flattering to Mother's appearance either, but according to Mother she got compliments on how good it looked on her. The downside of this of course was that Mother, being convinced that the hat was a winner, began wearing the hat everywhere she went. I was relieved when she found another that actually did look good on her.

It's apparent that this matter of truth and falsehood isn't as simple as lie or don't lie. While there have been times when I've lied and deeply regretted it, there have also been times when I've just as deeply regretted having told the truth.

I told just such a truth when I was sixteen, a sophomore in high school. Now sixty-three years later I still regret it. The event has a history that helps explain the nature of the truth I told and the forces that led up to it. My father, a Danish immigrant, raised turkeys for a living. At twenty-seven years of age, he arrived in Orange, California, where he met my mother and they were married before her eighteenth birthday. They'd married on the eve of the Great Depression, and so began the long struggle to make a living and get the farm to pay off. Perhaps these very real hardships contributed to my father's sternness, a man who would never allow my brother Rowland and I to talk back or cross him in any way. And when we did, he'd strip us and beat us with a lath stick he kept for such occasions.

He also put Rowland and me to work on the farm when we were still in elementary school, and so I spent all my childhood spare time working in the fields along with the few farm hands Father hired over the years. Pete Haney, Bob Townsley, and Fay Elam were part of the exodus from Oklahoma and Arkansas to California. Hector was a poor immigrant from Belgium. Al Messeral, the only locally born farm hand, had come to Father during the Depression seeking whatever employment he could get. These five were my closest companions. Since we were all subject to my father's will, I identified with them as one of the underdogs.

When I was sixteen, Father got a letter from Ikle Pedersen, a young countryman in Denmark, interested in modern methods of turkey production. He wanted to know if he could he come to California and study under Father's guidance. He'd like to work in the fields, he wrote, so as to get a firsthand feel of turkey farming. And so he came and went to work, though it was noticeable that he was spared any crawling around on his knees in the nest houses to gather eggs or any raking or shoveling of turkey manure. This irritated the rest of us, but worse was Ikle's air of arrogance and superiority around the other hands who knew that he was a guest in the house and ate at Father's table where none of them had ever been invited. Once when we were all at the barn, Ikle asked the others what they were being paid. It's not the sort of question one asks, and I was surprised when Pete spoke up and told him what he was earning and the others followed suit. "Really!" Ikle exclaimed, and then told them his own salary, which was half again more than any of the others were being paid and far more than the small hourly wage Father paid me.

Shortly after that disclosure, Father and I by chance encountered each other one early morning in the hallway between his bedroom and the bathroom. I was in work boots and jeans on my way to work and Father was in pajamas and slippers and probably on his way to pee. The hallway was narrow and I didn't step aside, which left us facing each other. Neither of us could move unless the other gave way. Father looked puzzled. "The men are angry about the wage you're paying Ikle," I said. Father looked surprised that I knew what Ikle was earning. "He's only here for a few months," Father said. I'd already gone further toward contention with my father than ever before, and I could feel my heart beating in my temples. And then I told him the truth. "The point is Ikle Pederson's not just another okie," I said. "He's a Danish countryman. You're ashamed to pay Ikle what you've been paying Al and Pete and Bob and Fay and Hector all these years."

For just a moment his face turned stern, and he tried to rally to his own defense. But then he caved in. I'd defeated him with the truth. I'd waited in ambush and gunned him down. But didn't he deserve it? I was right, wasn't I? Had I spoken anything but the truth? I learned that morning that it doesn't help much to be right, the consequence of which played itself out in the pain and humiliation of a man cornered in the hallway in his pajamas.

Truth is a beautiful thing—the *only* thing that liberates us from the falsehoods ego fabricates in service of its own cause. One of the ancient and original precepts of the Buddhist path is the vow to tell the truth and not lie. There are good reasons for this, but the real truth is that of the inborn buddha, the one who transcends all rules and who invariably speaks and acts with a wisdom tempered by kindness.

Every day.

Report from the Field:

BEING AN AMERICAN ZEN BUDDHIST MINISTER

Steve Kanji Ruhl

MERICAN ZEN BUDDHIST ministry is an audacious and unprecedented experiment.

How does a Zen Buddhist minister devise a workable practice of service and care? What kinds of challenges confront a Zen minister, and what kind of rewards might sustain him or her? How does personal Dharma practice enhance ministry and allow it to flourish?

As the first ordained "Zen House" minister in the Zen Peacemakers Order, an international socially engaged Buddhist order founded by Roshi Bernie Glassman and based in Montague, Massachusetts, these questions have functioned as my koans of daily life. They followed me when I founded a community ministry of pastoral care and counseling in struggling, hard-pressed villages in the central Appalachian Mountains of Pennsylvania, and currently confront me, as I explore an ordained

Rev. Steve Kanji Ruhl is an ordained Zen Buddhist minister in the Zen Peacemakers Order, a Dharma holder in Green River Zen Center, Greenfield, Massachusetts, and former director of Appalachian Zen House, in the mountains of rural Pennsylvania. His ministry focuses on pastoral care and counseling in a Buddhist context, feeding underserved people, and working on environmental issues through interfaith alliances. He received his BA in religious studies from Pennsylvania State University and his master of divinity degree from Harvard Divinity School. He is also a writer and former journalist and editor whose work has appeared in *The Boston Globe*, *Massachusetts Review*, *Santa Fe Reporter*, and elsewhere, and who has been awarded a nonfiction writing fellowship from the Pennsylvania Council on the Arts. A poet as well, he has been awarded a Massachusetts Artists Fellowship in poetry, and his poems have been published in numerous literary magazines nationwide.

ministry suitable for a small-town soup kitchen and zendo in western Massachusetts.

When I landed at Harvard Divinity School in 2005, with a degree in religious studies, I became one of a tiny cohort of Buddhist students in the master of divinity program, which functioned primarily as the school's track for ministry training. While I was earnestly committed to Zen practice, I was also called to a ministry based on the traditional Protestant Christian model I knew from my childhood—in which a minister cares for a congregation, offers pastoral counseling, provides service to his or her community, and delivers sermons from a pulpit. I felt challenged in trying to combine the two vocations.

If I mentioned to my peers that I might want to become a "Zen Buddhist minister," the term baffled them. With some reluctance I decided that I might aspire to become an interfaith chaplain instead, and I fantasized that perhaps I could serve on a college campus following my graduation. Soon after my arrival at the Divinity School, however, watching my mostly Protestant Christian classmates prepare for their own Baptist or Methodist, Presbyterian, or United Church of Christ or Unitarian Universalist ministries, I began to wonder: why can't I, as a Zen Buddhist, go through a similar training? Why can't I give sermons and offer pastoral care and counseling and serve a congregation, but in a Zen context of Dharma talks and dokusan interviews and a sangha?

As I see it now—living it daily, improvising it and field-testing it—Zen ministry offers a vital complement to Zen Buddhist priesthood and chaplaincy. Priests and chaplains in America who follow the Zen Buddhist Way fulfill essential roles. Zen priests perform liturgies. They lead rituals. They serve temple functions. Many, if authorized, provide Dharma instruction and meditation and present talks and train students. Zen chaplains also fulfill commendable and necessary roles. They sit at bedsides of dying patients in hospices, or share the Dharma with inmates in prison cellblocks, or offer comfort to bedridden patients in hospitals and solace to loved ones. They also may conduct weddings and funerals and rites of passage. (Some American Zen Buddhist priests, of course, perform such chaplaincy functions as well, volunteering to serve in hospices or prisons or hospitals, and conducting ceremonies for sangha members.)

As a Zen House minister in the Peacemaker Order, I have found myself acting in similar roles, and more. Some of my work I consider, essentially, "priestly." For example, on Sunday mornings or Tuesday evenings in our Green River Zen Center, located in Greenfield, Massachusetts, I might offer a *teisho*, similar to what Christians would call a sermon, under supervision of my Zen teacher, Roshi Eve Myonen Marko. I sometimes serve as *jikido*, or zendo monitor, opening an altar and lighting a candle and incense as I bow, then leading a chant of the Heart Sutra. As a teacher of Zen precepts in the zendo, I sometimes help teach a class to sangha members, discussing guidelines for ethical behavior in our daily lives. I sometimes deliver talks for "Renewal of Vows" ceremonies.

I recently conducted an evening memorial service for the deceased father of one of our sangha members, in which I led a ritual procession and guided a service of candlelit chants, music, and reminiscence. In my ministry I also complement these "priestly" temple functions with what I consider "chaplaincy" functions; for instance, I regularly visit an inmate at the county jail in Northampton to chat about his week, share personal experiences in anger management, and discuss his Zen meditation practice. I also assist with a soup kitchen "cafe" that serves meals to needy people in our area.

Yet while I sometimes act in roles familiar to a Zen priest or Zen chaplain, my personal calling as a Zen minister leads me to emphasize pastoral care and counseling. As a Zen minister, I am interested in being available to a wide community of people. The Zen ministry I find myself creating is the ministry of a listening heart. My ministry serves the elderly man in chronic, debilitating pain, hunched on the couch inside his trailer while telling me he contemplates suicide; a woman despairing in her feckless search for a job as a math teacher; a young Hispanic man struggling to avoid homelessness and the lure of reentry into a life of street gangs and random violence; a woman distraught over the recent death of her fiancé who languished for months in prison, his body destroyed by cancer; a man grappling with the unpredictable scourges of multiple sclerosis; a woman tearfully facing the crumbling of her marriage. Ordinary people, in other words, dealing with the challenges of ordinary lives—lives that have come abruptly to seem bewildering and overwhelmingly fraught with challenges. These people seek a minister as their first point of contact, someone who can listen attentively and respond with compassion.

When I begin a session of pastoral counseling, I recall to myself that the person in front of me has the inner ability and wisdom to work with their problems. Sometimes we all have confusion in our minds, and it can help to talk to someone who will deeply listen, who also offers some guidance to finding that inner wisdom.

This reflects a process that I devised in "Pastoral Care and Counseling" classes facilitated by Cheryl Giles at Harvard, as I tried to adapt standard ministerial techniques of counseling to Zen Buddhist principles. Those principles include spacious silence, mindful listening, and a conviction that each of us—beneath our perplexity and hurt and resentment—harbors original Buddha nature and the sagacity of pure mind. This method of pastoral counseling also implies the truth of a common Zen maxim: that the teacher has nothing to "give" the student. The student already possesses the answer; the teacher merely strives to help the student realize it. Similarly, as a Zen minister engaged in pastoral counseling I have nothing to "give" the other person. At best I assist in guiding the person to his or her own uniquely marvelous understanding and solutions.

In practice this means that I tend to leave open the space of silence, allowing the other person to grope his or her way through a process of assaying possibilities, backtracking and moving forward again while I offer as much presence and focused listening as I am able. I also may pose clarifying questions. If appropriate, I sometimes share observations or point out themes or linkages between statements the person makes. It becomes a mutual exploration.

When I counsel, I often stay quiet in the opening of the pastoral counseling session in order to prevent foreclosing on the other person. My intent is to guard against cutting the flow of speech by interposing my own thoughts or interpretations. My method is to listen intently to allow the person boundless freedom in discovering his or her own personal realization. As a Zen minister I employ the Zen Peacemakers' Three Tenets. These tenets consist of: *Not-Knowing*; that is, I try to enter each counseling situation freshly, without preconceptions or prejudices. *Bearing Witness*; that is, I try not to separate from any person or from anything arising in the instant. *Loving Action*; manifesting compassion that naturally and spontaneously opens from the act of bearing witness.

I also participate in each pastoral counseling session by approaching it as a "plunge." In Zen Peacemakers' parlance, a *plunge* is an experience—such as undertaking to live as a homeless person in the gritty hardship of a city for several days during a Zen Peacemakers "street retreat"; or directly encountering the barbed-wire death camps of Auschwitz and Birkenau during a Zen Peacemakers "Bearing Witness Retreat"; or engaging a Zen koan—that plummets a person into not-knowing. Each pastoral counseling session does this for me.

I never know what to expect. When a session begins, I never can anticipate what a person might present. A woman seated in a chair across from me shares our silence for a few moments, gazes at me, then jolts me by saying, "I feel so frightened, I feel so afraid that I might do something to harm myself. How do I open my heart? How do I conquer my fear? How do I feel less isolated?" and I experience the whoosh of the plunge. With that initial jolt I enter unknown territory. The work begins.

My Zen teacher, Roshi Eve, discusses with me koans, some of the teaching stories of Zen, when we meet for dokusan, probing each of these classic riddles within the context of ministry practice. In that context, we have talked about the tension in pastoral counseling of "boundaries and no boundaries." As a senior Zen student in training, in certain ways I must *forego* certain types of boundaries, become one with the suffering in front of me. And also, conducting pastoral counseling as a Zen Buddhist minister I must *keep* boundaries—careful to note issues of transference and countertransference, as any scrupulous professional counselor must—while at the same time bearing witness completely to a person's anguish, letting go of dualistic separation of "self" and "other" and in effect "identifying with the client's pain." It provides a dynamic challenge.

A Zen minister, however, will use a pastoral care and counseling session to help a person, in a process combining silence with guided inquiry, to see for himself or herself precisely where the stuck place is manifesting. The minister then assists that person in discovering his or her own resource of innate wisdom—all of this in order to aid in facilitating development of a healthier *self*.

In this and other ways, my Zen practice refreshes and bolsters my Zen ministry. Investigating koans enriches my understanding of pastoral care, while sitting zazen helps me to foster the spaciousness of mind and the effortless familiarity with silence so necessary for pastoral counseling. It also helps me continue developing the ability to jettison preconceived ideas and to remain present with moment-by-moment developments in my immediate environment. The ability to let go into not-knowing, and to remain present through bearing witness, are critical to my providing pastoral care.

In April 2011, after three years of serving in lay ministry, I became the first formally ordained Zen House minister in the Zen Peacemakers. This has strengthened my belief in the importance of ordination, and my respect for authentic ordination paths. Zen Peacemakers maintain rigorous standards for ordaining as a Zen House minister. To meet those standards I have needed to: obtain a master of divinity degree; complete the intensive five-month Zen Peacemakers Seminary in Socially Engaged Buddhism; work for a year in a Zen House offering service to people in need; train and become empowered as a preceptor in Green River Zen Center; learn our "Gate of Sweet Nectar" liturgy and other ritual formulations ranging from the Heart Sutra to funeral services; and train to become a senior in the zendo, authorized to give Dharma talks under the supervision of the roshi.

Formal ordination is important for Zen ministers to overcome two disadvantages that can present themselves when we are not ordained. First, without ordination, we are not recognized by other religious traditions as authentic ministers. Second, lack of ordination prevents greater access to institutions such as prisons and hospitals. For example, when I tried to contact prison officials to advocate for a dying prisoner or to help an inmate in his attempts to move from maximum to minimum security, it would have helped enormously, as a practical matter, if I had already received ordination and thus could have introduced myself as "Reverend Ruhl." The title of "reverend" carries power in American society and allows a minister to assist those in need by striding through institutional doors that otherwise remain barred.

For these reasons I strongly endorse legitimate ordination for Zen Buddhist ministers, and I look forward to seeing many other men and women accept this vocation. Yet challenges remain for many of us.

The first of these challenges is lack of personal support. Serving as an

American Zen Buddhist minister often requires going solo if only because the job category remains so small and we are so spread out. Once our training ends, the onus is on us to find mentors for ongoing professional consultation or feedback, and the need for such support is critical. Christian clergy have long enjoyed formal support from their superiors in the clerical hierarchy, from their congregations, from deacons and from other officers of the church. Without such support, and without appropriate boundaries established by the minister him or herself, the work can become acutely demanding, lonely, and, perhaps for some, unsustainable. Exacerbating the lack of support is lack of salary. It remains difficult for an ordained Zen minister to earn a livelihood. According to a recent issue of *U.S. News and World Report*, the average annual salary for an ordained Christian minister in America is $52,000. This hardly ranks as a princely sum, yet it can be sufficient to allow a modestly comfortable family life and repayment of school loans. The month that I graduated from Harvard I visited a Baptist classmate who had graduated the year before; in her freshly appointed ministry she led her own large, thriving church north of Boston and her congregants rewarded her with a decent income. The Zen Buddhist community does not have these kinds of salary systems in place. This calls into question how we, as Zen Buddhists, will compensate our ministers for services rendered.

I, for example, receive no money at all for performing my ministry vocation. Precisely because I consider it a vocation—a calling, in the true sense, and a pressing mission that I feel impelled by moral and spiritual necessity to honor—and because I harbor few material needs, I feel willing to proffer ministry without paychecks. Yet I do need to repay large school loans. Until recently I supported my ministry by working as executive director for Zen Peacemakers, earning a less-than-modest salary, plus minimal room and board in an old communal farmhouse. At the time of this writing, however, I am unemployed due to layoffs in the organization caused by economic recession and financial downturns. My school loans remain in temporary forbearance due to economic hardship. In order to meet my financial obligations I must find a way to remedy this. Other people who may wish to ordain as Zen ministers should be aware of the potential financial challenges.

Another challenge for me as a Zen minister is that of trying to meet non-Buddhist members in our local community where they are, people broken and seeking wholeness. A person distraught from the loss of a teenage daughter in a car crash may plead in wild, keening grief, "Tell me where my daughter is. I need to know. Please." A Christian minister can respond by offering solace, saying, "Your daughter is with the Lord Jesus, who has called her home to be with Him. Be assured that someday you will see her again in heaven." As a Zen minister I do not feel I can even answer her question, but I can offer my presence. I can sit with her in her grief. Each moment I can be fully present with her deep pain and her deep love. But our beliefs are different, and being a Zen minister entails navigating these differences.

Yet I believe that the role of the American Zen Buddhist minister is vitally important and offers extraordinary promise. The minister serves a broad range of people directly and unstintingly in the ordinary sufferings and emergencies of their daily lives, where they need it most. The Zen minister's job offers, despite the challenges, profound rewards. These rewards include the satisfaction of helping others, of using all of one's spirit and mind and heart in that service and bringing one's practice into the world. As an American Zen minister I feel delighted and fortunate to live as part of this historic adventure.

Buddha, Dharma, and Community Ministry in the City

Rebecca O. Johnson

NEWCOMERS attending the monthly practice session of the Boston People of Color Buddhist Meditation Group for the first time frequently describe the attraction to the practice in familiar, ordinary terms—"I'm anxious." "I need some peace." "My blood pressure is so high and I can't sleep at night." "My job is driving me crazy." "I feel so alone." They hope meditation will lift them out of themselves, to a place of bliss, calm, and happiness. They may not have found what they need in the religious practices of their youth, or increasingly, they grew up without any home religion. As we get to know each other, sangha members reveal deeper levels of pain, including what feels like the unrelenting burdens of racism, whether it manifests as isolation in overwhelmingly white academic settings, the frustration of social change workers, or the struggle to make ends meet in poor urban neighborhoods.

Are we looking in the right place? Are the various Western interpretations of Buddhism the right place for people of color, especially people of

Rebecca O. Johnson, MSCED, MFA, is a cofounder and core group member of Boston People of Color Buddhist Meditation Group. Rebecca began practicing meditation in the early 1990s. She continues to practice in the Theravadan tradition. She has worked for almost forty years as a community organizer, popular educator, and writer. These experiences inform her organizational development practice with grassroots social and environmental justice organizations. Rebecca is also graduate faculty with the Health Advocacy Program of Sarah Lawrence College. Her nonfiction has appeared in *Obit Magazine*, *Race-Talk*, *Callaloo*, *Women's Review of Books*, and *Sojourner: The Women's Forum*. Her meditation on the death of her father, *Love's Bright Fire*, received recognition from the Rubin Museum as a response to the exhibit *Remember You Will Die: Death Across Cultures*. Rebecca lives and writes in Akron, Ohio.

African descent, to find the practices that will provide a path to liberation, liberation from internal oppression and reactivity to external oppression? I have come to understand the possibilities for building community that offers healing and addresses injustice through the various practices that are part of our Buddhist tradition.

My teacher, Kamala Masters of the Vipassana Metta Foundation, has insisted on the centrality of learning a set of practices that lead to the development of qualities known as the *brahma viharas*, or the sublime abidings. The four brahma viharas are loving-kindness, compassion, sympathetic joy, and equanimity. Described by the Buddha as both antidotes to fear and a tool for developing concentration, the most well known of the brahma viharas is metta, or loving-kindness.

The practice involves visualizing beings with whom you want to share your loving friendship, beginning with yourself, then a benefactor—that is, someone who has taught you or made your life possible, such as a parent, a teacher, an important relation—moving on to a dear friend, a neutral person, and finally ending with a difficult person, then offering each of them safety, peace, wellness in body and mind, and ease of well-being. Eventually you are offering metta to all beings in all conditions everywhere. It took me a while to understand why these qualities are important. I, perhaps like most other yogis, came to practice seeking to be awake, to end this wheel of suffering through the attainment of enlightenment. Metta seemed a distraction until I realized how difficult it was to offer metta to myself in a nonjudgmental, open, and, well, loving way. Some of the difficulties that plagued my sitting practice—fear, self-judgment, anger—could only be addressed by letting Rebecca be Rebecca, that is the unconditional acceptance of myself. I learned one couldn't let go of a self that one does not love.

I also learned that one couldn't be awake if one's heart/mind didn't make room for as many beings as could fit. While metta is helping build concentration it is providing that other tangible benefit, the visualizing and holding oneself and an increasing array of others as worthy of love and concern. The contemplations that shape the other brahma viharas are similar. Let me suggest other benefits of these contemplations that take us beyond the personal to our experiences as people of color.

As both our mindfulness and metta practice grow, we begin sorting through attachments, aversions, and judgments, slowly arriving at a fundamental experience of our own goodness. That expands out to the world infusing life, both on and off the cushion. We begin to experience the well-loved community right where we live, in our town, neighborhood, and workplace. Our identification with particular forms soften and dissolve, allowing heartfelt love and concern for the well-being of those we encounter in our daily activities. Eventually (I have been told) we experience ourselves as loved well enough to allow the attachment to self to disappear, wearing away the most nuanced defensive barriers that seem to necessitate those attachments.

As our practice progresses we become able to face that which oppresses us—internally and externally—with less fear. For people of color this is especially important. It is an increasingly accepted notion that the unexamined racism of our society regularly exposes us to little incidents that are called microaggressions. These exposures are debilitating because they are so confusing. One can feel, and be led to believe, these experiences are in your head or because you have a chip on your shoulder or because you like to "play the race card." Frequently, it's these types of incidents at white majority practice and retreat centers that move yogis of color to seek out people of color groups. As fear abates our sense of compassion grows, especially if we have added karuna or compassion to our brahma vihara practice.

Karuna offers the wish that others be free of pain in whatever form they may be experiencing. It also urges yogis to allow the pain of others to touch and soften their heart. When I offer "may you be free of this pain, may you be free of this sorrow" or "may I touch your pain, may I touch your sorrow" I am expressing a willingness to acknowledge that all of us suffer, all of us seek relief from suffering.

Metta and karuna are powerful practices when realized in our lives and through us in the lives of our communities. I believe they, along with mindfulness practice, are a powerful source for individual and cultural healing.

In conversations with other yogis of color, I've discovered many of us approach our practice in just this way. Many of us are reluctant to talk about it, share our experience, or question our teachers about its efficacy.

I have come to accept that most of us are householders responsible for our own well-being and the well-being of others. For those of us who are activists and social service workers, we are karma yogis who have made a commitment to use our practice—that is all the activities and opportunities of our daily lives—to help end the personal and systemic suffering of others.

Our practice begins right where we are. The healing of our communities begins in our home neighborhoods, among our own and other people of color. A few years ago I was asked to introduce mindfulness to a group of young neighborhood activists who were doing peer-based harm reduction (sexually transmitted diseases) and past trauma (family and community violence) work. They were stressed out. It was during one of those summers when the city decided the best way to address youth crime was to pick up any African American young man standing on a street corner, including these young people distributing condoms and safe sex literature.

I had my doubts about the endeavor, mostly since our POC group is careful to not present ourselves as teachers. But we had been encouraged to offer the practice of "spiritual friendship," so I agreed to give it a try. I wasn't sure how the group, mostly young men of Afro-Caribbean descent, would respond to me.

As I began explaining mindfulness and what we were going to do, first an exercise to find our breath, then a brief sit (really brief, just three minutes), then a movement meditation that included walking with full cups of water that, inexplicably, causes teenage boys to giggle uncontrollably. As I was holding forth, one of the older youth (he was about eighteen) expressed doubts. He had grown up in the church, and straight up stated:

"All these words you say. That's devil worship!"

I think he was referring to the tradition that Tina Turner practices, one that is quite popular with African Americans and Latinos, in which practitioners chant the Lotus Sutra, *Nam Myoho Renge Kyo*. In response I began reciting the metta chant I had learned on retreat, the one chanted in Burmese monasteries:

Avera hontu,
Abyapajja hontu,
Anigha hontu,
Sukhi attanam, pariharantu.

And asked, "You mean like that?"
And the young man replied, "Yes ma'am."
"Can I tell you what it means?"
"Yes ma'am."
Taking a little liberty with person and tense, I translated:

May you be free from enmity and danger,
May you be free from mental suffering,
May you be free from physical suffering,
May you take care of yourself happily.

"Really? No one has ever wished that for me before."
"Well I wish it for you every night."
That young man became one of the most ardent meditators in the group and a great help in controlling those giggling thirteen-year-olds.

Family Programming in Buddhist Community

Sumi Loundon Kim

UDDHISM IS NOT, compared to other faith traditions, very child- and family-friendly. Our revered founder began his path to awakening by ditching his wife and newborn son. Among Westerners, the focus on silent, seated meditation leaves little room for doing things children would enjoy or communicating the tradition in a broad and rich way. As a result, many parents with Buddhist inclinations have been unable to find a local center or temple that will nurture the whole family. Often these centers are comprised of a majority of adult members in pre- and post-family phases of life: students and baby boomers. Yet, we should ask, who will carry the tradition forward after our generation dies off?

If Western Buddhists wish to see our children inherit the Buddhist way, then we need commence a larger-scale effort to provide them with opportunities to learn and practice. But creating a family-centered Buddhism in the West will not be easy. We are hampered from the get-go by a fundamentally ascetic and celibate tradition. This philosophical basis permeates every aspect of Buddhist culture and practice, from the

Rev. Sumi Loundon Kim, MTS, is the Buddhist chaplain at Duke University and minister for the Buddhist Families of Durham (BFD). She has published two anthologies about young Buddhists, *Blue Jean Buddha* and *The Buddha's Apprentices*, among other articles and chapters. After receiving a master's degree in Buddhist studies and Sanskrit from the Harvard Divinity School, she was the associate director for the Barre Center for Buddhist Studies. Originally brought up in a Zen community, she has been practicing in the Theravada lineage for the past twenty years. Sumi and her husband, a native of Korea and professor of Korean Buddhism and culture, have two young children.

prioritization of monastics in institutional Buddhism to the messages that sex and the products of sex (i.e., children) are the results of desire and attachment. One of the most common questions from parents is, "How do I practice nonattachment with my children?" This question evokes the painful dilemma householders feel between trying to be a good Buddhist and the natural feelings of attachment and protection that come with healthy parental instincts.

Of course, there are ways around these core values, and many temples in Asia, as well as Asian temples in the West, have found ways to include children and families for centuries. Westerners, however, are still in an experimental phase: some of the larger, more established organizations have long-running children and family programs while smaller, local groups rarely do. As a testament to this formative period, when I contacted these larger institutions, each had internal documentation detailing their programs for children but these remain unpublished. However, in the last five years, a number of books have indeed been published on Buddhist parenting, Buddhist books for children, and meditation for children. In many ways, this pioneering phase provides an exciting opportunity for creativity and adaptation. At the same time, with few ready-made materials, cultivating a community or program takes enormous work, research, and time for trial and error.

This chapter discusses first my experience of creating a program for the Buddhist families of Durham, in North Carolina. Second, I reflect on how Buddhism can be experienced from a child's perspective to provide a philosophical foundation for the religious education of children and families.

CREATING A FAMILY COMMUNITY

I did not see the need for children's programs in Buddhist settings, like so many others who have started ones themselves, until I myself became a mother. At the time, I lived in Tucson, Arizona, and wanted to join a Sunday morning meditation group at a Vietnamese temple nearby. My daughter, then two years old, loved being at the temple, too, but how could she endure a forty-minute meditation followed by chanting and a Dharma talk?

One Sunday morning, a Taiwanese woman approached me. Sherry and I had the same problem. In order to do meditation, we needed some way to keep our kids busy. But we didn't want to just keep them busy: we wanted them to start learning about Buddhism, too. The abbot, an elderly white American and Chan monk, suggested we start a Sunday school so that the children had lessons while the parents meditated. One mom taught the kids while the other joined the adult sit, and we alternated weeks.

It wasn't long before the Vietnamese American kids began coming, too. They liked learning about meditation, playing games, and talking about Buddhism in English, their primary language. Sherry and I drew on a lifetime of both practicing and studying Buddhism, with some supplementation from books, to create weekly lesson plans. But we were both intimidated by the prospects of teaching because neither of us had managed a group of kids before. However, we found that with a little trial and error, we got the hang of it pretty quickly. An example of an activity: we had each child learn one of the different mudras, or symbolic hand gestures, of the Buddha. Then we went into the Dharma hall when the adults had ended meditation and demonstrated each one. All of the adults were happy to learn these, too!

A year later, my family relocated to Durham, North Carolina. I looked around for a situation like the one in Tucson. A Won (Korean) Buddhist temple had sporadic offerings but not on Sunday morning, the only time during the week when our family had nothing scheduled. A Zen center also had bi-monthly Sunday morning lessons for kids, but because most adult members arrived, meditated, and departed without much interaction among each other, there was not a strong sense of community. I wanted my children to be free to develop relationships with adults who might some day be an inspiration, model, or mentor for them.

Thus I decided to start a new community that came to be called the Buddhist Families of Durham. About five families, who saw the posting for this new group on the neighborhood list-serve, attended the very first Sunday morning meeting, which was held at the home of one family. The children colored in line drawings of the Buddha that I printed from Buddhanet.net and listened to a reading of *Zen Shorts* by Jon Muth, while the other adults practiced meditation and talked about applying

Buddhism to parenting. Within a few months, we were twelve families large. All of the parents are hugely loving, thoughtful people, most of whom had had some exposure to meditation through hatha yoga, stress-reduction classes, or retreats. Very quickly, the parents settled into a comfortable schedule of meditation and discussion, which I found easy to lead. Addressing the needs of the children, however, became an enormous challenge. I was uncertain as to both what to teach and who should teach it.

The early lesson plans were drawn up from my own knowledge of Buddhism, but I quickly ran out of books and ideas. When I looked at the curricula from other organizations, they tended to either be lineage- or organization-specific, centered on foreign language terms, or draw from particular Asian cultures. Nonlineage curricula, on the other hand, framed teachings in terms of values, mindfulness, or stress reduction and did not have content related to Buddhist ideas, ethics, and rituals. I have found myself cobbling together bits and pieces. I often use library books that are not Buddhist but represent a Buddhist idea such as *The Bear with the Sword* by Davide Cali, which is essentially about karma. I have taken ideas from the Unitarian Universalists' extensive and online religious education program. And I sometimes just randomly opened up a book on Buddhism for kids and decided, okay, today we're going to talk about the Buddha's footprint, outline our own foot, and then draw all the things we wish to leave in the world (kindness, flowers, rainbows) in the footprint. For music, I have stumbled on a number of Buddhist CDs such as *Calm Down Boogie* and *Paramita: American Buddhist Folk Music*, or I will find something that sounds Buddhist enough from, say, Jack Johnson's *Curious George*.

In the early days, I would draw up lesson plans and then parents would do their best to teach it, but after a while I thought it would be good if the parents could teach it, as well as contribute from their own spiritual knowledge. Two parents taught as a team, with a different team each Sunday. The problem with this system was that parents themselves were not familiar with Buddhist teachings. The kids went along with this but eventually complained that the curriculum lacked continuity, with very different topics each Sunday, and some of the kids expressly stated they wanted to learn more about Buddhism as a religion. In addition, different parents had different expectations on behavior and after a while the kids began taking advantage of the chaos. To adjust for these problems, parents began team-teaching for four consecutive Sundays, and I provided the curriculum for them.

This new system did indeed provide content continuity and a shorter learning curve for managing the personalities among the children. However, parents provided feedback that during the time they were teaching they felt isolated, even exiled, from the adult group. Moreover, preparing an hour of activities that was both educational and entertaining took considerable time for both the teaching team and I. Each week, I needed to train the teachers on the material and they had to buy supplies, think through the activities, and coordinate with their coteacher. At some point the issue crystallized: we parents realized that what we really wanted on Sunday mornings, after a week of shuttling kids to school and sports, groceries, cleaning, laundry, appointments, was *to do nothing*. In short, the needs of the kids—to have a rich, activity-filled morning—and the needs of the parents—to meditate—were diametrically opposed. The only solution, therefore, was to hire teachers.

I polled the parents, informing them that hiring teachers would be expensive. Still do it? The overwhelming response was "yes." We hired a seasoned meditator to more or less babysit our three- to four-year-olds and a graduate student of Buddhism to teach the five- to twelve-year-olds. So far, this system has been working wonderfully well, but I have noticed that the two groups feel more separate than before, with adults and kids each doing "their thing." My hope is to shift toward a more integrated model in which the whole family engages Buddhist practice together. We will begin a unit on the five precepts, consciously taking up one precept each week both in the meetings and at home.

In talking with others who run family programs elsewhere, I found we have in common the challenge of finding qualified teachers. Often parents are either too new to Buddhism themselves to teach or, if they have had some training, they may not have confidence or skills in teaching itself. In some situations, older, more seasoned community members have been able to commit to teaching the children for terms at a time, but this comes at the cost of their own limited time for personal practice. As I have done, these other programs have managed to create their own curricula by scavenging from a range of sources. My sense is that there is a great deal out there, but little of it has been published or put online. It is my hope that in the not-distant future those of us running family programs can come together with the best of what we know to create a flexible but clearly Buddhist curriculum useful to a diversity of Western Buddhist family programs.

Children relate to Buddhism in a very different way than do adults. To figure out how to teach kids Buddhism, I have had to think back on my own childhood. What did I remember from life at the Zen community where my family lived in the late '70s and early '80s? What lessons have remained with me today? Some reflection has provided a few insights on possible ways to teach my own children, ages three and five.

When I turned seven years old, I was given my own meditation spot on the women's side of the meditation hall. I was expected to get myself up at 5:30 in the morning and join the adults, who had already been sitting for half an hour, and meditate for the remaining half-hour. I didn't complain about having to get up at this ungodly, dark time of morning or about facing a wall with nothing to do except breathe. Why? Because everyone else in the community did it, too. Following the schedule, along with hundreds of other expectations such as sharing the work and cleaning up after oneself, was not just reinforced by two adults, my parents, but an entire community of people. To me, this speaks to the value of situating children in community to learn Buddhism. Of course, we learn a tremendous amount at home from our own parents, but a community's culture and expectations can shape children greatly. For this reason, both my children are BFD students so that they can see that we are not the only ones who value this gentle, reflective way of life.

During morning meditation, I could not follow my breath for more than a minute and I often spent most of the half-hour blinking my eyes rapidly to see how many spots I could make. Nonetheless, even though I was bored at times, I loved this special time of quiet and stillness. The smell of the incense, the glow of the candles on the altar, the warm smile of the Buddha statue, the way the chanting of the Heart Sutra filled my whole mind with sound and rhythm: these aspects of the meditation hall created a feeling of sacredness. Today, if I smell the same cedarwood incense, I feel calm and happy because it returns me to the magical qualities of the morning meditation. Reflecting on this childhood experience, I now see that incense, candles, visual materials, and chanting were the ways that I related to the Buddhism of my parents. Children feel wonder when they hear the sound of a gong or are invited to drink tea in a ceremonial way. Through art, music, scent, food, and stories, we can connect our children to Buddhism by connecting to their finely attuned senses.

Likewise, children experience spirituality in their bodies. In the Zen community of my parents, we followed the fairly elaborate forms of the Japanese tradition. For example, I was trained in how to enter a hall properly. It began with a bow to the hall. Take one step in, starting with the left foot. Bow to the altar, the men's side, and then the women's side. Turn left . . . etc. To me as a child, this training was not meaningless subjugation. Rather, following the forms of worship felt like a choreographed dance that created equanimity and poise. I remember learning how to do a full bow to the floor when I was about seven, and I have been bowing on and off ever since. Today, when I take a bow, my body remembers this form and it feels entirely natural and even reassuring. A bow can be a refuge on difficult days.

I also remember that during intensive meditation retreats, during which the adults would do sitting and walking meditation almost all day, the children of the community were asked to help with the normal workload. For example, at lunch one other child and I would ladle soup into the bowl of each adult sitting in his or her meditation spot. At other times, I would be asked to sweep the meditation hall or set out meditation cushions. These kinds of tasks made me feel like an important part of the community and the retreat. For this reason, I now believe that adults should ask children to be actively involved in family and community Buddhist events. Children love to light candles. Teenagers feel valued when asked to ring the bell at the end of a meditation. College students are proud to use their computer skills to design a poster for an event. In my adult years, I have too often seen that young people sit passively on the sidelines. My son and daughter fight over who gets to light the incense and place it before the Buddha at our home!

There may be other ways to teach children about Buddhism, but making them study the Four Noble Truths or listen to a Dharma talk is like making them eat chalk—dry and tasteless. For children, learning and memorization are not the doors to the Buddha's Way. Rather, young people develop themselves as Buddhists through strong community relationships, through their senses, through kinesthesia, and by becoming an active part of worship and events.

If Buddhism is to continue beyond the baby boomer generation in the West, there are two options. The first is to draw from young adults who convert or incline toward Buddhist practices and thought. Certainly this is how earlier generations of Western Buddhists formed. These converts bring great dedication and sincerity to their practice, qualities that immigrant Asian teachers have found refreshing. The downside of converts, though, is that they tend to prioritize practice and study over culture and community. Yet these latter two elements are essential to creating vibrant and enduring religious traditions. For example, Buddhist teachers often complain that it is challenging to get their members to understand *dana* or generosity and that it takes decades to acculturate their members on the financial aspects of their center. The other downside of converts is that they are frequently the only person in their family to pursue the path: the parents or spouse or children are of different religions or none. This isolation can lead to a fractured spiritual life in which a fully expressed Buddhist way of thinking only comes out in special settings and not at home or with the people one is closest to.

The second option for bestowing Buddhism to another generation is to focus on the education and cultivation of children. Although many will not take it any further upon reaching adulthood, a good number, after a nearly required period of rebellion, do return to their roots. When the seeds planted in childhood are watered with adult capacities, the fruit can be enormously sustaining for the whole community. We can see the fruition in the likes of Noah Levine, Ethan Nichtern, Diana Winston, Will Kabat-Zinn, and Hanuman Goleman, to name a few!—all grown children of baby boomer Buddhists (some famous) and each is doing remarkable work.

For the well-being of the Buddhist way of life in generations to come, it is perhaps time for more centers to create a welcoming space for families.

When a community supports the whole family, there is greater benefit to both the children and the parents than if just the parents are attending. Not only do the families benefit, but the joy, presence, and sincerity of the children strengthens and enlivens the community, as well.

Internet Resources for Buddhist Chaplaincy and Ministry

TRAINING PROGRAMS

The following is a list of vocational programs that offer specific training for Buddhist chaplains and ministers. All of these programs are intended as supplements to the traditional forms of Buddhist training.

Graduate Theological Union: http://www.gtu.edu/
Harvard Divinity School: http://www.hds.harvard.edu/
Institute of Buddhist Studies: http://www.shin-ibs.edu/
Maitripa College: http://www.maitripa.org/
Metta Institute: http://www.mettainstitute.org/
Naropa University: http://www.naropa.edu/
New York Zen Center for Contemplative Care: http://zencare.org/
University of the West: http://www.uwest.edu/site/
Upaya Zen Center: http://www.upaya.org/index.php
Sati Center for Buddhist Studies: http://www.sati.org/
Shogaku Zen Institue: http://www.shogakuzen.org/pages/
    mission.php
Spiritual Care Programme: http://www.spcare.org/
Buddhist Society for Compassionate Wisdom: http://www.zenbuddhist-
    temple.org/seminary.html

OTHER LINKS OF INTEREST

American Association of Pastoral Counselors: http://aapc.org/
Association for Clinical Pastoral Education: http://www.acpe.edu/
Association of Professional Chaplains: http://www.professionalchaplains.org/

Buddhist Chaplains Network: http://buddhistchaplainsnetwork.org/

Buddhist Chaplains.org: http://buddhistchaplains.org/cmsms/
index.php?page=about-us

Connecticut Coalition to Improve End-of-Life Care: http://www.ctend
oflifecare.org/

Family Hospice: http://www.familyhospice.net/index.html

Healthcare Chaplaincy: http://healthcarechaplaincy.org/

Human Kindness Foundation: http://www.humankindness.org/

International Conference of Police Chaplains: http://www.icpc4
cops.org/

Karuna Hospice Service: http://www.karuna.org.au/

List of Buddhist Hospices: http://www.buddhanet.net/hospices.htm

Medicine Horse: http://www.medicinehorse.org/

Military Chaplains Association: http://mca-usa.org/

National Association of College and University Chaplains:
http://www.nacuc.net/

National Conference on Ministry in the Armed Forces: http://ncmaf.org/

National Hospice and Palliative Care Organization:
http://www.nhpco.org/templates/1/homepage.cfm

Prison Dharma Network: http://www.prisondharmanetwork.org/

Project Clear Light: http://projectclearlight.org/index2.html

The Ratna Peace Initiative: http://www.ratnapeaceinitiative.org/

Sarah House: http://sarahhousesb.org/

Spiritual Care Programme: http://www.spcare.org/

Veterans Peace of Mind Project: www.veteranspeaceofmind.org

Windhorse Family and Elder Care: http://www.windhorsecare.com/

Zen Hospice Project: http://www.zenhospice.org/

Zen Peacemakers: http://zenpeacemakers.org/

Selected Bibliography

Aronson, Harvey B. *Buddhist Practice on Western Ground: Reconciling Eastern Ideals and Western Psychology.* Boston: Shambhala, 2004.

Balboni, M. J., A. Babar, J. Dillinger, A. C. Phelps, et al. "It Depends: Viewpoints of Patients, Physicians, and Nurses on Patient-Practitioner Prayer in the Setting of Advanced Cancer." *Journal of Symptom and Pain Management* 41 (2011).

Baldoquín, Hilda Gutiérrez ed. *Dharma, Color, and Culture: New Voices in Western Buddhism.* Berkeley: Parallax Press, 2004.

Bernhard, Toni. *How to Be Sick: A Buddhist-Inspired Guide for the Chronically Ill and Their Caregivers.* Boston: Wisdom Publications, 2010.

Bidwell, Duane R. *Short-Term Spiritual Guidance.* Minneapolis: Augsburg Fortress, 2004.

Biegel, G. M., K. W. Brown, S. L. Shapiro, and C. M. Schubert. "Mindfulness-Based Stress Reduction for the Treatment of Adolescent Psychiatric Outpatients: A Randomized Clinical Trial." *Journal of Consulting and Clinical Psychology* 77 (2009).

Blackman, Shushila. *Graceful Exits: How Great Beings Die.* Boston: Shambhala, 2005.

Boyle, Gregory. *Tattoos on the Heart: The Power of Boundless Compassion.* New York: Free Press, 2011.

Brady, Mark. *The Wisdom of Listening.* Boston: Wisdom Publications, 2003.

Chodron, Pema. *The Places That Scare You: A Guide to Fearlessness in Difficult Times.* Boston: Shambhala, 2001.

———. *The Wisdom of No Escape.* Boston: Shambhala, 2010.

Coleman, Graham, and Thupten Jinpa. *The Tibetan Book of the Dead: The First Complete Translation.* New York: Penguin Classics, 2007.

Collett, Merrill. *At Home with Dying.* Boston: Shambhala, 1995.

Cooper-White, Pamela. *Shared Wisdom: Use of the Self in Pastoral Care and Counseling.* Minneapolis: Fortress Press, 2004.

Covell, Stephen G. *Japanese Temple Buddhism: Worldliness in a Religion of Renunciation.* Edited by George J. Tanabe, Jr. Topics in Contemporary Buddhism. Honolulu: University of Hawai'i Press, 2005.

Dalai Lama. *Healing Anger: The Power of Patience from a Buddhist Perspective.* Ithaca: Snow Lion, 1997.

de Hennezel, Marie. *Intimate Death: How the Dying Teach Us How to Live.* New York: Vintage, 1998.

Doehring, Carrie. *The Practice of Pastoral Care: A Postmodern Approach.* Louisville: Westminster John Knox Press, 2006.

Dogen. "Bukkyo the Buddha's Teaching." In *Master Dogen's Shobogenzo.* Edited by Gudo Nishijima and Chodo Cross. London: BookSurge Publishing, 1994. Reprint, 2006.

Dimidjian, Victoria Jean. *Journeying East: Conversations on Aging and Dying.* Berkeley: Parallax, 2004.

Edelstein, Scott. *Sex and the Spiritual Teacher.* Boston: Wisdom Publications, 2011.

Esack, Farid. *On Being a Muslim: Finding a Religious Path in the World Today.* London: Oneworld Publication, 2009.

Foster, Charles R. *Educating Clergy: Teaching Practices and Pastoral Education, Preparation for the Professions.* San Francisco: Jossey-Bass, 2006.

Fozzard S. *Surviving Violence.* Geneva: BICE (International Catholic Child Bureau), 2002.

Grassman, Deborah L. *Peace at Last: Stories of Hope and Healing for Veterans and Their Families.* St. Petersburg: Vandamere Press, 2009.

Greenspan, Miriam. *Healing Through the Dark Emotions: The Wisdom of Grief, Fear, and Despair.* Boston: Shambhala, 2003.

Griffith, James L. and Melissa Elliot Griffith. *Encountering the Sacred in Psychotherapy: How to Talk with People about their Spiritual Lives.* New York: Guilford Press, 2002.

Guenther, Margaret. *Holy Listening: The Art of Spiritual Direction.* Cambridge: Cowley Publications, 1992.

Gunaratana, Bhante. *Mindfulness in Plain English.* Boston: Wisdom Publications, 1996.

Halifax, Joan. *Being with Dying: Cultivating Compassion and Fearlessness in the Presence of Death.* Boston: Shambhala, 2008.

Kendel, Paul M. *Walking the Tiger's Path: A Soldier's Spiritual Journey in Iraq.* Aurora: Tendril Press, 2011.

Kearney, Michael. *A Place of Healing: Working with Suffering in Living and Dying.* New York: Oxford University Press, 2000.

Koenig, H. G., M. E. McCullough, D. B. Larson. *Handbook of Religion and Health*. New York: Oxford University Press, 2001.

Lief, Judith L. *Making Friends with Death: A Buddhist Guide to Encountering Mortality*. Boston: Shambhala, 2001.

Longaker, Christine. *Facing Death and Finding Hope*. St. Louis: Main Street Book, 1998.

Lozoff, Bo. *We're All Doing Time: A Guide to Getting Free*. Durham: Human Kindness Foundation, 1998.

Malone, Calvin. *Razor-Wire Dharma*. Boston: Wisdom Publications, 2008.

McRae, John R. *Seeing through Zen: Encounter, Transformation, and Genealogy in Chinese Chan Buddhism*. Berkeley: University of California Press, 2003.

Mipham, Sakyong. *Turning the Mind into an Ally*. New York: Riverhead Books, 2003.

Miura, Isshu, and Ruth Fuller Sasaki. *Zen Dust: The History of the Koan and Koan Study in Rinzai (Lin-Chi) Zen*. New York: Harcourt, 1966.

Monroe, Barbara, and David Oliviere. *Resilience in Palliative Care*. London: Oxford University Press, 2007.

Newman, T., with T. Yates, and A. Masten. *What Works in Building Resilience?* Barkingside: Barnado, 2004.

Nuland, Sherwin B. *How We Die: Reflections of Life's Final Chapter*. New York: Vintage, 1995.

Petersen, Marilyn R. *At Personal Risk: Boundary Violations in Professional-Client Relationships*. New York: W.W. Norton, 1992.

Phillips, Jenny. *Letters from the Dhamma Brothers: Meditation Behind Bars*. Onalaska: Pariyatti Press, 2008.

Podvoll, Ed. *Recovering Sanity: A Compassionate Approach to Understanding and Treating Psychosis*. Boston: Shambhala, 2003.

Richmond, Lewis. *Healing Lazarus: A Buddhist's Journey from Near Death to New Life*. New York: Atria, 2003.

Rinpoche, Anyen. *Dying with Confidence: A Tibetan Buddhist Guide to Preparing for Death*. Boston: Wisdom Publications, 2010.

Rinpoche, Sogyal. *The Tibetan Book of Living and Dying*. San Francisco: Harper, 2002.

Rinpoche, Zopa Lama. *Ultimate Healing: The Power of Compassion*. Boston: Wisdom Publications, 2001.

Rinpoche, Lama Zopa, and Kathleen McDonald. *Wholesome Fear: Transforming Your Anxiety about Impermanence and Death*. Boston: Wisdom Publications, 2010.

Rosenberg, Larry. *Living in the Light of Death: On the Art of Being Truly Alive*. Boston: Shambhala, 2001.

Safran, Jeremy D. *Psychoanalysis and Buddhism: An Unfolding Dialogue*. Boston: Wisdom Publications, 2003.

Sapolsky, R. *Why Zebras Don't Get Ulcers: An Updated Guide to Stress, Stress-Related Diseases, and Coping*. New York: W.H. Freeman and Company, 1998.

Saunders, Cicely, and David Clark. *Cicely Saunders: Selected Writings 1958–2004*. New York: Oxford University Press, 2006.

Schneider, David. *Street Zen: The Life and Work of Issan Dorsey*. Cambridge: Da Capo Press, 2000.

Seigen Yamaoka, *The Transmission of Shin Buddhism in the West*. Wahiawa: Federation of Dharma School Teachers League, 2005.

Shapiro, S. L., K. Brown, and G. M. Biegel. "Teaching Self-care to Caregivers: Effects of Mindfulness-Based Stress Reduction on the Mental Health of Therapists in Training." *Training and Education in Professional Psychology* 1 (2007).

Simmer-Brown, Judith and Fran Grace. *Meditation and the Classroom: Contemplative Pedagogy for Religious Studies*. Albany: State University of New York Press, 2011.

Smith, Rodney. *Lessons from the Dying*. Boston: Wisdom Publications, 1997.

Tanaka, Kenneth T. "The Individual in Relation to the Sangha in American Buddhism: An Examination of 'Privatized Religion.' *Buddhist-Christian Studies* 2007.

Taylor, S. E., L. J. Burklund, N. I. Eisenberger, B. J. Lehman, C. J. Hilmert, & M. D. Lieberman. "Neural bases of moderation of cortisol stress responses by psychosocial resources." *Journal of Personality and Social Psychology* 95 (2008).

Thondup, Tulku. *Peaceful Death, Joyful Rebirth: A Tibetan Buddhist Guidebook*. Boston: Shambhala, 2006.

Trungpa, Chogyam Rinpoche. *Training the Mind and Cultivating Loving-Kindness*. Boston: Shambhala, 2003.

VandeCreek, Larry. "Ministry of Hospital Chaplains: Patient Satisfaction." *Journal of Healthcare Chaplaincy* 6 (1997).

Wicks, Robert. *The Resilient Clinician*. New York: Oxford Press, 2007.

Zajonc, Arthur. *Meditation as Contemplative Practice*. Aurora: Lindisfarne Books, 2009.

Reprint Permissions

Index

as the full expression of Buddha
nature, 36
See also community
Sangye, Phadampa, 46
Sarah House, 231–41
Sati Center for Buddhist Studies, 14
Saunders, Cecile, 250
Schireson, Grace, 27, 187
scholarly study of Buddhist literature, 23
Seigen Yamaoka, 15
self, study and forgetting of in CPE,
99
self-acceptance, 177
selflessness in Buddhist caregiving,
82–87
seminary training
Buddhist equivalency, certification
and, 69–70
changes in, 19–20, 25–26
problems with, 25
September 11, 2001, commemora-
tive services, 181–82
sexual assault prevention, in military
chaplaincy, 195
Shambhala Buddhism, 124
Shambhala Prison Community
(SPC), 134
Shantideva, 121, 125
shila (moral discipline) as skill for
Buddhist chaplains, 108–9
Shin Buddhism, 292–94
shock, in a military setting, 194–95
sickness, the Buddha on caring for
others, 183
silence, chaplains and, 270
skills needed in Buddhist chaplaincy,
106–10, 221, 222

Sluyter, Dean, 113
social model hospice, 231–41
social workers, role of in hospice,
266
sociopathology, 130
Sogyal Rinpoche, 244–45, 251
soldiering skills, for Buddhist Army
chaplains, 194
Soto Zen Buddhist Association
(SZBA), 21
Soto Zen ordination requirements,
23
spaciousness, cultivation of, 248
speech, right, 294–95
"spiritual bypassing," 34
spiritual care
Buddhist perspective on, 7, 255–57
Casita Model of, 257–60
vs. contemplative care, xvii–xviii
in death and dying care, 225–26,
245–46
listening as, 281–90
patient-practitioner prayer, 42
practice in action, 262–63
role of, 260–62, 265–66
spiritual maturity as basis of SPOT
training, 34
spiritual needs, universal, 246
SPOT training program
East meets West curriculum, 34–37
methodology of, 33–34
misunderstandings and challenges,
31–33
origins of, 28–31
Suzuki Roshi and, 27–28
training day, example of, 37–39
staff officers, Buddhist Army chaplains as, 194–95

About Wisdom Publications

WISDOM PUBLICATIONS is dedicated to offering works relating to and inspired by Buddhist traditions.

To learn more about us or to explore our other books, please visit our website at www.wisdompubs.org.

You can subscribe to our e-newsletter or request our print catalog online, or by writing to:

Wisdom Publications
199 Elm Street
Somerville, Massachusetts 02144 USA

You can also contact us at 617-776-7416, or info@wisdompubs.org.

Wisdom is a nonprofit, charitable 501(c)(3) organization, and donations in support of our mission are tax deductible.

Wisdom Publications is affiliated with the Foundation for the Preservation of the Mahayana Tradition (FPMT).